PROCESSES, BELIEFS, AND QUESTIONS

SYNTHESE LANGUAGE LIBRARY

TEXTS AND STUDIES IN
LINGUISTICS AND PHILOSOPHY

VOLUME 16

PROCESSES, BELIEFS, AND QUESTIONS

Essays on Formal Semantics of Natural Language and Natural Language Processing

Edited by

STANLEY PETERS

Dept. of Linguistics, The University of Texas at Austin

and

ESA SAARINEN

Dept. of Philosophy, University of Helsinki, and Center for Cognitive Science, The University of Texas at Austin

SPRINGER-SCIENCE+BUSINESS MEDIA, B.V.

Library of Congress Cataloging in Publication Data

Main entry under title:

Processes, beliefs, and questions.

(Synthese language library ; v. 16)
Includes indexes.
1. Semantics—Addresses, essays, lectures.
I. Peters, Stanley, 1941– . II. Saarinen, Esa, 1953– . III. Series.
P325.P7 415 81–13785
ISBN 978-90-481-8366-1 ISBN 978-94-015-7668-0 (eBook)
DOI 10.1007/978-94-015-7668-0

Originally published by D. Reidel Publishing Company, Dordrecht, Holland in 1982
Softcover reprint of the hardcover 1st edition 1982

TABLE OF CONTENTS

STANLEY PETERS AND ESA SAARINEN

INTRODUCTION

SECTION I

In 1972, Donald Davison and Gilbert Harman wrote in the introduction to the volume *Semantics of Natural Language*:

"The success of linguistics in treating natural languages as formal syntactic systems has aroused the interest of a number of linguists in a parallel or related development of semantics. For the most part quite independently, many philosophers and logicians have recently been applying formal semantic methods to structures increasingly like natural languages. While differences in training, method and vocabulary tend to veil the fact, philosophers and linguists are converging, it seems, on a common set of interrelated problems."

Davidson and Harman called for an interdisciplinary dialogue of linguists, philosophers and logicians on the semantics of natural language, and during the last ten years such an enterprise has proved extremely fruitful. Thanks to the cooperative effort in these several fields, the last decade has brought about striking progress in our understanding of the semantics of natural language.

This work on semantics has typically paid little attention to psychological aspects of meaning. Thus, psychologists or computer scientists working on artificial intelligence were not invited to join the forces in the influential introduction of *Semantics of Natural Language*. No doubt it was felt that while psychological aspects of language are important in their own right, they are not relevant to our immediate semantic concerns.

In the last few years, several linguists and logicians have come to question the fundamental anti-psychological assumptions underlying their theorizing. Some have gone so far as to conclude that notoriously recalcitrant phenomena such as propositional attitudes cannot be accounted for without changes in the foundations.

Over approximately the last decade, some computer scientists working in the areas of computational linguistics and artificial intelligence have developed a procedural theory of semantics, which is apparently quite different from the truth-conditional and generally model-theoretic approaches of the logicians and linguists.

Psychologists concerned both with comprehension of language and with

S. Peters and E. Saarinen (eds.), Processes, Beliefs, and Questions, vii–xxxi.

reasoning have been attracted by the potential of procedural semantics to illuminate features of human linguistic performance and verbal memory.

Can these different approaches to semantics in any way be reconciled? Are their differences due merely to differences in training and vocabulary, like those between linguists and logicians working on semantics in the late 60's and early 70's? A growing number of scholars have come to face these questions in the last few years, calling for a common enterprise not just by linguists and logicians, but by psychologists and computer scientists as well.

The emerging interdisciplinary field of cognitive science is the background for the present collection of articles. The volume, based on a conference held at the University of Texas at Austin in March 29–31, 1979, brings together some of the leading linguists, logicians, psychologists and computer scientists working on semantics. The main issue to be addressed in this collection is the same as faces the whole of cognitive science in the field of semantics: is it possible to find a synthesis of the apparently different formal (model-theoretic) and psychological or procedural approaches to semantics? While at the present time we are not in a position to answer this question in anything like a conclusive manner, the articles in this collection at least pave the ground for further work in this area.

SECTION II

The contrast between formal and psychologically oriented approaches to semantics can be put in a number of different ways. Since this contrast is fundamental to all of present-day semantic theorizing and since it will come up repeatedly in the articles below, we shall now try to outline some of the main issues in this controversy.

Semantics: Mathematics or Psychology

One fundamental disagreement between formal and psychological approaches to meaning concerns the general nature of basic semantic concepts: are they 'mentalistic' ('psychological') or are they ones that do not allude to (or depend on) the human mind? Formal semantics has chosen the latter course. It has studied meaning in terms of structures that have had little or no psychological motivation. The anti-mentalistic philosophy underlying model theoretic work on meaning has seen semantics as part of mathematics, rather than psychology, and has started off from the basic conviction that there is no intrinsic difference between natural languages and logicians' formal languages.

As a working hypothesis, the logical approach to the study of natural language has made possible an exact and fully explicit treatment of the semantics of natural language. The standard of rigor in the epoch-making work of Richard Montague has been that of modern mathematical logic. The formal clarity of model-theoretic semantics is undoubtedly the single most important factor facilitating breakthroughs in this conduct of inquiry.

Until recently, the anti-mentalistic convictions underlying formal semantics have not been investigated in any detail. The main stream of formal semanticists has not found its anti-psychological assumptions problematic. Is this tacit, seldom argued conviction unfounded? Do the abstractions of formal semantics point at an intrinsic limitation of the very enterprise, thus calling for revisions in the very foundations of it? These crucial questions are discussed in several essays in the present collection.

One key difficulty in comparing formal and psychological approaches is that the two seem to operate with distinct adequacy conditions (criteria of success). In order to make the different approaches commensurable it is therefore important to explicate just what the distinct theories purport to explain – to locate a common 'date base' – and to see whether a common goal and common set of criteria can be found.

Here the situation is more complicated than might appear at first glance. The reason is that choice of a 'data base' has considerable theoretical consequences. The problem is not merely how to design a theory to match a certain data base, but whether that data base itself is biased and arbitrarily defined. The latter question, however, is one that is often impossible to settle in any conclusive manner. It hinges on various, often tacitly assumed, methodological assumptions that represent belief and scholarly taste more than any carefully argued conviction.

By way of illustration, consider the definite noun phrase *the Swedish tennis star that lives in Monte Carlo* in the following two sentences:

(1) The Swedish tennis star that lives in Monte Carlo was complaining about his backhand.

(2) Björn Borg and John McEnroe were discussing their games. The Swedish tennis star that lives in Monte Carlo was complaining about his backhand.

Should one and the same semantic theory account for the intuitive import of *both* these occurrences in one fell swoop? The way a formal semanticist has traditionally answered this question is somewhat as follows. He first suggests that the contribution of the noun phrase in (1) is that, in any given model M, it designates the one and only one object that in the model *M* is a Swedish tennis star that lives in Monte Carlo. Thus, on this account, the truth of (1) implies that there is one and only one Swedish tennis star who lives in Monte Carlo.

Things are different with (2), where under the most natural reading the noun phrase picks out an object among those mentioned in the first clause. Thus the most natural understanding of (2) does not commit us to the claim that there is just one and only one Swedish tennis star living in Monte Carlo. Intuitively, we might say that the noun phrase is not evaluated with respect to the whole domain of discourse of the model *M* but instead with respect to a subset of it determined by the previous discourse.

While this line of thought is intuitive enough, it calls for features going beyond the formal semanticist's immediate resources. His theory has not been designed to account for such phenomena of 'sentential cohesion', any more than to characterize other phenomena of text linguistics. Thus the formal semanticist's standard reaction to (2) has been to say that the reading of (2) characterized is not in his 'data base' and, consequently, the meanings of the noun phrase in (1) and in (2) are two quite different things.

A theorist less impressed by straightforward model-theoretic semantics is not likely to buy this line of thought, however. In particular, he will find the formal semanticist's definition of the 'data base' arbitrary. For this critic, any satisfactory account of definite noun phrases should yield a unified treatment for both (1) and (2). Thus, his *desiderata* are different from the formal semanticist's, the very success conditions are not the same.

The choice of 'data base' is clearly quite crucial. Nevertheless a given choice is seldom argued for. It should, however, be backed up with theoretical assumptions concerning such basic questions as what a semantic theory ought to explain or whether the object of semantic investigation is an abstract semantic competence. Answering questions such as these is the key to comparing psychological and formal semantical approaches with one another.

Semantics: Dynamic or Static

Should a semantic theory try to 'simulate' the actual psychological processes that take place when a speaker comprehends a sentence, at least in the minimal sense of providing a semantic model which is in some direct way related to actual semantic comprehension? Formal semantics has answered in the negative. This approach has paid hardly any attention to meaning-related *processes* at all. The underlying assumption has been that notions such as 'understanding', 'comprehension' and 'semantic processing' do not lie within the formal semanticist's domain of investigation.

The psychological and procedural semanticists take a wider view of the domain of semantic theory. According to them, semantic theory should acknowledge from the outset the 'dynamic' nature of semantic computation and use a formalism in which semantic processing finds a straightforward expression. In as much the formal semanticist defines his area of investigation more narrowly, he is bound to leave important aspects of meaning untouched.

Thus, the issue of whether a semantic theory should provide a 'static' or a 'dynamic' picture of language is to a large extent an issue about the very aims of the semantic theory. The situation is analogous to what we found in connection with definite noun phrases. The reader will have noted that the model-theoretician's adherence to a 'static' theoretical framework was an impediment to his accounting for 'anaphorically' used noun phrases, as in (2). In contrast, a theoretician who started with a process-based model would naturally seek a unified treatment for (1) and (2). (For early process-based models of these and related phenomena, see Isard, 1975 and Winograd, 1972.)

Thus, an element of incommensurability is introduced at the outset by the different success conditions on which the different enterprises are based. The model-theoretician remains unconvinced by the arguments of a procedure-oriented semanticist because he does not think procedures and concepts of that ilk are needed to cope with the semantic phenomena *he* is concerned with.

To take another example, consider natural language anaphora, as exemplified in the interplay of *a present* and *it* in

(3) John wants to buy a present and give it to Barbara.

A formal semanticist might suggest that all that is needed in order to characterize the anaphoric relation is to note that the pronoun is a variable bound to the quantifier in the noun phrase *a present*. This would suffice to characterize the contribution of the pronoun to the truth conditions and entailment relations of (3).

Intuitively, however, when (3) is processed by a human speaker, the noun phrase *a present* and the pronoun *it* are two distinct semantic units, a fact reflected in the obvious truth that the former is processed first and the latter only later. Semantic comprehension as well as syntactic parsing proceeds from left to right; in computing the meaning of (3), the anaphoric pronoun refers to an individual somehow 'already picked out'.

The straightforward intuitive idea just mentioned does not find expression in terms of the formal semanticist's apparatus of quantifiers and bound variables. For a procedure-oriented scholar this fact along indicates a severe inadequacy in the formal semanticist's proposal. But the formal semanticist set aside the relevant features of semantic processing quite deliberately; he is operating with different criteria of success.

At the present time, it seems to remain an open problem whether the 'dynamic' picture of language implicit in psychological and other procedure-oriented approaches is needed to explain semantic data even in the model-theoretician's sense. (Some scholars working in the tradition of formal semantics have argued for a 'dynamic' semantic model. See, e.g., the work on game-theoretical semantics in Saarinen, 1979, or Kamp's approach in Kamp, forthcoming.)

In the present collection, procedural semantics and the dynamic semantic theories suggested by computer science will be discussed in the contributions of Johnson-Laird, Partee, and Moore and Hendrix.

Is There a Semantic Competence-Performance Distinction?

Formal semantics has been designed to capture in a rigorous way (a certain type of) intuitive entailment-relation. It has not been concerned with psychological limitations in grasping entailments, questions such as what kind of inferences are difficult for humans to comprehend, which ones easy. This abstraction may seem harmless enough. It would seem that as far as truth conditions and entailment-relations are concerned, no reference to the speaker's psychological limitations need be made. Thus, it could be argued, human limitations in grasping entailment relations are comparable to their limitations in grasping syntactic structures. Since operating on a level of abstraction where such human limitations are dispensed with has turned out to be fruitful in the study of syntax, it can be expected to help in semantics also.

A theorist thinking along these lines would accordingly endorse in semantics something like the familiar competence-performance distinction. The formal semanticist's notion of semantic competence would not only abstract away from human memory limitations and similar phenomena that by any standards are part of 'semantic performance', but also from all phenomena connected inextricably to 'understanding', 'semantic comprehension' and 'semantic processing'.

In some areas of semantics the hypothesis of such an abstract semantic competence seems to work very well. For instance, after ten years of extensive work we now have a fairly clear understanding of the semantic behavior of natural language quantifiers and sentential connectives. This work, moreover, has operated on a level of abstraction which assigns to sentences properties that go vastly beyond anything an actual speaker can immediately verify by his own intuition. For instance, it is well-known that humans have difficulties in grasping sentences with even three consecutive conditionals (*if-then* connectives). Few scholars have suggested that this kind of human (performance) limitation would be of direct relevance for a study of the truth conditions and entailment relations involved in the *if-then* conditional of natural language.

In such areas of investigation, the working hypothesis of a semantic competence thus seems vindicated. Furthermore, because the object of investigation is an idealized, abstract entity free from vague parameters, it is possible to formulate one's theory in a precise, mathematical manner. The assumption opens the door for using the rigorous methods of logic in this area of research.

However justified the formal semanticist's notion of semantic competence is elsewhere, it runs into trouble as we move to propositional attitudes and other psychological contexts.

The problem could be stated in a number of ways, one of which is the following.

The formal semanticist's notion of semantic competence abstracts away from various human limitations, e.g. from limitations in making logical inferences. From his point of view all entailments are on a par and the only interesting question concerns the characterization of the whole class of them. The formal semanticist aims at a characterization of all of the logical consequences of a given sentence, even if some of them are so complex that hardly any humans realize that they follow from the sentence. Such human limitations are considered performance phenomena, not of relevance of the formal semanticist's competence model.

However, propositional attitude attributions explicitly talk about mental states of agents who are not logically omniscient. Thus propositional attitude attributions can be sensitive to distinctions that an abstract competence model has no way of dealing with, precisely because it abstracted away from the psychological limitations that give rise to the distinctions in the first place. For instance, a competence model of the semantics of a sentence S may perhaps disregard the fact that most human speakers do not realize that S entails Q – but an adequate treatment of the sentence "John believes that S" cannot. Thus the abstract level of competence that seems to do useful work elsewhere in semantics appears to be an impediment in connection with propositional attitudes.

The issue, therefore, is this: Does the semantic competence-performance distinction make sense in the field of propositional attitudes and other psychological contexts? Or, putting it slightly differently, what is the 'data base' for a competence theory of propositional attitudes? No generally accepted answer to these questions is in the offing. It is for this sort of reason that one can say without exaggeration that the semantics of propositional attitudes and belief-sentences is the deepest and most consequential open problem in the field of semantics at the present time. It is therefore appropriate that propositional attitudes and belief-sentences be discussed in several essays in the present collection.

One might think that such considerations straightforwardly show how ill-founded the formal semanticist's notion of semantic competence was in the first place. But to dispense with an abstract notion of semantic competence altogether will not do either. As we have already noted, there are areas of investigation where the hypothesis has led to major insights. For one thing, it is hard to see how those insights could be accounted for by a theory tied exclusively to semantic performance, or even by a theory that operates with a significantly less stringent notion of 'semantic competence'. In the areas where the formal semanticist's approach works, it appears to work better than any rival account. (Below, Janet Fodor proposes a psychologically motived semantic treatment of quantifiers; as the reader will see, part of her problem is to make the theory score on the home field of the model-theoretician's 'competence model'.) Even more telling, however, is the fact that when one sentence entails another, they stand in that relation because of the meanings that speakers know the two sentences to have; this ensures that the entailment relation holds between the sentences, whether or not speakers realize it holds. Precisely this possibility of failing to be aware of consequences of one's knowledge is characteristic of the distinction between competence which a person has and performance that imperfectly reflects it.

What further complicates matters is that some of the psychologically-oriented theories of procedural semantics *do* endorse a semantic competence-performance distinction. The distinction, however, is not identical with the one with which formal semanticists operate – a fact which has led some formal semanticists to conclude that process-based models are *per definitionem* performance models. A process-based formalism does not necessarily indicate a performance model, however, and procedure-related notions need not be lumped together with full-fledged performance notions (such as those dealing with memory limitations). It remains an open problem at the present time whether a notion of semantic competence acceptable to both traditions can be found.

The Semantics-Pragmatics Distinction

Another methodological controversy in present day meaning-theory concerns the legitimacy of a sharp semantics-pragmatics distinction. Here a terminological precaution is in order: often 'semantics' is taken as synonymous with the theory of meaning itself. In discussions of the semantics-pragmatics distinction 'semantics' is taken, however, as a level of description at which meaning is considered independently of the *use* of language. The controversy concerns the legitimacy of 'semantics' thus understood.

Formal semantics has assumed that there is such a level of the study of meaning. Some have even suggested that in order to characterize the notions the model-theoretician is most interested in – truth conditions and the entailment-relation – it is imperative to abstract away from language use. One argument takes note of the fact that some entailment-relations obtain between sentences so complex that no human speaker could comprehend, much less use, any of them. Thus restricting the attention to sentences as used would restrict the entailment-relation in an undesirable way.

Abstracting away from the use of language has turned out to be a useful strategy. It has proved useful even in studying such expressions as demonstratives and indexicals, whose key features evidently are highly context- and use-dependent. (Cf. e.g. Kaplan, 1977.)

The situation is somewhat more controversial in the area of questions and answers, which is the topic of Nuel Belnap's paper below. Belnap's treatment is in the tradition of formal semantics, and it presupposes that there is a context-independent notion of question- and answerhood. In this light Belnap's paper is of potential methodological consequence, even apart from its interest as a contribution to formal semantics.

However well the hypothesis of a use-independent level of abstraction may work elsewhere, it runs into trouble in the field of propositional attitudes. It is far from obvious whether we can talk about truth and falsity of propositional attitude attributions *without* reference to essentially pragmatic, context-dependent parameters.

One way to see the point is to observe how uncertain our intuitions are concerning the truth conditions of even the simplest of propositional attitude attributions. This matter is discussed at length in Partee's and Johnson-Laird's papers below and we shall not repeat it here. Notice, however, that if we try to sharpen our intuitions about the truth conditions of a propositional attitude attribution by considering its entailments, we are not much better off. In fact, it is hardly possible to list *any* uncontroversially valid inferences from, say, one belief-attribution to another (apart from such lexicon-related inferences as "knowledge implies belief"). Thus, putting it slightly differently, it can be argued that for belief-sentences and other propositional attitude sentences there is no genuine notion of entailment for a semanticist to characterize.

This is not to say that there is no interest in the various 'logics of propositional attitudes' that have been proposed. (Cf. e.g. Hintikka, 1962, 1969.) The proposed logics of belief (say) are interesting as attempts to characterize (something like) the logic of completely rational belief. But belief-attributions in natural language do not speak about rational and logically omniscient agents.

The Epistemological Status of Meaning

A controversy analogous to that between psychological and formal semantics can be located in recent philosophical discussions about meaning. There the contrasting positions arise as distinct stands on the epistemological status of the notion of meaning.

Does the theory of meaning concern what the speaker knows when he knows the meaning? Is meaning basically an epistemological concept, one connected intimately with what a speaker can know? The modern followers of Frege – philosophers such as Dummett, Castañeda and Schiffer – have answered in the affirmative and have stressed meaning as an epistemological concept. (See their works listed in the bibliography.)

The mainstream of modern philosophers, however, takes a different line. They build on the influential work of the so-called theorists of direct reference (Kripke, Kaplan et al) and argue that an epistemological difference does not imply a difference in meaning. Thus, these theorists hold, "Tully is short" and "Cicero is short" mean one and the same thing even though a competent speaker may not know this. According to these theorists, meanings are not 'in the head'.

The reader will readily discern that these anti-epistemological theorists of the modern philosophy of language are philosophical counterparts to anti-psychologistic model-theoreticians of linguistic semantics.

In the present collection the philosophical issues concering meaning will not be discussed in detail. However, Johnson-Laird's and Partee's discussion of the meanings-are-not-in-the-head thesis show how closely these philosophical issues are related to foundational issues of linguistic semantics.

It is interesting to note in this connection what the single most important problem area is that has made philosophers doubt the celebrated anti-epistemological theory of direct reference, to wit: propositional attitudes, especially belief-sentences. Propositional attitude and other belief-sentences remain the outstanding open problem both in model-theoretic semantics for natural language and in the philosophical theory of 'direct reference'.

SECTION III

We shall now sketch the contents of each of the contributions.

1. Philip Johnson-Laird's lengthy essay 'Formal Semantics and the Psychology of Meaning' compares in detail the formal and psychological approaches to semantics. The paper, seeking a link between the work on semantics in linguistics and philosophy on the one hand, and psychology on the other, serves as an excellent introduction to the basic problems facing cognitive science in this area.

Johnson-Laird notes that various superficially diverse psychological theories of meaning have one important assumption in common: they presuppose that meaning is represented by *an expression in a mental language* (a language of thought as it were). These expressions in the mental language provide what is called *propositional representation* of sentences (and other expressions in the language we are studying). It is part and parcel of the very starting point of this kind of psychological approach that it operates with concepts that are 'in the head'. In this respect, they sharply differ from the basic concepts of formal (logical) semantics.

Contrary to what some other scholars have argued, Johnson-Laird holds that there is a fundamental distinction between propositional representations (expressions in a language of thought) and so-called *mental models*. The former are *descriptions* of structures that satisfy a given sentence whereas the latter are themselves such structures of evaluation. Thus on the level of mental models, one's mind represents the meaning of a given expression directly, simply by constructing a model that satisfies the expression. Johnson-Laird argues that such mental models, as distinguished from sentences in a mental language, could be used to explain psychological differences between different logically indistinguishable inferences: the construction of mental models calls for extra-logical principles that can help to explain phenomena left untouched by logic. Johnson-Laird also presents experimental evidence in support of his general conviction.

Given the independent status of mental models and their need in psychological semantics the question naturally arises: what is the relation of these models to the models of formal (model-theoretic) semantics? This question is theoretically important, because it links together the two divergent enterprises of cognitive science.

Why not assume that the two types of models are wholly analogous? Why not simply assume that the models of formal semantics deal with *what* is computed when a sentence is understood whereas mental models concern *how* it is computed? Johnson-Laird locates four types of problems with this straightforward line.

(a) The problem of lexical semantics. Firstly, formal semanticists typically consider lexical semantics to lie outside their domain, whereas according to psychological semantics it is an integral part of the whole enterprise. Secondly and more importantly, it has been forcefully argued by Putnam and others that the meanings of certain crucial lexical items – most notably so-called natural kind terms – are not 'in the head', and thus any adequate meaning-theoretic analysis of lexical items would have to call for concepts psychological semantics cannot provide. Putting it slightly differently, it would seem that Putnam's arguments show that lexical semantics is not knowable and that therefore it is fundamentally different from the structural semantics which formal semantics is concerned with.

This conclusion, Johnson-Laird suggests, is premature. He argues, *pace* Putnam, that the meanings of lexical items are in the head and that lexical semantics is as knowable as structural semantics. (Though we cannot review Johnson-Laird's detailed and sophisticated discussion in detail here, please take note of our further comments below in discussion of Partee's paper.)

(b) The second main problem, Johnson-Laird notes, in associating mental models with the models of formal semantics is that the latter often employ the notion of a possible world. How this notion could be built into mental models is far from obvious. Furthermore, since psychology tells us that humans have difficulties in manipulating several alternatives at once, in processing modal statements a human can be expected to construct perhaps just one mental model, not a whole collection of 'alternative' ones. This surely indicates that from the psychological viewpoint, possible-worlds-oriented formal semantics is off the track, thus shaking the hopes of a direct link between the two notions of model.

(c) The third problem that Johnson-Laird discusses about identifying formal and mental models with one another is due to the fact that mental models are *incomplete*. Mental models are characteristically partial ones – not all sentences of the language can be evaluated with respect to them (not even those with the same primitive vocabulary). This undermines, Johnson-Laird suggests, the possibility of identifying mental models with the models of formal semantics. (It is not altogether obvious to us, however, why the conclusion would follow. Surely a formal semanticist is not compelled to operate with complete models. In fact, recent work by Barwise and Perry shows how useful partial models can be in model-theoretic semantics.)

(d) The fourth issue Johnson-Laird discusses is one that several other writers in the present collection also address: the problem of propositional attitudes. Johnson-Laird argues that none of the proposed refinements of formal semantics are adequate. Attitude attributions are sensitive to the psychological limitations of the agents to whom the attitude is attributed – limitations including even some ignorance of language itself. These psychological limitations must be taken into account in analyzing discourse about propositional attitudes, a fact which requires rejection of the basic anti-psychologistic and realistic convictions of formal semantics. Instead, Johnson-Laird recommends a 'constructivist' approach to propositional attitudes, an approach that would be explicitly psychological and would emphasize the communicative aspects of language. (For, as Johnson-Laird points out, communication is possible even in the presence of considerable ignorance of the language itself. This fact is seldom appreciated in model-theoretical approaches to meaning.)

Johnson-Laird ends his discussion by calling for a meaning-theoretic analysis that would be mentalistic and that would concentrate on the mental processes through which language links with reality.

2. M. J. Cresswell's paper 'The Autonomy of Semantics' contrasts with Johnson-Laird's in emphasizing model-theoretic semantics as opposed to more psychological approaches. Cresswell, one of the leading logicians working in semantics, argues for the basic conviction underlying all model-theoretic semantics: the key role of the concept of truth in the theory of meaning.

Cresswell raises the question of whether semantics can be considered an autonomous discipline, a discipline based on the notion of truth and *not* concerned with a 'language of thought' or anything of that nature. The way the very question is put illustrates the basic issue of the present collection (and of cognitive science as concerned with meaning more generally) – the status of mentalistic (psychological) elements in semantics.

Cresswell first argues that if the behavior of propositional attitude locutions is disregarded, a truth-based, model-theoretic semantics can plausibly be assigned the status of a special science. According to this position, although possible worlds (or what have you) which are alluded to in specifying truth conditions presumably have *some* mental representation, it would not be a semanticist's concern to explicate the nature of that representation. Thus the key conceptions underlying the model-theoretician's approach would be vindicated and the need to enrich the theory with more psychological ingredients abolished.

However, Cresswell notes, this comfortable picture is blurred by the behavior of propositional attitude locutions, most notably by belief-sentences. The reason, of course, is that no adequate way is known of dealing with propositional attitude using the resources of model-theoretic (truth-based) semantics.

Unlike Johnson-Laird, Cresswell thinks that the situation does not call for a radical change of fundamentals in formal semantics. Cresswell goes on to review some of the proposals to correct model-theoretic semantics so as to deal with propositional attitudes. (The proposals are: the suggestion to postulate 'propositions' as separate, primitive entities, which are not reducible to the notion of truth; the suggestion to introduce so-called impossible possible worlds; the suggestion to treat attitude locutions as metalinguistic.) Cresswell argues that all the proposed solutions are defective, however.

Cresswell then goes on to make his own suggestion, based on the following two ideas.

First, Cresswell suggests that propositional attitude attributions involve various 'levels of construal', different ways to understand the sentence in question. Only some levels of construal make the attitude attribution sensitive to substitution of logically equivalent expressions.

Secondly, Cresswell brings in David Lewis' notion of a 'structured meaning', which explicates the meaning of a sentence partly as a function of the way the meaning is composed of its various constituents. (That is, structured meanings are sensitive to syntactic structure also.) The proposal is, then, that the meaning of an attitude attribution depends not just on the meaning of the complement-clause but on the 'structured meaning' of it. (To refer to 'structured meanings' in connection with attitude attributions is of course not a new idea; Carnap suggested it already with his notion of 'intensional isomorphism'.)

Cresswell is not altogether happy with his solution to the problem of propositional attitudes, in particular he is uncomforable with having have to postulate various levels of construal. But he argues that such levels are needed on other proposals to remedy the model-theoretic approach as well.

3. Barbara Hall Partee's paper 'Belief-Sentences and the Limits of Semantics' demonstrates how intimately the problems of belief- (and other attitude) sentences are bound with basic methodological issues in current semantic theory.

The paper begins with a survey of the problems facing formal semantics in the field of propositional attitudes. Partee notes that the failure of logical omniscience for human speakers is the reason, not just for the failure of substitutivity of logically equivalent sentences in attitude contexts, but also for the limits on our knowledge of the semantics of our language. This reflects a basic line of thought of Partee's paper: she argues that there is an intimate connection between our semantic competence and the semantics of propositional attitude locutions.

Could model-theoretic semantics be interpreted as providing a super-competence model, one that would characterize the semantics of an omniscient speaker of English? Partee argues that the answer is in the negative. The omniscient speaker would know that the human agents whose attitudes we are talking about are *not* logically omniscient and therefore may not recognize the logical equivalence of two syntactically distinct sentences. Thus the super-competent omniscient speaker would *not* infer "John believes that *Q*" from "John believes that *S*" on the basis that he, the omniscient speaker, knows that *S* entails *Q*.

Partee next goes on to discuss the 'raw data' that a semantics of belief-sentences (and other attitude attributions) should explain. She notes that a straightforward answer is not in the offing. In particular, the criteria that apply elsewhere in semantics do not seem applicable for belief-sentences. Thus for instance synonymy judgements and judgements of entailment relations are highly controversial and hardly provide any clear-cut positive data. It is much easier to provide inferences involving belief-sentences that are *not* valid than inferences that are.

Partee's discussion lucidly pinpoints the basic problem of belief- and other attitude sentences. As long as we do not agreed even about the phenomena our semantic theory should account for, we can hardly expect that anything like an adequate theory can be presented. Putting it slightly differently, since formal semantics is designed to capture intuitive judgements of entailment and truth conditions, it is clear that the approach runs into trouble in an area where those pretheoretical judgements are themselves vague and controversial.

Partee next discusses the notion of semantic competence. This question, she notes, is crucial because it appears that the notions of semantic competence implicit in formal semantics and psychological semantics are *prima facie* incompatible. Any 'common goal' position must come up with a notion of semantic competence compatible with both enterprises.

Many entailment-relations are recursively undecidable. How then could the 'semantic competence' that captures such undecidable inferences be finitely represented in the head of a finite creature? This would be possible only if we take semantic competence to be about what is determined by what is known by the speaker, not about what he knows in any such sense as being present to his mind (whether consciously or tacitly). However, she goes on to argue, this would mean that semantic competence should be kept free of psychologically flavored notions such as judging or understanding.

But can a complete, finitely representable semantics be given at all? In the next section of her paper Partee proposes that it cannot and she argues for this in the sequel. Her point is that one can reconcile the two seemingly incompatible approaches to semantics precisely by abandoning the assumption of a fixed, finitely representable semantics.

Partee's main evidence comes from belief-sentences involving theory-laden lexical items (such as "semantics" or "psychology"). The behavior of such expressions has been largely ignored in discussions to date.

An example is

(4) Loar believes that semantics is a branch of psychology but Thomason believes that semantics is a branch of mathematics.

The point is that the relevant features of the theory-laden expression "semantics" do not concern anything like the meaning of the expression "semantics". In explicating what is involved in (4) it won't do to appeal – as one might be inclined to do in view of Putnam's (1975) work on natural kind terms – to 'experts' or to an eventual 'correct theory' of scientific disciplines. As far as (4) is concerned, there simply is *no* way to fix the meaning of the expression "semantics" that would not destroy the intuitive meaning of the sentence.

Here it is useful to recall a point Johnson-Laird made in his paper. He argued that the extension of certain lexical items is *not fixed at all.* Johnson-Laird emphasized the point, often not appreciated by model-theoreticians, into any necessary and sufficient conditions at all.

Let us contrast Johnson-Laird's move with that of Putnam. What Putnam did was put the meaning of certain lexical items outside the head of an average speaker. But he still assumed that *there is* a fixed meaning and a fixed extension are definable only by the relevant 'experts'. Johnson-Laird in contrast argues, à la the later Wittgenstein, that for some lexical items there is simply no fixed extension at all. *Nobody* need know the precise meaning! This is essentially Partee's point: no fixed interpretation of the language is in the offing. As she points out, this means that any model-theoretic approach to semantics which starts off with a fixed set of basic semantic entities is doomed to failure.

This conclusion may seem startling but Partee points out that what we face here is a "remarkable adaptation" for coping with our all too familiar intrinsic limitations. We are better off not restricting ourselves to a fixed and rigid metaphysics and a fixed language.

Partee concludes her paper by suggesting that the formal and psychological approaches to meaning are in fact compatible and that their apparent conflicts result from a seemingly natural and harmless but in fact fallacious assumption: the assumption that human language must have a finitely representable (fixed) semantics.

4. Robert C. Moore and Gary G. Hendrix's paper 'Computational Models of Belief and the Semantics of Belief Sentences' approaches belief-sentences from a computational viewpoint. The idea is to present a computational system that would provide a model for human belief-structures and the semantics of belief-sentences.

The computational approach to meaning shares important basic assumptions with psychological semantics. In both cases, a 'language of thought' plays a key role. Thus, Moore and Hendrix argue that since belief is a psychological state, the corresponding expressions in natural language should semantically be treated in terms of psychological processes and states.

In keeping with this, their basic conviction is that to possess a belief is to stand in a computational relation to the appropriate expression in an internal language. A 'belief set' is the set of expressions of the internal language to which the system is related in the appropriate way.

Moore and Hendrix take the internal language as the language of ordinary quantification theory, together with intensional operators for propositional attitudes.

The language is assumed to have a well-defined deduction relation defined over it "since people clearly draw inferences from their beliefs". Since Moore and Hendrix do not elaborate on this we do not know just what kind of logic the deduction relation of the internal language provides us with. Notice, however, that if the deduction relation is anything like that studied in ordinary logic – and therefore transitive – the well-known problems of logical omniscience would seem to crop up immediately. Since the authors suggest that beliefs are individuated "more or less as are formulas in the internal language" – which *would* avoid the problem of logical omniscience – it seems that the deduction relation of the internal language does not correspond to any familiar logic. (Or, alternatively, that the 'logic' depends on the agent in question.)

The basic semantic proposal Moore and Hendrix make is that a belief sentence '*a* believes that *S*' is true if and only if *a* "has the formula in his internal language that corresponds appropriately to '*S*' in his belief set, or can perhaps be derived in his belief set with limited effort". This proposal, apart from obvious terminological differences, is very much like so-called quotational theories of belief-sentences. According to them, a belief-sentence says that the agent in question stands in a certain relation to a sentence, indicated by the complement clause. In this sense, Moore and Hendrix's computational approach to belief-sentences can be viewed as an effort to put that old suggestion on the firm footing of computer science.

The problem they discuss next is how sameness of meaning should be defined for the expressions of different people's internal language's. (The authors suggest that the syntax itself is innate and universal.) While they do not point it out explicitly, it is clear that this question is of crucial import here. Moore and Hendrix have reduced the truth conditions of the belief-attribution '*a* believes that *S*' to *a*'s standing in a certain relation to a formula *P* of *a*'s internal language. But as long as we don't know what the expression *P* of *a*'s internal language *means* – as long as we have no inter-subjective semantics for that expression *qua* an expression in *a*'s internal language – we have no grasp of the truth conditions of the belief-attribution, either.

The issue at hand vividly illustrates the paradox of belief-sentences: propositional attitude psychology has means to make very fine discriminations, but only at the expense of difficulties in adjusting to the social (inter-subjective) nature of language and semantics. It is hard to reconcile the 'objective' nature of semantics with the 'subjective' aspects of propositional attitude attributions.

Moore and Hendrix have an elaborate proposal to give their notion of 'meaning for an individual' inter-subjective meaning. The reader is referred to their paper for details.

Here we shall only point out a connection between their paper and Partee's. Partee argued that there is no way to fix a semantic interpretation for even a single dialect of English in a way that would not do injustice to propositional attitude locutions. This point could be put in Moore's and Hendrix's terms by saying that, assuming their basic proposal for handling belief-sentences is right, there is *no way* to fix a cross-agent synonymity-relation between the internal languages of different agents.

5. Janet Dean Fodor's paper 'The Mental Representation of Quantifiers' sketches a system of semantic representations which aims to be psychologically realistic. The idea is to develop a system of semantic representations in terms of certain types of mental models. Fodor's paper links closely with

Johnson-Laird's essay, which also discusses in detail the status of mental models in semantics.

Fodor is concerned mainly with representing the usual existential and universal quantifiers. Thus she attacks the model-theorist's abstract, anti-mentalistic system of representation on its home ground.

Recall that a model-theoretic semanticist is not opposed to the idea of 'mental representations' or such *per se*. His conviction is only that such psychologically motivated concepts are of no semantic utility (in his sense of 'semantics'). In order to convince the model-theoretician, Fodor must demonstrate that her system of representations will account for the data *he*, the model-theoretician, is interested in.

Thus, she sets out to show how the most elementry semantic features of quantifier sentences – quantifier dependence – can be accounted for on her theory. Towards the end of her paper she also outlines how entailment relations could be accounted for in her system.

The main target of Fodor's theory, however, is the psychological data – phenomena a model-theoretician's system of representations was never intended to account for. These are phenomena such as that certain entailment relations are easy others difficult, for speakers to discern, and that certain types of sentence are easy, others difficult, for speakers to process. One of the basic foundational issues of the cognitive science of meaning is precisely whether it is possible to hit all these targets at once.

Before expounding her own theory, Fodor reviews various proposals that have been made for handling the most obvious psychological data concerning quantifier processing. Her extensive review includes discussions of 'prefixed quantifier representations', the representations in terms of hierarchical structures and 'feature representations'. Fodor argues that none of these approaches are adequate and that they do not account for the relevant psychological data.

Fodor calls her own system 'model-of-the-world representations'. The idea is to work in terms of models that are constructed step-wise as a sentence is processed from left to right. Fodor represents the models using diagrams that indicate the relative scope of the quantifiers. For instance the two readings of 'Every child saw a squirrel' are represented by the following two diagrams:

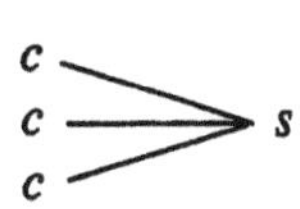

saw

c ——— *s*
c ——— *s*
c ——— *s*

saw

Thus, a universal quantifier introduces a family of 'individuals' to the mental model, an existential quantifier just one, unless the quantifier is in the scope of a universal quantifier. In the latter case the quantifier introduces an 'individual' for each 'individual' introduced to the mental model by that universal quantifier.

Fodor does not state the precise rules for constructing her mental models on the basis of the surface form of a sentence. The basic idea is clear, however. The model is constructed directly from the surface structure of the sentence and no intermediary 'logical form' is postulated. In particular, quantifier scopes are *not* represented by employing an intermediary structure which reorders the quantifiers, to yield the right logical force. Rather, what logicians indicate by reordering the quantifiers, Fodor represents by a *change* in the mental model. The quantifiers themselves are processed in exactly the same order in each case (for each reading).

The mental model is constructed through various transition-stages which may change the model quite drastically. These changes in the mental model are precisely the ingredients Fodor needs for her psychological measure predicting which readings are easy to process and which ones are not.

For instance, the model construction corresponding to the ∀E reading of "a child saw every squirrel" is more complex than that corresponding to the E∀ reading of the same sentence. In the former case the construction proceeds from

c ———

saw

to

(5) *c* ——— *s*
c ——— *s*
c ——— *s*

saw

and thus requires changes in a part of the model already constructed. The transition is more complex than the one corresponding to the E∀ reading, which is the preferred one:

(Recall that since the quantifiers are 'evaluated' from left to right even in the ∀E reading, the first stage of model construction is provided in each case by an individual introduced by "a child".)

Fodor argues that in this way one can explain the relative difficulty of readings where a universal quantifier extends backwards (leftwards), as well as the relative easiness of readings where a universal quantifier extends forwards (to the right).

We cannot discuss Fodor's rich paper in more detail here but must be content to note the following general objection a model-theoretician is likely to make concerning the kind of proposal Fodor presents. In order to satisfy the model-theoretician's criteria of adequancy Fodor's theory should define a function from 'semantic representations' (in her sense) to something like truth conditions. It is not immediately obvious how that could be done, however. For instance, why is the mental model (5), above, a representation for a reading of 'every child saw a squirrel' rather than a representation for a reading of 'three children saw a squirrel' or of 'three children saw three squirrels'? Possibly Fodor will allude to 'the derivational history' of the mental model; if so, it remains to be seen how the details are worked out. The problem is that a 'mental model' – even together with its 'derivational history' – seems insufficient to serve as a semantic representation satisfying a logician's criteria of adequacy. These require that a characterization of the semantics of a sentence should (at least indirectly) provide a *class* of models – all the models in which the sentence is true. It is not immediately obvious that Fodor's system achieves this, in spite of its explanatory power on the psychological side of the fence.

These remarks are not intended as criticism of Fodor's paper, but rather serve to illustrate just how difficult is it to satisfy both the adequacy criteria of psychologically oriented semantics and those of formal semantics. Once again we not that in the present state of the art, we are not in a position to say whether the goal is achievable even in principle. This remains one of the outstanding foundational problems in semantics at present.

Nuel D. Belnap, Jr's paper 'Questions and Answers in Montague Grammar' is concerned with presenting and defending a model-theoretic analysis of the semantics of questions. In the present context, the topic of questions is important for reasons of several different kinds. One is the inevitable association of questions with answers. Concerning semantics, one of the more important roles that a question's meaning has is in determining what constitutes an answer to the question. Virtually all theories about the semantics of questions trade heavily on the relationship between questions and their answers, which leads once more to some fundamental issues we have met already.

For some questions there seems to be considerable variability from one speaker to the next in what is acceptable as a satisfactory answer. Does this indicate that these questions have no fixed, determinate meaning? Or is the variation traceable to a different origin? It seems to be the case that a major source of the variability is differences in the amount and content of shared knowledge and beliefs on the part of questioner and respondent – echoing the factor which complicates propositional attitude attributions. Human imperfection in drawing out logical consequences also makes itself felt in the domain of question-answer acceptability. For instance, no one who asks "Is the square root of two a rational number?" is likely to feel his question has been adequately answered if the respondent merely states the definitions of "square root", "two" and "rational number", though these do logically imply a negative answer. Thus it is crucial for Belnap to characterize clearly the relationship between what a question means and what constitutes an answer to it, as he in fact does.

Another reason that questions are important here is the allegation which is sometimes made that model theory, with its roots in the notion of truth, is inescapably bound to declarative or statement-making sentences and cannot yield a semantic analysis of questions or other nondeclarative sentences. If correct, this objection would be a crushing blow against model-theoretic semantics. But as Belnap and in fact others before him have shown, model theory does provide semantic analyses of questions which attain a high degree of adequacy. (See his paper for a clear exposition of one such analysis, resulting from joint research by him and the late Michael Bennett.)

This point is significant in connection with an interesting observation Belnap makes about the relationship of formal or model-theoretic semantics to the mental processes by which people actually understand questions and other sentences. He considers the absence from existing model-theoretic semantics of process-oriented concepts a virtue rather than a failing. This very freedom from procedural concepts allows a model-theoretic characterization of, say, English semantics to provide a test of correctness for any proposed processing theory about meaning in English. To the extent that the model-theoretic description gets the meanings right, any procedural account must produce the same meanings for sentences or be seen to be an incorrect account of the language's semantics. This is no moot point, as procedural descriptions exist for the semantics of English questions. In fact, question-answering programs for computers are where procedural semantics originated. How correct then are these programs? This question unfortunately remains unanswered, for the comparison of results given by model theory with those of procedural theory has not been made. When it is made, of course, it will be important to check each area of disagreement between the two theories to see which is closer to the actual facts as given by speakers' intuitive judgements.

Belnap's account of the semantics of questions is couched in a version of model theory that has come to be called Montague Grammar. He argues that this has the additional virtue of employing an auxiliary formal language which perspicuously displays the particular semantic resources his model theory make use of, thereby facilitating the task of seeing that the model theory really does get the semantics of English sentences right. This feeling of perspicuity presumably explains the perennial popularity of 'regimented' formal languages in semantic theory (even when the meanings of the formalized expressions are left unclear). We have seen that auxiliary languages are popular both as media of mental representation and as computer-internal representations. When clear interpretations are given for these languages, they can indeed aid perspicuity.

In addition to discussing these issues and presenting a precise model-theoretic semantics for a fragment of English including many questions, Belnap offers insightful and stimulating observations concerning a variety of question types not included in his formal treatment.

7. Willem J. M. Levelt's paper 'Linearization in Describing Spatial Nelworks' deals with problems in psycholinguistics and discourse analysis. The key notion of the paper is that of 'linearization', the ordering of clauses to a (linear) left-to-right structure.

Levelt's underlying hypothesis is that linearization has functional properties which are similar for various types of discourse. Some general features of linearization which do not depend on the content of the discourse are formulated by Levelt in the paper. The most basic is what Levelt calls 'Principle of Minimal Effort': everything else being equal, the speaker prefers to use descriptions which minimize the number and duration of elements on store (memory) and the length of the description.

Levelt argues for his general conviction in terms of a case study involving a well-defined type of discourse, the discourse concerning (certain very simple) spatial networks. The speaker is required to describe a network of a two-dimensional nodes which are related to one another by arcs, in such a way that hearer can reproduce the structure of the network on the basis of the description.

The main problem here is characteristic of all of linearization: how to represent multi-dimensional (in this case two-dimensional) information in speech, which characteristically is linearly ordered.

Levelt formulates two theoretical models for linearization. The first one of these he calls the 'speaker-oriented model' and the second the 'listener oriented model'. (We shall not describe these models here.)

Levelt tests the two models of linearization *vis-à-vis* experimental data. The data strongly support Levelt's models. The 'speaker-oriented model' characterizes the linearization patter of 'jumpers', speakers who, when describing the spatial networks, jump back to choice points. The 'hearer-oriented model' in turn characterizes the linearization pattern of 'movers', speakers who, when describing spatial networks, move back to choice points by retracing their earlier steps. ('Jumping' and 'moving' is here understood by reference to the spatial networks under description by the speaker.)

It is not immediately clear what 'linearization' entails for *semantics*. More generally, it remains to be seen whether the kind of psycholinguistic facts that linearization and the like are based on are reflected at the level of semantic structure. There is no doubt, however, that in choosing words to express an intended meaning, we must often choose a left-to-right order for the words on the basis of cognitive factors not uniquely determined by the meaning.

The University of Texas at Austin (S. P. and E. S.)
University of Helsinki (E. S.)

BIBLIOGRAPHY

Castañeda, H.-N.: 'On the Philosophical Foundations of the Theory of Communication: Reference', *Midwest Studies in Philosophy* 2 (1977), 165–168.

Davidson, D. and G. Harman (eds.): *Semantics of Natural Language*, D. Reidel, Dordrecht, 1972.

Dummett, Michael: *Frege*, Duckworth, London, 1972.

Hintikka, Jaakko: *Knowledge and Belief*, Cornell University Press, Ithaca, New York, 1962.
Hintikka, Jaakko: 'Semantics for Propositional Attitudes' in Hintikka's *Models for Modalities*, D. Reidel, Dordrecht, 1969.
Isard, S. D.: 'Changing the Context' in E. L. Keenan (ed.), *Formal Semantics of Natural Language*, Cambridge University Press, Cambridge, 1975.
Kamp, Hans: 'A Theory of Truth and Semantic Representation', forthcoming.
Kaplan, David: *Demonstratives*, unpublished UCLA mimeo, 1977.
Kripke, Saul: 'Naming and Necessity' in Davidson and Harman (1972).
Montague, Richard: *Formal Philosophy*, edited with an introduction by R. H. Thomason, Yale University Press, New Haven, 1974.
Putnam, Hilary: 'The Meaning of "Meaning"' in Putnam's *Philosophical Papers*, Cambridge University Press, Cambridge, 1975.
Saarinen, Esa (ed.), *Game-Theoretical Semantics*, D. Reidel, Dordrecht, 1979.
Schiffer, S. R.: 'The Basis of Reference', *Erkenntnis* 13 (1978), 171–206.
Winograd, T.: *Understanding Natural Language*, Edinburgh University Press, Edinburgh, 1972.

P. N. JOHNSON-LAIRD

FORMAL SEMANTICS AND THE PSYCHOLOGY OF MEANING

I: INTRODUCTION

Logicians have only related language to models in various ways; psychologists have only related it to the mind; the real task, however, is to show how language relates to the world through the agency of the mind. This task is, at present, beyond the resources of Cognitive Science, but there is some chance of success by pooling the skills and knowledge of its contributing disciplines. The aim of this paper is accordingly to try to bring together formal and psychological semantics in order to determine the nature of the relations between them. In writing it, I have found myself in effect attempting to make a tunnel that would link up the heights of formal semantics, where the light has an unreal clarity, to the low lying realities of psychology, where the atmosphere is, to say the least, somewhat murky. Like a tunneler, I have tended to work first from one direction to the other, and then, when I reached an *impasse*, to switch round and work from the other direction. Whether or not the two halves would in the end join up – and I would, as it were, be able to shake hands with myself – was something that was unforeseeable at the outset. The project was an experiment: how could I tell what to think until I read what I wrote? Fortunately, there were a number of excellent surveys to guide me, and indeed it would be as well to begin with a brief exploration of the two areas with a view to finding some potential routes between them.

Formal Semantics

A language can be provided with a semantic interpretation with respect, not to the world, but to a model that has an assignment function from the well-formed expressions of the language to elements in the model structure. For readers who are unfamiliar with model-theoretic semantics, Table 1 presents a very simple example for a very small fragment of English. The example illustrates the fact that the model structure belies its name and consists simply in a structureless set of entities; in what follows, I shall for simplicity often refer to it as a model, but the reader should bear in mind

S. Peters and E. Saarinen (eds.), Processes, Beliefs, and Questions, 1–68.

that logicians use that term to refer to both the model structure and the assignment function. The example also illustrates the fact that there are two main sorts of semantic rule used to specify an interpretation. First, there are rules for *lexical* semantics, which provide an interpretation for the basic lexical items of the language. Second, there are rules for *structural* semantics, which build up the interpretations of complex expressions from the interpretations of their constituents, and which may introduce further words such as *and*. These rules are generally contrived to operate in parallel with the syntactic rules of the language, e.g. a syntactic rule in the example specifies how to form a conjunction using *and*, and the corresponding semantic rule specifies its interpretation. Logicians, of course, are seldom interested in a single model for a language, but rather in principles that hold over any arbitrary model.

In many formal languages and in certain fragments of natural language, the structural rules can establish what a complicated expression picks out in a model as a function of what its constituent expressions pick out in the model. But, as Frege (1892) established long ago, no such rules can work for natural language as a whole, because different expressions that refer to the same entity cannot be freely substituted in a sentence *salva veritate*. For example, the assertion that "William Buckley wants to meet the leader of the Conservative party" is not necessarily equivalent to the assertion that "William Buckley wants to meet Mrs. Thatcher." The first assertion could be true and the second one false if its subject, Mr. Buckley, does not know that Mrs. Thatcher is the leader of the Conservative party. From such considerations, Frege distinguished between the sense (or intension) of an expression and its reference (or extension), and argued that in certain contexts the interpretation of an expression should be not its extension but its intension; in drawing this distinction he laid the foundations for a formal semantics of natural language.

Subsequently, Tarski (1956) showed how the notion of truth could be defined for a formal language. In particular, he specified how to cope with expressions of the form, "Every man loves a woman who loves him," where the constituent, "who loves him", cannot have a truth value in isolation. Tarski's ingenious idea is to introduce a more general notion, *satisfaction*, which applies to such constituents, and to use it in turn to define truth. An ordered pair of elements in a model, say, Mary and James, satisfies an expression such as "who loves him" if and only if the pair is in the extension of "loves" in the model.

Logicians have argued about whether or not there is a definite contrast to be drawn between analytic and synthetic sentences, that is, whether or not

TABLE 1

A simple model-theoretic semantics for a very small fragment of English

The syntax of the fragment of English

Lexical items:

(1) There are three nouns: "John," "James," "Mary."
(2) There are two verbs: "loves," "hits."

Syntactic rules:

(1) If α and β are nouns and γ is a verb, then $\alpha^\frown\gamma^\frown\beta$ is a well-formed sentence, where "$\frown$" denotes a simple concatenation of lexical items.
(2) If ϕ and ψ are sentences, then $\phi^\frown$ "and" $^\frown\psi$ is a sentence.

The semantics of the fragment of English

There is a model structure containing the following individuals: John, James, Mary. There is a model assignment consisting of the following lexical rules:

(1) "John" is assigned the extension, John, in the model.
(2) "James" is assigned the extension, James, in the model.
(3) "Mary" is assigned the extension, Mary, in the model.
(4) "loves" is assigned as its extension the following set of ordered pairs: {⟨John, Mary⟩, ⟨James, Mary⟩}. We can equivalently treat such a verb as function from the set of ordered pairs of individuals to a truth value.
(5) "hits" is assigned as its extension the following set of ordered pairs: {⟨John, James⟩, ⟨James, John⟩}.

There are structural rules for building up the interpretation of sentences:

(1) A sentence of the form $\alpha^\frown\gamma^\frown\beta$ is true with respect to the model if and only if the ordered pair comprising the extension of α and the extension of β is a member of the set comprising the extension of γ.
(2) A sentence of the form $\phi^\frown$ "and" $^\frown\psi$ is true with respect to the model if and only if ϕ is true in the model and ψ is true in the model.

Examples

The strings of words, "John loves Mary" and "Mary loves John", are both well-formed sentences of the fragment. The model corresponds to the familiar 'triangle' in which two men love the same woman: "John loves Mary and James loves Mary" is true with respect to the model, but both "Mary loves John" and "Mary loves James" are false with respect to the model.

there really are sentences that are necessarily true simply in virtue of the meanings of the words they contain. A sentence such as, "All bachelors are unmarried", certainly appears to be analytic, but sceptics such as Quine (1953) have argued that the concept of analyticity is ultimately without foundation. Carnap (1956, Appendix) proposed a useful mechanism for stipulating that relations between such predicates as *bachelor* and *unmarried* support analytic truths: an assertion of the form, *for any x, if x is a bachelor, then x is unmarried*, is simply added to the formulation of the semantics of the language. He termed such assertions, "meaning postulates". One consequence of a meaning postulate is to restrict the set of models for a language to those that are in conformity with it, e.g., there can be no models in which an individual is both a bachelor and married, since bachelors are necessarily unmarried.

Natural languages also make an explicit use of the modal notions of necessity and possibility. The essential Leibnizian doctrine is that an assertion that is *necessarily* true is true in all possible worlds including the real world, and an assertion that is *possibly* true is true in some possible world(s). This idea lies at the heart of Kripke's (1963a, b) model-theoretic semantics for modal logics. What he introduced was the notion of an accessibility relation between possible worlds: an assertion is necessarily true in a particular world if and only if it is true in all possible worlds that are *accessible* to that world. It can be helpful to think of accessibility as analogous to conceivability (Hughes and Cresswell, 1968) – a world is accessible to us if we can conceive of it – but the analogy should not be pushed too far and is resisted by some theorists. Different assumptions about the relation of accessibility can be made, and depending upon them so the resulting semantics corresponds to different modal logics (see Part III of this paper).

The advent of a formal "possible worlds" semantics has illuminated Frege's distinction between sense (intension) and reference (extension). The intension of a sentence – the proposition that it expresses – can be treated as a function from the set of possible worlds onto the set of truth values;[1] the extension of the sentence is its truth value with respect to the particular "possible world" under consideration. Analogous distinctions can be drawn between the intensions and extensions of other expressions, such as noun phrases. Hence, the reason why one cannot freely interchange co-referential noun phrases *salva veritate*, such as substituting "Mrs. Thatcher" for "the leader of the Conservative party", is that although they have the same extension in the actual world at this moment, they do not have the same intensions. At other times, or in other possible worlds, their extensions differ.

The application of model-theoretic semantics to natural language by Montague (1974) and his associates, and by other like-minded theorists (e.g., Lewis, 1972; Parsons, 1972), has relied on the use of "possible worlds" semantics in order to cope with modal expressions, with verbs expressing such propositional attitudes as wants or beliefs, and with other "intensional" expressions. The word *alleged*, for example, is intensional in that when it modifies a noun, the resulting extension is not necessarily a function of the extension of that noun: *an alleged thief* is not necessarily a *thief*. Montague, in particular, has extended the apparatus of formal semantics in order to cope with various fragments of natural language, and shown how an elegant system of different semantic categories (or types) can be constructed to run along parallel lines with the grammatical categories of the fragment. In order to ensure maximal generality, his system initially interprets expressions intensionally; if a construction is extensional, then he introduces further machinery in order to capture that aspect of it.

There are a number of important methodological differences between model-theoretic semantics and theories of meaning proposed within the immediate tradition of transformational generative grammar (e.g. Katz and Fodor, 1963; Gruber, 1965; McCawley, 1968; Lakoff, 1971; Jackendoff, 1972). However, from the standpoint of psychology, there are three major aspects of formal semantics that it is necessary to concentrate upon:

(1) The intension of a declarative sentence is a function from a set of possible worlds, and a set of times, to a truth value.

(2) This function is derived from the intensions of the basic expressions in the sentence according to structural rules that work in parallel to the syntactic rules governing the sentence.

(3) The intensions of the basic expressions are taken as primitive: the interpretation function directly assigns intensions to each basic expression in the language.

What we shall be ultimately looking for is a relation between these principles and those of psychological semantics. There is no reason to suppose that there will be any direct connection, but the comparison could be revealing.

Psychological Semantics

Psychological theories of meaning are superficially diverse, but reflect some common underlying preoccupations. Whether they are based on semantic networks (e.g. Collins and Quillian, 1972; Norman and Rumelhart, 1975), decompositions into semantic features (e.g. Smith, Shoben, and Rips, 1974; Clark and Clark, 1977), or mental instantiations of meaning postulates (e.g. Kintsch, 1974; Fodor, Fodor and Garrett, 1975), they effectively suppose that meanings are represented by expressions in a mental language. In essence, they diverge only on the vocabulary of that mental language, and accordingly on how inferences based on the meanings of words are captured.[2] They provide what psychologists call ***propositional representations*** of sentences, and many theorists have argued that the same sort of representations – expressions in a mental language – also correspond to images, whether perceived or imagined (see e.g. Pylyshyn, 1973; Palmer, 1975; Anderson, 1976, 1978; Norman and Rumelhart, 1975).

Although a model structure in model-theoretic semantics can consist of a set of sentences with respect to which the sentences of the language under analysis are evaluated (see Hintikka's, 1963, use of such model sets), it is clear that the psychologists' propositional representations are to be taken, not as models, but as *descriptions* of models – a view that will be substantiated below. Moreover, their prime explanatory function is to explain phenomena that do not depend upon extensions, e.g. the way in which subjects evaluate analytic sentences such as "all canaries are birds". The theories are correspondingly weak or deliberately silent on the question of how language relates to the world. There is a nice irony in the fact that formal semantics *finesses* this problem by taking the intensions of basic expressions as primitive givens, while psychological semantics avoids the problem by concentrating its attention on other issues. (I cannot resist adding that *Language and Perception* was deliberately intended, not to shirk this issue, but to try to provide a basis for a psychological theory of meaning that dealt with extensions as well as intensions.)

If psychologists have generally dealt with meaning by proposing systems for representing propositions, then their theories are obviously radically incomplete. They have followed Montague (1974), on the proper treatment of quantification, only half way. They have provided a (semi-) formal language into which sentences of a natural language can be translated, but, while Montague went on to provide a model-theoretic interpretation for his intermediate language, which is a tensed intensional logic, psychologists have merely maintained a discreet silence. Logically speaking, there is no need to translate a natural language into an intermediate language: a model-theoretic semantics can be provided for it directly, as Montague (1974) did for the fragment characterized in his paper on English as a formal language. A cynic might accordingly characterize the psychologists' efforts in the words of the poet: they use the snaffle and the bit all right, but where's the bloody horse?

This is not quite fair, of course. The task for psychological semantics is neither to relate language to a model nor to relate it directly to the world. It is rather to show how language and the world are related to one another in the human mind, to show how the mental representation of sentences is related to the mental representation of the world. Hence, a reasonable research strategy for a psycholinguist is to concentrate upon the representation of sentences and to leave the representation of the world to those who study perception. This strategy depends on the assumption that relations between intensions are autonomous and can be characterized independently from questions of extension. It assumes, in other words, that a satisfactory account can be given of semantic properties such as ambiguity, and of semantic relations such as synonymy, without considering the way in which sentences are mentally related to their extensions in the world. As I have argued elsewhere, however, the assumption turns out to be false (see Johnson-Laird, 1979a), and it is necessary to recognize that a number of intensional phenomena can be accounted for only on the assumption that speakers and hearers build mental models of the extensions of linguistic expressions. Much of comprehension consists in constructing, not a representation of the propositions being expressed (i.e. a description of a model), but an actual mental model.

Mental Models and Propositional Representations

What is the difference between a mental model and a propositional representation? This question, or rather a specific version of it, has haunted psychologists ever since their interest in mental imagery revived in the mid-1960's. A mental image is perhaps the most striking subjective experience suggesting that we are able to construct and to manipulate internal models of the external world. Not long after the dramatic demonstrations by Shepard and his colleagues that one could estimate the amount of time taken to rotate an image in the mind's eye – about 60° per second for fairly simple three-dimensional objects (Shepard and Metzler, 1971) – several critics argued that the underlying representation of an image was nevertheless propositional (e.g. Pylyshyn, 1973; Palmer, 1975). Anderson (1976, 1978) has similarly argued that a theory making use of one sort of representation can be mimicked by another theory making use of the other sort of representation provided that the two theories encode stimuli into corresponding sets of equivalence classes. Such arguments have led many people to suppose that there is no fundamental difference between mental models (or their perceptible counterparts, images) and propositional representations. However, this view seems unwarranted.

The gist of an argument that can be made against it (see Johnson-Laird, 1979b) runs as follows. Either the claim that all representations are propositional in form is trivially true, or else it has empirical content but turns out to be false. The first horn of the dilemma is established by the fact that if a behavior can be modelled by an effective procedure, then it can be modelled by a Turing machine, and such a device can be described propositionally, i.e. by a set of propositions that characterize its transitions from one state to another, etc. The second horn of the dilemma arises from the concept of a propositional representation that we have already encountered, the idea of a formula in a mental language that expresses the intension of a sentence in a natural language. A contrast can be drawn between this sort of propositional representation and a mental model. Propositional representations and meaning postulates are unable, in principle, to give a satisfactory account of the uncertainties of transitivity associated with such spatial relations as *on the right of* and *at*, whereas the vagaries of these terms can be accommodated within a theory based on mental models (Johnson-Laird, 1979b). However, the simplest way to draw the distinction is by examining some empirical phenomena.

If you were reading a story, then you might very well come across the following sort of passage:

> It was a good fire and the room was illuminated by it. At one side of the fireplace was a heavy curtain, which covered the bay window we had seen from outside. On the other side was the door which communicated with the veranda. A desk stood in the centre, with a turning chair of shining red leather. Opposite was a large bookcase, with a marble bust of Athene on the top. In the corner between a bookcase and the wall, there stood a tall green safe, the firelight flashing back from the polished brass knobs upon its face.

You would be likely to form only a hazy idea of the exact layout of the room: a few details would stand out, the shining red chair, perhaps, or the firelight glinting off the knobs on the safe. But your representation would be very partial – indeed, it would have to be unless you were prepared to go beyond the information given and assign specific values to certain indeterminate relations. However, if you had been asked to form a clear impression of the layout, then you would probably have been able to construct a rather more complete mental picture of the room. There appear to be different levels of comprehension. It might be argued that the difference is simply one of detail, the extent to which you furnish the representation of the room with all the details that are alluded to, as opposed to imagining merely a typical room lit by firelight. No doubt there are such differences. What I am trying to establish, however, is that there is also a difference in kind: there are different ways in which an expression, a sentence, or a paragraph, are mentally represented as a result of understanding them.

One sort of representation, reflecting a deep level of comprehension, consists in the construction of a mental model, and the other sort of representation, reflecting a more superficial understanding, consists in a propositional representation, i.e. the representation of a description. I surmise that such descriptions are really functions that, if evaluated by the procedure for constructing models, would indeed yield a model. Hence, it may be useful to think of a propositional representation, not as a description *simpliciter* which would require a model for its evaluation, but as an argument that can be used by the procedure for generating models. This procedure, of course, goes beyond the specification laid down in a propositional representation: it is forced to make assumptions about matters unspecified in the description, and it can rely on general knowledge or knowledge of other specific cases in order to assist it. It can even, if need be, make an arbitrary assumption.

There is some experimental evidence in support of the distinction between mental models and propositional representations. Kate Ehrlich and I asked subjects to listen to some assertions about the spatial relations between entities, e.g.

The knife is in front of the spoon.
The spoon is on the left of the glass.
The glass is behind the dish.

and then to make a simple drawing of the corresponding layout using the names of the objects (see Ehrlich, Mani, and Johnson-Laird, 1979). The task was relatively easy, with 69% of the drawings correct, if the premises were arranged like those above so that a model could in principle be built up continuously. The task was much harder, with only 42% of the drawings correct, if the premises were discontinuous in that the first two assertions had no item in common:

The glass is behind the dish.
The knife is in front of the spoon.
The spoon is on the left of the glass.

It might be argued that the subjects were simply re-ordering propositions in their minds in order to build up an integrated propositional description, and then converting it all-of-a-piece into a drawing. However, this assumption seems to be inconsistent with the relative ease (60% correct) of semi-continuous premises where the third sentence has nothing in common with the second:

The spoon is on the left of the glass.
The glass is behind the dish.
The knife is in front of the spoon.

Such premises would require a considerable amount of re-ordering to yield an integrated propositional description, but they would allow a model to be built up continuously.

Kannan Mani and I have obtained a further piece of evidence in support of two distinct modes of representation. The subjects in this experiment again heard similar sorts of premises, but this time they described either a determinate layout (as in the previous examples) or else they were indeterminate, e.g.

The knife is in front of the spoon.
The spoon is on the left of the glass.
The fork is on the right of the spoon.

where the relation between the glass and the fork is undetermined. After each presentation, the subjects were shown a picture of a layout and had to decide whether or not it corresponded to the information in the premises. Our idea was that subjects would be inhibited from forming a model of the indeterminate premises since they might easily form the 'wrong' one, that is, one that failed to correspond with the picture, though it was consistent with the premises. At the end of the experiment, the subjects received an unexpected recognition test of their memory for the premises. They remembered the determinate premises significantly better than the indeterminate premises: only two out of the 18 subjects were against this trend. However, there was an interesting incidental finding: given that a subject picked out a set of premises that were synonymous with the originals (whether the premises were determinate or indeterminate), then it is possible to assess the likelihood of the subject selecting first the premises with the *exact* wording of the originals. The proportions of these trials went, if anything, in the opposite direction: 63% for the indeterminate premises, which was significantly better than chance, but 57% for the determinate premises, which was not significantly better than chance. Hence, given that the indeterminate problems could be remembered at all, their exact wording was more likely to be recalled. What this finding suggests, of course, is that the subjects originally utilized a propositional representation for the indeterminate premises, but constructed a model for the determinate premises. Certainly, such a distinction explains the large overall difference in the memorability of the two sorts of problem.

The contrast between mental model and propositional representation can also be illuminated by considering the interpretation of quantifiers. When people make inferences based on quantified assertions, their performance shows certain systematic biases and errors. Given a pair of premises about the hypothetical occupants of a room, such as:

Some of the authors are poets
All of the poets are professors

the overwhelming majority of subjects draw the conclusion:

Some of the authors are professors.

It is a rare individual indeed who draws the equally valid converse conclusion:

Some of the professors are authors.

On the other hand, if the occupants of the room are characterized by premises of the following form:

All of the musicians are drivers
All of the scientists are drivers

then some subjects draw the invalid conclusion:

All of the scientists are musicians

or its equally invalid converse, and some subjects draw the invalid conclusion:

Some of the scientists are musicians

or its equally invalid converse, and only about half the subjects that we have tested – they were college students – realize that no valid conclusion can be drawn about the relation between the scientists and composers. These phenomena and others like them (see Johnson-Laird, 1975a; Johnson-Laird and Steedman, 1978) are difficult to explain on the assumption that the premises are represented propositionally and then rules of inference are applied to them.

A much more plausible account can be given on the basis of the following argument. Suppose that you were to interpret the premises in the last example by actually gathering together a number of individuals in a room, and then assigning them the roles of musician, driver, and scientist, in a way that was consistent with the premises. Moreover, suppose that in order to derive a specific conclusion, you worked according to the heuristic principle of always trying to establish identities between the different roles. Hence, you get together, say, six friends, and arbitrarily assign three of them to be musicians. The first premise stipulates that they must all be drivers. Of course, there may be drivers who are not musicians, and so you arbitrarily assign that role to the other three of your friends, but since the premise does not establish their existence definitively, these individuals represent only a possibility. You have accordingly interpreted the first premise by establishing the following scenario:

$$\begin{array}{l} m = d \\ m = d \\ m = d \\ \quad\;\; (d) \\ \quad\;\; (d) \\ \quad\;\; (d) \end{array}$$

where "*m*" denotes a musician, "*d*" denotes a driver, "=" denotes an identity, and the parentheses indicate that the relevant individuals may not exist. In interpreting the second premise, "All of the scientists are drivers", you are guided by the heuristic and attempt to establish as many identities as possible between scientists and musicians. Hence, you set up the following situation:

$$\begin{array}{l} m = d = s \\ m = d = s \\ m = d = s \\ \quad\;\; (d) \\ \quad\;\; (d) \\ \quad\;\; (d) \end{array}$$

At this point, you may well conclude, like some of our subjects, that *all of the musicians are scientists* or conversely that *all of the scientists are musicians.* However, if you are prudent, you might refrain from drawing a conclusion until you have checked out whether the identities between the various roles are secure: you attempt to destroy them without doing violence to the interpretation of the premises. Moreover, you may well discover that you can break at least one of the identities between a musician and a scientist without violating the premises:

$$\begin{array}{l} m = d = s \\ m = d = s \\ m = d \\ \qquad\;\; d = s \\ \quad\;\; (d) \\ \quad\;\; (d) \end{array}$$

At this point, you may be tempted – again like some subjects – to conclude that *some of the musicians are scientists* or conversely that *some of the scientists are musicians*. However, if you are really prudent, you may try to extend your destructive manoeuvre to all the identities. This step leads to the following re-assignment of roles, in which all of the identities are destroyed:

$$\begin{array}{ll} m = d & \\ m = d & \\ m = d & \\ & d = s \\ & d = s \\ & d = s \end{array}$$

Since you have been able to arrange matters so that none of the scientists are musicians, and hitherto you had arranged them so that all of the scientists are musicians, you should now appreciate that you cannot draw any valid inference about the relation between the scientists and the musicians.

The theory of mental models for quantifiers (Johnson-Laird, 1975a; Johnson-Laird and Steedman, 1978) simply assumes that you can carry out an exactly comparable "thought experiment". You construct a mental model and submit it to the same sorts of destructive tests. There are always many – infinitely many, wholly trivial but valid inferences that can be drawn from a set of premises: logic countenances all of them, but has no machinery to single out an 'informative' conclusion as opposed, say, to a mere disjunction of the premises. The mental construction of a model, however, naturally calls for such extra-logical principles, and the heuristic that I have proposed readily accounts for the sorts of errors that people make. Mental models can obviously be generalized so as to represent any sort of quantifiers, including numbers and quasi-numerical terms such as "most", "several", "few"; they can represent multiply-quantified assertions such as, "every man loves a woman who loves him"; they can even represent sentences that are claimed to demand "branching" representations that go beyond the resources of the ordinary quantificational calculus.[3] They can also be generalized into the notion of a "discourse model" in order to accommodate the referential phenomena based on definite and indefinite descriptions and other anaphoric expressions (Johnson-Laird and Garnham, 1979).

What is more important, however, is the contrast between a mental model and a propositional representation of a quantified sentence. A propositional representation is some formula in the mental language. Kintsch (1974, p. 50) suggests, for example, that the assertion, "All men die", is represented by:

(DIE, MAN) & (ALL, MAN).

The system contains meaning postulates to capture the inferential consequences of quantifiers. E. Martin (in press) has also advocated a similar sort of system. As far as I can determine however, no one has specified the required set of meaning postulates, or indeed a heuristic that would enable people to *make* specific inferences.

A propositional representation is, as Steve Isard (1978) has emphasized, a description of a model rather than a model itself. This claim can be vindicated by comparing Kintsch's proposal with the way in which quantified assertions are represented in PLANNER-like languages (see Hewitt, 1971; Winograd, 1972). Programs written in PLANNER-like languages have a model structure (or data-base) that consists of a set of assertions, written in a predicate-argument format, such as:

(LOVES JOHN MARY)
(LOVES JAMES MARY)

This use of assertions in a model is equivalent to Hintikka's (1963) use of model sets. The sentence, "John loves Mary", is accordingly true with respect to this model, and PLANNER enables the programmer to implement procedures that work in a way that corresponds to the interpretations of model theory. They can be used to evaluate a sentence with respect to the assertions in the data-base and to return its truth value. PLANNER also enables the programmer to devize procedures for inserting assertions in the data-base. However, if the assertion is of the form "All men are mortal", then rather than tamper with the model, PLANNER allows a representation in which the model is *described*. For example, a procedure known as a consequent theorem, can be set up:

(CONSEQUENT(*X*) (MORTAL ?*X*)
(GOAL (MAN ?*X*)))

and in effect added to the data-base. What this procedure says is that *x is mortal* is true for any *x* provided that the goal of showing that *x is a man* is achieved. It is just one of the ways in which the assertion *all men are mortal* can be represented in a PLANNER system. Rather than go through the model and add to every assertion about a person the further assertion that the person is mortal, PLANNER allows this information to be directly represented as a description, but a description that can be put to use directly: if the program's goal is to show that John is mortal, then the procedure can be called if there is no simple assertion to that effect in the data-base. Hence, as Isard (1978) points out, PLANNER allows one to operate with a hybrid system, part model in the model-theoretic tradition, and part description in what I would characterize as the propositional-representation tradition. Thus when Kintsch proposes to represent a quantified assertion by some such formula as: (DIE, MAN) & (ALL, MAN), he, too, is using the formula as a description. The theory of mental models, however, is very different: it represents quantified assertions directly by constructing a corresponding model that satisfies the assertion. Perhaps, we will not have too far to travel to establish a link between the theory of mental models and model-theoretic semantics.

The Obstacles between Formal and Psychological Semantics

The shortest route from formal to psychological semantics would be simply to assume that human beings have models in their minds that are wholly analogous to the models postulated in formal semantics. Formal semantics would accordingly provide an abstract template against which performance could be matched. The relation between the two fields would indeed be in accordance with Stanley Peters' suggestion of an 'ecumenical principle': formal semantics characterizes *what* is computed when a sentence is understood, whereas psychological semantics characterizes *how* it is computed.

As so often with the shortest route between two places, there are direct obstacles that prevent one from following it. Here, they take the form of four major problems:

(1) The nature of lexical meanings and whether the mental lexicon is compatible with the rules of formal semantics.

(2) The concept of possible worlds and how they could be mentally represented.

(3) The contrast between the completeness of model structures and the incompleteness of mental models.

(4) The problem of 'propositional attitudes'.

The remainder of the paper is devoted to discussing each of these problems in turn.

II: THE PROBLEM OF LEXICAL SEMANTICS

A major obstacle to the project of linking formal and psychological semantics has been independently discovered several times in this century. It hinges on the formal use of a direct assignment of interpretations to the basic expressions of the language. This step seems plausible granted that when theorists lay down the law about meanings, they generally attempt to stipulate the necessary and sufficient conditions for the application of a term. If the vocabulary of a natural language is similarly explicable, and simple lexicography will indeed turn up the relevant necessary and sufficient conditions, then taking basic intensions as primitive is a sensible way to avoid the problems of lexical analysis.

As Thomason wrote in his introduction to Montague's (1974) papers:

> . . . *we should not expect a semantic theory to furnish an account of how any two expressions belonging to the same syntactic category differ in meaning*. 'Walk' and 'run', for instance, and 'unicorn' and 'zebra' certainly do differ in meaning, and we require a dictionary of English to tell us how. But the making of a dictionary demands considerable knowledge of the world. The task of explaining the particular meanings of various basic expressions will obviously presuppose, if not factual information, at least a minutely detailed terminology for classifying things of all kinds. Perhaps even pictures or a museum of representative specimens would have to be counted as "terminology" – after all, there are words in English such as 'meter' and 'yard'.

To a psychologist, Thomason is here making a surprising claim. The major part of psychological semantics *is* to explicate differences in meaning between 'walk' and 'run', and to show how such words are organized in the mental lexicon. Of course, Thomason is right in supposing that the lexicon makes use of factual information, representative specimens, and embraces all areas of knowledge. But, the argument that it is therefore not a semanticist's task to investigate lexical meanings, seems spurious to a psychologist. What one wants to know are the *principles* underlying the acquisition, organization, and use, of this knowledge in the mental lexicon. Principles can be studied without having to deal with the whole encyclopedia. One can indeed mimic Montague's strategy and investigate a fragment of the lexicon, and how the terms within it are semantically interrelated. There is a respectable tradition of studying such "semantic fields" in linguistics (see Ullmann, 1962), and psychologists have more recently followed the same practice (e.g. Osgood, 1970; Miller, 1972; Miller and Johnson-Laird, 1976).

Likewise, Thomason is unfortunately wrong in supposing that one should look to lexicographers, and to dictionaries of English, to find out the difference in meaning between such words as 'walk' and 'run'. Dictionaries can provide us with clues, but their limitations have certainly been known to dictionary-makers for a very long time (cf. Dr. Johnson's satirical definition of *horse* as 'an equine quadruped'). In a series of experiments, we have found that certain words resist useful definition; that they are the most frequently used words in the language; and that they come closest to expressing semantically primitive notions (see Johnson-Laird and Quinn, 1976). They also have a greater number of different meanings than those words that are easier to define, as Dave Haw and I have established in an unpublished experiment in which dictionaries, rather than human beings, served as our subjects.

The burden of these and other psychological studies is that not all the expressions in the lexicon can be analyzed into sets of necessary and sufficient conditions. Indeed, in my view, these investigations provide convincing evidence that not all expressions can be linguistically analyzed, that is to say, there are certain terms that cannot be usefully decomposed in any way within the object language itself, e.g. *possible, see, at, have, true*. They correspond to semantically primitive notions.

The impossibility of specifying necessary and sufficient conditions for the applicability of certain terms has, of course, been pointed out before, most notably by Wittgenstein. In his *Philosophical Investigations* (1953), he argued that the meaning of many terms is more properly thought of as a set of family relationships or as conforming to a stereotype. This thesis was in part a reaction to his own earlier Fregean views in the *Tractatus* (1922) – views which of course are embodied in Montague's (1974) method of basing semantics on two *types* of notion: entity and truth value. In particular, Wittgenstein in his later philosophy, according to Hacker (1972), was reacting against Frege's view that concepts are defined by their characteristic 'marks' (Merkmale), that is, the essential properties of the items falling under them.[4]

The fact that the meanings of many words resemble stereotypes has a potentially profound consequence for our project of linking formal and psychological semantics. Putnam (1970, 1975) has argued that the phenomenon can be pushed one step further to reach the conclusion that the intensions of terms cannot be mental objects: *meanings are not in the mind.*[5] Hence, as Partee (1981) has emphasized, there is a serious hiatus between the structural and the lexical rules of model-theoretic semantics. Structural semantics, which determines the intensions of phrases and sentences as a function of the intensions of their constituent expressions, is evidently knowable, at least according to the well-known views of Chomsky (1965). Lexical semantics, which assigns the interpretations of the basic lexical expressions, is unknowable. This major and unexpected obstacle to progress certainly merits closer inspection before we modify our plans and attempt a new route.

Putnam (1970) starts with the observation that indeed there are words whose meanings cannot be analyzed into sets of necessary semantic components. The meaning of *lemon*, for instance, might be decomposed into such characteristics as: round, yellow, having peel, having a tart taste, and so on. Yet none of these components is essential: a green lemon is still a lemon, a sweet peelless lemon is still a lemon. The nature of lemonhood is evidently a matter to be elucidated by a theory – presumably the naive everyday 'theory' of fruits – and Putnam dubs those words whose meanings depend on such sorts of theory, "natural kind terms".[6] In telling someone what a lemon is you generally sketch your theory of lemonhood; you describe a typical lemon, a normal member of the class of lemons. This stereotype, Putnam argues, does not specify the extension of the word. That, he suggests, is determined by some test, though no one particular test may be necessary, or by providing a sample. There are tests, for example, for establishing whether or not something is *gold*. However, these tests are known only to experts, and are not part of the stereotype governing the ordinary use of the word. If the tests were added to the stereotype, then according to Putnam they would thereby change it – along with the concomitant 'theory' of gold.

In subsequent papers, Putnam (1973, 1975) tackles the question of what determines the extension of a natural kind term in the first place. He adopts a position similar to that espoused by Kripke (1972): the extension is fixed by the ostensive reference that accompanied the original giving of the name, that is, the actual properties of the object(s) used in defining a natural kind term for the first time fix its extension. This fixing occurs regardless of whether the underlying properties of the object were known to the original users. One immediate consequence of this state of affairs is that the stereotype associated with a term may get attached to the wrong extension. Putnam considers a number of hypothetical instances of the phenomenon. One example is based on a world that is a counterpart to ours except that the extension of *water* is not H_2O but a different substance. Speakers in both this world and ours may have exactly the same stereotype for *water*, especially if one considers their state of mind in, say, the seventeenth century, yet the extension of the term is totally different in the two worlds. An analogous example rests upon common ignorance. Putnam (1975) writes:

> Suppose you are like me and cannot tell an elm from a beech tree. We still say that the extension of 'elm' in my idiolect is the same as the extension of 'elm' in anyone else's, viz., the set of all elm trees, and that the set of all beech trees is the extension of 'beech' is *both* of our idiolects. Thus 'elm' in my idiolect has a different extension from 'beech' in your idiolect (as it should). Is it really credible that this difference in extension is brought about by some difference in our *concepts*? My *concept* of an elm tree is exactly the same as my concept of a beech tree (I blush to confess).

The remainder of Putnam's argument is straightforward. The extension of a term is specified by its intension. Since a stereotype does not determine an extension, it is not an intension; and since a stereotype is the only concept of many terms that speakers possess, it follows that speakers do not possess intensions. Intensions cannot be mental objects.

If meanings are not in the mind, then how can a coherent semantic theory be constructed? How can lexical semantics be combined with structural semantics to form a theory of a language that human beings could actually know? Partee's (1981) answer is that what we have in our minds are semantic representations that reflect our *beliefs* about intensions, not intensions themselves; hence, what we have in our minds does not determine the extension of words. She concedes to Putnam that the intension of a term is in part determined by the underlying properties of the actual objects used in the original ostensive introduction of the term, even if these properties were not then known. She claims only that Putnam may have underestimated the role of psychological factors, since people seem to have a shared disposition to make the same generalizations, and to see the same perceptual similarities.[7] This tentative solution of postulating beliefs about meanings instead of meanings does not seem to do justice to the psychology of beliefs. There is a distinction to be drawn between having a word in one's command, especially one expressing a primitive notion, and having a belief about its meaning. One might argue, of course, that Partee's solution merely embeds an additional level of 'unconscious' belief into the characterization of both of these states. Yet I remain unhappy with such a formulation. The moment would seem opportune for a switch in the direction of exploration, and for an examination of some psychological phenomena concerning the meanings of words.

Psychological Aspects of the Meanings of Words

It is commonly held that communication is possible provided the participants in discourse have sufficient similarity in their knowledge of the meanings of words. In fact, it is perfectly possible to communicate with little or no such similarity – or else children would never learn their native tongue. Moreover, accurate communication relatively rarely depends upon speakers' possessing complete and identical representations of the meanings of the terms they employ. A simple example establishes the point:

Speaker A: Where's the Henry Moore bronze?
Speaker B: Opposite the hotel.

These two individuals may understand each other perfectly without either of them knowing that bronze is an alloy of copper and tin. Furthermore, it is very easy to establish, as Graham Gibbs and I have shown experimentally, that speakers have systematic gaps in their knowledge of the meanings of infrequent words. Our subjects tended to know, for instance, that *pemmican* is a consumable solid but they tended not to know whether it is a natural or a manmade substance, they knew that *turpentine* is a non-consumable liquid but they thought erroneously that it is a manmade substance. With few exceptions, people tend to know whether or not something is consumable, and solid or liquid, but they know less well whether it is manmade or natural; the same pattern can even be detected in the latencies with which subjects make decisions about highly frequent words (see Johnson-Laird, 1975b). An incomplete knowledge of the meaning of a word need be no barrier to communication.

One reason for this perhaps surprising state of affairs is the way in which words are originally acquired. Children learn words at so great a rate – around nine new words per day on average up to the age of six (see Templin, 1957; Miller, 1977a) – that one cannot seriously suppose that they are learning either their complete intensions or fixing their extensions from encountering actual objects to which they refer. They must be able to gather a considerable amount about the meaning of a word from the linguistic context and the social and physical circumstances of the utterance (see Carey, 1978). Indeed, my colleagues and I have found that 3–4 year old children can pick up and retain for at least a week semantic information from merely hearing a story such as: "John stepped out of the boat and the water mibbed his trousers, so he went home to change into some dry clothes. The water had mibbed his trousers right through so Simon made him some hot tea. But John dropped his cup and the tea mibbed over the floor." The novel verb, *mib*, has a transitive meaning similar to that of *soak* and an intransitive meaning similar to that of *spill*. Children evince no surprise on hearing it – there is no reason why they should since many words they encounter they will never have heard before – and hence it is unlikely that they merely translate it into some word that they do know. The details of this study are reported in Wykes and Johnson-Laird (1977); Jon Davies has carried out a complementary study in which he found that children could likewise readily pick up information about nouns from their linguistic context, particularly from the verbs with which they occurred. Perhaps the most dramatic finding was obtained by Susan Carey (1978). She found that six weeks after a nursery school child has complied with the request, "Bring me the chromium tray, not the red one, the chromium one," a child is likely to show a change in his or her spontaneous use of color terminology, being much less likely to refer to an olive color (the original referent for *chromium*) as *green*.

The studies of language acquisition certainly bear out Putnam's (1978) recent remark that *reference and truth have less to do with understanding language than philosophers have tended to assume*. He goes on to argue:

> ... one does not need to *know* that there is a correspondence between words and extra-linguistic entities to learn one's language. But there is such a correspondence none the less, and it explains the *success* of what one is doing. *After* one has learned one's language one can talk about *anything* – including the correspondence in question.

Somehow, behind the scenes – perhaps by relying on the experts – the extensions of terms are fixed. But, according to Putnam, the intensions that do the job are not mental entities. Let us now return to a more direct confrontation with this hypothesis.

Effective Intensions are Mental Objects

In order to maintain that a stereotype is an effective intension, and that meanings are indeed in the mind, I shall have to rebut some of Putnam's arguments. On the central point, however, there is no disagreement: stereotypes rather than sets of necessary and sufficient conditions are our only mental baggage for many terms. What I want to show are the following four points:

(1) There are no intensions other than stereotypes for many terms in the language.

(2) If a natural kind term has a 'true' intension, then it is in principle impossible for us to know whether we know it. Hence, as semanticists we need not worry about true intensions.

(3) The social division of linguistic labor is entirely consistent with the thesis that meanings are in the mind.

(4) The extensions of natural kind terms are not necessarily fixed.

If these arguments are sound, then they clear away one obstacle between linking up formal and psychological semantics: lexical semantics is just as knowable as structural semantics.

What is the difference between your semantic representations of the terms *unicorn* and *zebra*? You presumably possess a stereotype for both: a zebra has a certain sort of shape, stripes, four legs and a tail; a unicorn is similar except that it has no stripes, and it has a single horn on its head; you know how to recognize a unicorn just as well as you know how to recognize a zebra. The difference is that you have probably seen a zebra in a zoo, whereas you have never seen a unicorn, only a picture of one. Indeed, like the lady in Thurber's story, you do not believe that unicorns exist. Nevertheless, there are no necessary and sufficient conditions for what it is, or would be, for something to be a unicorn. A unicorn that has lost its horn, or that only has three legs, would still be a unicorn.

Of course, unicorns *may* exist; they may have existed long ago; they may exist in the future. Hence, the term should have a non-empty extension at some times in some possible worlds. What determines this extension? One can hardly reply: the actual properties of those unicorns that were ostensively referred to when the term was first introduced. Likewise, the answer that it is the actual properties of the unicorns that exist in certain possible worlds when the term was, or will be, introduced in those worlds fails to provide *us* with an extension for the term. The safe answer, of course, is that we cannot know the extension of the term as it applies to those possible worlds. But, how then is it possible for us to recognize a unicorn if one should stroll into our garden? It seems there can be only one answer to this question: the effective intension of the term *unicorn* is [determined by] the stereotype that we possess for unicorns. Moreover, there are no grounds for supposing that there is any essential difference between *unicorns* and *zebras* on this point: speakers possess a stereotype in both cases, which provides them with an effective intension.

One immediate retort that could be made on behalf of Putnam is that there *is* a difference: there are expert zoologists who have tests to determine precisely whether or not something is a zebra, but there are no experts and no such tests for unicorns. Before I deal with the social division of linguistic labor, let me first present a very different lexical item, the spatial preposition, *at*. We all know the meaning of this word, yet none of us can say precisely what it means. As Miller and I discovered to our cost in writing *Language and Perception, at* is one of those words that is sufficiently close to being a semantic primitive as to resist ready analysis. There are indeed a number of erroneous analyses in the literature. The problem is to determine what has to be the case for the following sorts of assertion to be true:

John is at the window.
The chair is at the table.
The bicycle is at the garage.

There appear to be no necessary conditions for the applicability of *at*.

Moreover, as Lucy Velicogna and I found (in a mercifully unpublished experiment), even with simple circular discs there is a region of uncertainty between those arrangements for which subjects will definitely accept an assertion of the form *a is at b* and those for which they definitely reject it; there is a region where they will fail to make a clear distinction between *a is at b* and *a is near b*. Plainly, the relation is one that depends on the nature of the entities that are interrelated – in the experiment, it depended on the relative sizes of the discs – and a semantics for *at* should probably depend on the notion of a *region* of an object. As Miller and Johnson-Laird (1976, p. 388 *et seq.*) argued: "to say '*x* is at *y*' is to say that *x* is included in the region of *y*, that is, *x* is where it can interact with *y* socially, physically, or in whatever way *x*'s conventionally interact with *y*'s." If this analysis is on the right lines, then underlying the semantics of *at* are a whole series of prototypical relations. For many, if not most of them, there are no experts to advize us: the intension of the term is founded solely on stereotypes. Other spatial prepositions, and indeed other sorts of word in the language, have the same type of semantics. *There are no intentions other than stereotypes for many terms in the language*.

Putnam in effect distinguishes three different sorts of putative extension for a natural kind term such as *water*. First, there is what ordinary individuals consider to be water, which depends on their respective stereotypes. Second, there is what experts with access to the appropriate tests identify as water, which certainly provides a more uniform extension. Third, there is what water really is, which according to Putnam and Kripke, is the same in all possible worlds (*water* is a rigid designator), and whose extension is fixed by the actual properties of the stuff that was used ostensively when the term was introduced for the very first time.

There is no reason to suppose that the chemical tests for water are infallible. Some ingenious chemist, for instance, may discover that what we have hitherto been calling *water* is really two very different, though apparently similar, substances. The discovery naturally raises the interesting question: which of the two substances is the 'real' water? According to Putnam and Kripke, the question can only be answered if it is possible to find out which of the two substances – it could be both – was used in the original dubbing ceremony that introduced the word into the language. Such information seems most unlikely to be forthcoming and, I submit, can never be established definitively. It follows that no one will ever be able to discover whether or not the true extension of *water* is known.

To some extent, Putnam (1975) has considered this problem. He writes:

Another misunderstanding that should be avoided is the following: to take the account we have developed as implying that the members of the extension of a natural-kind word necessarily *have* a common hidden structure. It could have turned out that the bits of liquid we call 'water' had *no* important common physical characteristics *except* the superficial ones. In that case the necessary and sufficient condition for being 'water' would have been possession of sufficiently many of the superficial characteristics.

But, following Kripke, he does not imply that water could have failed to have had a hidden structure: water is necessarily H_2O. Likewise, he considers the case of jade, which really is two different substances, jadeite and nephrite, with the same unique textural properties. The solution here, he says, is to say that there are two sorts of jade. And if *per impossible* water was two entirely different substances, then we would say there were two sorts of water. Indeed, we would. But this claim is hard to reconcile with the causal account, since only one sort of water might have been used in the original ceremony that introduced the term. "If there is a hidden structure, then generally it determines what it is to be a member of the natural kind, not only in the actual world, but in all possible worlds." That is the general claim that Putnam makes, but it is open to a Putnamian objection in the form of a science fiction scenario. Suppose there is a counterpart world to ours in which there is a liquid that the inhabitants drink, use for washing, and so on. They call it *mib*. One day their chemists discover that *mib* is in reality a variety of different substances with no important common physical characteristics. The same day their historians discover conclusive proof that the word was coined when one of their explorers first drank *mib* from a vast lake that he had discovered. Should the inhabitants now say that there are different sorts of *mib* or only one true *mib* (that from the explorer's lake) and a lot of stuff that merely looks and tastes like it? I think that Putnam is required to choose the second alternative to be consistent with his remarks that I have quoted above. But then of course it follows that speakers can never be certain that they know the real extension of any natural kind term. Even what an expert currently thinks to be the decisive tests can always turn out to be fallible and to conflate two different sorts of entity or substance. One is bound to conclude that since the real extension can never be definitely established, it can hardly be very important in the use of language. It is a philosophical idol. *If a natural kind has a 'true' intension, then it is in principle impossible for us to know whether we know it. Hence, as semanticists we need not worry about true intensions.*

Lay individuals often have an incomplete or erroneous knowledge of the meaning of a word, and Putnam is obviously correct in postulating a social division of linguistic labor. He has, however, failed to push through its implications far enough. He suggests that a test that an expert knows for establishing the extension of, say, *gold* is not part of a stereotype, and that if it were added to a stereotype then it would thereby change it. But, it can be argued that an expert simply possesses a different and more complete intension for the term *gold* than that possessed by a layman. The difference is analogous to that that holds between two people who disagree about the meaning of a term: they have different intensions for it. There is, however, one critical distinction: the majority of ordinary individuals know that they have an incomplete knowledge of the intension of *gold*, and indeed part of their stereotype for the term may well be that there are tests for it of whose nature they are ignorant, but which are known to metallurgists and other experts. Hence, they are happy to defer to experts for a definitive opinion about whether some item is made from gold.

One can know that one is ignorant. This phenomenon is entirely overlooked by Putnam in his example based on his ignorance of the difference between a beech and an elm. What he does know is that there *is* a difference between them, and that there are other people who know what that difference is. A crucial feature of the mental organization of the lexicon is that a category of terms, corresponding to some semantic field, may constitute a contrastive set. A child may know that basic color terms form such a set before he is able to identify all the colors correctly (see Miller, 1977a). Likewise, adults such as Putnam and the present author know that there is a contrastive set of terms for trees – beech, elm, oak, larch, pine, and so on – without knowing very much about the nature of the differences between them. If such domains of the lexicon are organized along the lines of a computer programmer's decision table, a view urged by Miller and Johnson-Laird (1976, Sec. 4.4.3), then a speaker may be aware of the contrasting set of 'actions', the items of vocabulary, without being very knowledgeable about the set of 'conditions', the intensions that govern their use. *The social division of linguistic labor is entirely consistent with the thesis that meanings are in the mind.*

If an ordinary individual acquires a knowledge that allows him to distinguish between a beech and an elm, then his intentions for the two terms are thereby of course modified. Hitherto, he knew only that the two terms had different extensions, now he is able, in principle, to assign the two sorts of tree to their appropriate extension. Likewise, if an ordinary individual has hitherto systematically confused the two species, and used *beech* to refer to elms, and *vice versa*, but is now disabused of his error, his intensions for the two terms are thereby modified. Neither of these cases is problematical.

However, in my view, what can happen to an individual can happen to a set of individuals. Indeed, it can happen to an entire linguistic community: the only difference is in the cause of the change of an extension of a term.

There are genuinely problematical natural kind terms, whose extensions may well change. The late Richard Asher's (1972) discussion of medical terminology provides some nice examples. According to the textbooks, Pel Ebstein fever occurs in certain cases of Hodgkin's disease, and is a fever that is high one week, low the next week, and so on. Asher, however, was convinced that there is no such fever, and that doctors believe in it only because its name and associated description exist. Obviously, if he is correct, then the term should either be abandoned or else a new extension found for it. I do not know its current status in medical circles, but perhaps a consensus has been reached about its re-deployment. Doubtless medical authorities have an unusual degree of power to enforce a range of reference, and so the occurrence of change in their terminology is good evidence for similar degrees of freedom for ordinary words. The cause of such changes is little understood, but their existence seems beyond doubt. Speakers can come to use words in ways that no longer coincide with their original uses: *tawdry* no longer refers to articles sold by St. Audrey; *tree* no longer refers only to oaks; *phlogiston* no longer refers to the substance of flames. *The extensions of terms are not necessarily fixed.*

How Is a Stereotype Mentally Represented?

One virtue in supposing that an intension can be a stereotype is that stereotypes are eminently knowable. Hence, the thesis bridges the hiatus between the lexical and structural parts of formal semantics that so worried Partee. However, one may still wonder how structural semantics marries with stereotypical intensions, particularly as Wittgenstein took their existence as an argument against the Fregean programme. Likewise, one may still worry about the nature of the extensions that are determined by stereotypes. Putnam (1975) has suggested that: "If one really wanted to formalize the notion of extension as applied to terms in a natural language, it would be necessary to employ 'fuzzy sets' or something similar rather than sets in the classical sense." What is needed to resolve these final obstacles is a closer look at the mental representation of stereotypes.

Psychologists are, indeed, familiar with the idea that the meanings of certain terms may be represented by stereotypes – or 'prototypes' as they tend to call them (see Fisher, 1916; Bruner, Goodnow, and Austin, 1956,

p. 64; Berlin and Kay, 1969). Rosch and her colleagues have shown, for example, that not all members of a class are equally good exemplars of it: a robin is a good example of a bird, a penguin is not. The difference is also reflected, as one might expect from Marbe's law (see Woodworth, 1938), in the times that it takes to decide that a robin is a bird, and that a penguin is a bird (Rosch, 1973).

One theory about the mental representation of prototypes is that they are images. Rosch (1976) makes this suggestion: "the most cognitively economical code for a category is, in fact, a concrete image of an average category member." It is difficult to reconcile this hypothesis with the decision that a penguin *is* a bird: the response could be made on the basis of an image of a typical bird, but more information about the process is needed than Rosch has so far formulated. A second hypothesis about the representation of prototypical information has been put forward by Smith, Shoben, and Rips (1974). They rely on a decompositional dictionary in which the meanings of words are broken down into *characteristic* features and *defining* features. A good exemplar of a category will have both sorts of feature; a poor exemplar of the category will have the defining features but not the characteristic features. The notion of a characteristic feature seems to be essentially some sort of an inductive generalization based on an analysis of cases. It is, for instance, a characteristic feature of British birds that they tend to have dull colors. However, this sort of feature seems to be intrinsically different from, say, the more conventional characteristic that birds have two wings. The discrepancy suggests a third approach to the problem.

Minsky (1975) introduced the notion of a 'frame' in order to account for certain aspects of perception. According to his theory, a frame is a structured piece of knowledge about a typical view of an object such as a room; and a whole set of frames, together with rules about how to move from one to another, is needed to perceive the room as one moves around within it. Frames contain two features that make them ideal candidates for the representation of prototypes. First, they contain variables (or 'terminals' as Minsky calls them) into which go the specific values of a given instance of the relevant entity. A particular bird, for instance, will have a specific size, a specific shape of head, a specific sort of beak, and so on. Second, the values of many such variables can be specified by default: if no information about them is available for a given instance, the frame specifies a 'default' value. Thus, the frame system for a bird would specify by default that a bird sings, flies, has two wings, lays eggs in a nest, and so on. In other words, as I have suggested elsewhere, a prototype is simply a frame system that takes all the default values for its relevant variables (Johnson-Laird and Wason, 1977, p. 342).

It turns out that the notion of a default value was anticipated in its essentials by Wittgenstein (1953). Hacker (1972, Ch. X) and Baker (1974) have argued that what emerges from a close examination of the relevant texts is that Wittgenstein's notion of a *criterion* corresponds to a relation that is weaker than entailment, but stronger than a mere inductive generalization. Criteria, in turn, appear to be the most plausible way of capturing what is meant by a prototype. Our grounds for believing that a certain object is a bird would include the satisfaction of the following criteria: it has wings, it flies, it sings, it is of a certain size, it lays eggs, and so on. Although criteria are part of the theoretical apparatus that Wittgenstein developed by way of his reaction against a Fregean semantics, the machinery of default values would make an excellent device for handling them,[8] and such a device may be entirely compatible with a special sort of formal semantics.

If the mental representation of an intension can be a prototype, defined by criteria, then what is the nature of its corresponding extension? Several linguists and psychologists have followed Putnam's precept and adopted fuzzy sets (e.g. Lakoff, 1972; Halff, Ortony and Anderson, 1976). This strategem is superficially appealing, but I suspect mistaken.

In orthodox set theory, on which model-theoretic semantics relies, an individual is either a member of a set or not; in fuzzy set theory, membership can be partial ranging over the real number continuum, or some less dense numbers, from zero to unity. It follows that truth values range over the same continuum, and hence any truth-functional connectives or operators must be appropriately re-defined. These revisions are a nuisance, but they also raise a problem for the meaning of "truth". What does it mean to say that a sentence such as "John is kind" has a truth value of 0.75?

It seems important to distinguish between three different states of mind:

(i) An uncertainty about something that is intrinsically determinate.

(ii) A certainty of the exact indeterminacy of something that is indeed intrinsically indeterminate.

(iii) An inability to decide an issue because it is outside the scope of the rules of the system.

If you are uncertain about whether Home existed then you are in the first state of mind. If you know definitely that the probability of your losing on 'red' on the next spin of the roulette wheel is 0.5, then you are in the second state of mind. If you cannot decide whether or not the size of the goal-keeper's gloves is permissible, because the laws of the game say nothing about the matter, then you are in the third state of mind. Likewise, you may be uncertain about the truth value of an assertion, e.g. "Homer existed", or you may be unable to decide the truth value of a sentence, because the meaning of a word does not cover the relevant case, e.g., "An electric light bulb is a piece of furniture." What seems incoherent is the idea that a truth value is something that is intrinsically indeterminate, and that you can be absolutely certain that a sentence has a truth value of 0.75. Of course, a generic assertion may be true three times out of four for the specific instances that it covers, but this condition is a very different matter. Indeed, one says, "Three out of four marriages end in divorce" rather than that, " 'Marriages end in divorce' has a truth value of 0.75."

In short, lexical semantics presents no essential obstacle to our project of linking formal and psychological semantics. Intensions *are* knowable, but very often they take the form of stereotypes. A stereotype is a special sort of intension, very different from the logician's idea of a set of necessary and sufficient conditions. It is essentially a partial function from possible worlds to extensions. Hence, what we possess in our minds simply fails to cover all the cases that nature presents us with – we may have no grounds or criteria for deciding whether a given entity is a piece of furniture, or whether one item is *at* another. The lexicon is open. Its phylogeny reflects its ontogeny: its present status reflects the way it is learnt. If sufficient problematical cases occur, then an intension may be modified, or a more precise 'test' may be introduced, in order to legislate about the problematical cases.[9] Natural language tolerates these uncertainties because it is used primarily for communication, which is largely a matter of conveying what you intend to refer to and what properties you intend to designate, rather than conveying precise extensions. Logicians often talk of the problem of vagueness; perhaps in reality it is a solution.

III: THE PROBLEM OF POSSIBLE WORLDS

Formal Semantics

In order to make sense of modal logics, as Kripke (1963a) pointed out, one needs to consider only certain possible worlds, namely, those that are *accessible* to a given world. This notion may be taken to mean that there are only certain possible worlds that can be conceived, and hence, a necessary proposition is one that is true in all conceivable worlds (see Hughes and Cresswell, 1968, for this interpretation). Clearly, an individual in one possible world w_1 may be able to conceive another possible world w_2; but it may not be that w_1 is conceivable by any individual in w_2, e.g. we can imagine a world in which human beings are unable to see, but the inhabitants of such a world may not be able to imagine our world of sighted individuals. In such a case, the only constraint on the relation of accessibility is that it must be reflexive: w_1 is always conceivable in w_1. If this principle is assumed in the formal semantics, then it yields an interpretation for a particular modal logic (System T). The rules defining well-formed formulae permit indefinitely long sequences of such operators as *necessarily* and *possibly*, e.g. *necessarily necessarily possibly p*. If we consider a sequence of such operators, including negation, to define a "modality", the question arises as to how many distinct modalities there may be in any particular modal logic. Two different modalities may well turn out to be equivalent, e.g. if we can show that *necessarily p* implies *necessarily necessarily p*. It is impossible to derive any such theorems in System T, and it accordingly contains an infinite number of logically distinct modalities: a sequence of n + 1 occurrences of a modal operator is always distinct from a sequence of n occurrences.

There are two variants of System T to which it is worth devoting a few words. If one stipulates that for any pair of possible worlds the accessibility relation holds at least one way between them, then the relation connects them up. Hence, if one further stipulates that accessibility is transitive, a sequence of worlds is obtained that can be interpreted as moments of time. The corresponding temporal logic was originally suggested by Prior (1957) as the basis of a 'tense logic' in which *necessarily p* is interpreted as true at a particular moment of time if and only if *p* is true at that moment and all subsequent moments. This particular logic involves a continuous treatment of time. A system in which time is discrete can be obtained by adding a further condition to the semantics. One way to make this addition is to stipulate, by way of the accessibility relation, that for any moment of time t there is always another later moment t', such that any moment of time that is later than t is either equal to or later than t'. (Another way would be simply to assume that the set of moments of time is the set of integers.) This "dis-creteness" condition yields the semantics for a modal logic known as System D. Montague (1974) regarded the structure of time as a contingent matter and assumed merely a simple ordering $\leqslant$, which is reflexive, transitive, and antisymmetric (i.e. if $x \geqslant y$ and $y \leqslant x$ then $x = y$).

To revert to the ordinary interpretation of modality, if we suppose that conceivability involves appreciating the imaginative powers of the individuals that we imagine, then the relation of accessibility would have to be treated as both reflexive and transitive. The resulting semantics corresponds to a different modal logic (System S4) in which if a proposition is necessarily true then this fact is itself a necessary truth. It is difficult to determine whether such a principle is sensible or not because modal operators are rarely concatenated in this way in ordinary discourse. However, the effect is to reduce the number of distinct modalities to fourteen. If, finally, we consider that accessibility is reflexive, transitive, and symmetric, i.e. we now assume that if w_1 is conceivable in w_2 then w_2 is conceivable in w_1, then accessibility becomes an equivalence relation, with the result that we can simply define necessary propositions as those that are true in all possible worlds in a straightforward Leibnizian way. This semantics corresponds to a modal logic (System S5) in which there is a simple set of three modalities: *necessarily p, p, possibly p*, and their respective negations.

There is clearly more than an elegant sufficiency of different modal logics. A psychologist is bound to wonder which system best captures the everyday sense of possibility and necessity. In my view, the issue of finding the "best" system is something of a red herring. Our ordinary use of modal terms is seldom made with any explicit set of axioms in mind. If we need to draw some tortuous inference, we could always invent the axioms on the spot, or formulate their corresponding semantics. Moreover, psychologists can be sure that a possible worlds semantics has only a remote relation to the mental representation of modal assertions.

One trouble with possible worlds is that there are too many of them to get inside one's head. They are infinitely many and hence, granted the criterion – decisive in other contexts (see Miller and Chomsky, 1963) – that human beings have only a finite mental capacity, there is no direct way in which they can accommodate them. One possible solution to this problem is simply to represent a description of a set of worlds rather than the worlds themselves. Hans Kamp (in a recent talk) has suggested an extremely interesting variant of this proposal in order to provide a more psychologically plausible semantics for time. Model-theoreticians, as I mentioned earlier, make use of a set of moments of time and a simple ordering relation over them, but of course it is most implausible that people really have a corresponding sequence of moments in their heads. Kamp proposes that there is a hierarchy of descriptions, with partial descriptions near the top that correspond to bundles of moments, i.e. events, and ever more precise descriptions lower down until ultimately at the limit there is the set of moments of time (cf. Russell, 1936). This set is accordingly an idealized abstraction. Exactly the same notion can be employed in order to represent possible worlds.

Isard (1978) has proposed a different approach based, not on descriptions of models, but on finite procedures for constructing them. He suggests that rather than postulating an isomorphism between the model and what it represents, a more fruitful idea is to argue that the two domains are "equivalent with respect to a language", that is, anything that can be truly said about one is true of the other. A mental model, however, is specified by a finite generative device, so that not all of its elements are actually explicitly represented in the brain. The complete model is again an abstract idealization. The analogy is clearly with a grammar, where the limitations of human performance render the complete language unrealizable. Partee (1979) has similarly argued that model-theoretic semantics represents a sort of supercompetence: "what we would be like if not limited by finite brains and finite experience (e.g. if we were God)."

My proposal for representing quantified assertions by mental models containing arbitrary numbers of elements is one way in which such a scheme might be implemented. Such a system is readily extended to deal with sets of an infinite cardinality (cf. the usual way of demonstrating a mapping between an infinite set and one of its infinite subsets). However, although this approach may be appropriate for handling assertions about infinite sets of simple entities, such as moments of time, it seems much less plausible for representing possible worlds. A possible world is intrinsically richer than an integer. Logicians can take a set of possible worlds as primitive, but psychologists worried about mental representation cannot afford to do so.

The Mental Representation of Modality

A possible world is in effect a state of affairs that is a conceivable alternative to some given state of affairs. It is not really necessary to consider the world as a whole in evaluating the truth or falsity of a modal assertion. Hence, a plausibility hypothesis, which I have advanced elsewhere (Johnson-Laird, 1978), is that people actively construct mental models corresponding to alternatives to a given situation. Indeed, since human beings find the systematic mental manipulation of even a few alternatives rather difficult (see Wason and Johnson-Laird, 1972, Chapters 13–15), they may construct only a single alternative model. According to this "constructive" approach, the evaluation of a modal sentence containing an infinitival complement, such as, "It is possible for John to leave," involves taking the situation that it concerns as the basis for an attempt to imagine a sequel in which the event of John leaving occurs. The process of construction utilizes general knowledge as well as a knowledge of the situation itself. Think of how you evaluate the assertion in a specific context such as John being bound in a strait-jacket. You do not passively evaluate it with respect to a series of states of affairs that pass magically before your mind's eye. You are actively engaged in the problem of constructing a scenario on the basis of what you know.

An unexpected bonus for this approach to modality is that it is no longer necessary to argue that modal auxiliaries such as *may, must*, and their cognates, are ambiguous between deontic and epistemic senses (see also Wertheimer, 1972). If the body of knowledge elicited by the sentence and its context concerns matters of fact, then the modal is interpreted epistemically, e.g. it is possible for John to leave because he studied with Harry Houdini; if the body of knowledge that is elicited concerns moral or social conventions, or rules of conduct, then the modal is interpreted deontically, e.g. it is possible for John to leave because the psychiatrist has approved it. The interpretation of modals also depends on a number of other aspects of the sentences in which they occur including their temporal schemata (see Steedman, 1977). However, according to the present theory, they are essentially deictic (indexical) in that their interpretation depends on knowledge. This view was anticipated by Frege (cited by Karttunen, 1973) who argued that modality should accordingly be excluded from logic proper. That the "constructive" analysis of modality is at least consistent with a model-theoretic approach is borne out by Kratzer (1977), who makes use of the same notion that modals are unambiguous and depend on bodies of knowledge for their interpretation.

The relation between psychological performance and a model-theoretic semantics remains a remote one. When you evaluate an assertion about a possibility as true, then you will either have succeeded in constructing a state of affairs in which it is realized, or at the very least failed to have shown that there cannot be any such state of affairs. These two outcomes are psychologically very distinct. Only if it is conceded that they are *logically* equivalent, may the outcome of your processing be characterized in model-theoretic terms: there is at least one accessible possible world in which the putative event occurs.

IV: THE PROBLEM OF COMPLETENESS

There remains a further obstacle to a total identification of mental and formal models. Any sentence in a formal language has a determinate truth value in relation to its model: an interpretation is precisely a device for assigning extensions to the expressions of the language. The model is, to use the technical term, *complete*. What we have in our minds is radically incomplete: we are often incapable of evaluating a sentence. Isard (1978) proposes that: "if we identify the mental model not with just the abstract model, but with the abstract model together with mechanisms for accessing it, the mental model need not be complete. The abstract model contains, in principle, an answer to any question, but the model's user can remain ignorant, or in doubt." Partee (1979) points out:

> Finiteness restricts us to constructing partial models, and in place of complete intensions of words we construct imperfect algorithms which yield partial functions on these partial models. Different individuals will have different partial models and different algorithms, since our brains and our real-world experience are not identical. Communication will be possible as long as there is sufficient similarity in our partial models and our imperfect semantics.

There is just one major obstacle to this thesis, she declares: the problem of propositional attitudes, which will be considered in the next section of this paper. Here, I want to deal in more detail with the notion of an incomplete model; the previous discussion should have convinced the reader that Partee is right in supposing that the intensions of basic expressions are often partial functions.

The earlier description of the use of mental models for representing quantified sentences is one way in which to implement a system of partial models. The model corresponding to the assertion, "All of the musicians are drivers," is a partial one since it is impossible to assign a truth value to, "Some of the drivers are not musicians", with respect to it. It is entirely characteristic of discourse that it fails to provide sufficient information for a complete model to be constructed. How do readers and listeners cope with this inadequacy? There are, in principle, a number of possible strategies.

First, if the information is indeterminate, then a number of separate models, each representing a different possibility, could be constructed in parallel, e.g. one model in which some drivers are not musicians and another model in which all the drivers are musicians. Human beings are poor at manipulating a number of models in parallel; hence, this strategy is of limited value since there is plainly a combinatorial explosion if each sentence of a discourse, as often happens, contains an indeterminate element.

Second, as George Miller (1977b) has suggested, a specific mental model or image may be constructed together with a representation of the set of possible states of affairs that are compatible with the discourse so far. The latter are selected from the set of possible states as each sentence is interpreted. The two forms of representation together constitute the reader's *concept* of the passage. Hence, its determinate aspects are represented in an image or model, whereas its indeterminate aspects are represented essentially in the form of a description of a set of possible worlds.

Third, the two forms of representation postulated by Miller could be combined in a hybrid representation in which conventional or propositional representations are an integral part of models. The models for quantified assertions use the convention of representing classes by an *arbitrary* number of elements. They use a parenthesis notation to represent that an element may or may not be present. This descriptive device is equivalent in force to the construction of several models in parallel, but it is more economical. The representation of negation plainly requires some sort of conventional or descriptive notation within a partial model, because otherwise ignorance of whether, say, a particular individual has a certain property would be readily confused with its specific denial. Davies (1974) has shown how a negative assertion can be represented within the hybrid scheme of a PLANNER-like language in the form of a procedure (analogous to a PLANNER procedure for representing a quantified assertion) which can be used to ensure that the correct answers to Yes/No questions are made, and which will erase itself if ever a subsequent assertion is added to the data-base that contradicts it. Davies' program, unlike Winograd's (1972) accordingly makes a clear distinction between "No" and "Dunno" in answering questions. An alternative is to introduce negative links directly into the model, that is, to use a notational convention that the system treats as negation. Such a convention can be used with representations of quantified assertions provided that the arbitrary numbers of elements are kept small.

It is difficult to resist the conclusion that human beings operate with more than one representational device. They can represent a negative assertion, for example, in the form of a propositional description – perhaps a procedure, or in the form of a model containing a link that by convention represents negation. The crucial point is that if a model is incomplete, then some such system for representing negation within it, or as an adjunct to it, is vital. The nature of the distinction between formal and mental models is accordingly in the relative amount of work done by the different components of the two systems. In a formal model, negation and quantification are handled by the structural rules of semantics, and the model structure is, as I remarked earlier, simply a set of entities. In a mental model, however, negation and quantification may be directly represented: the model is richer in structure, and in specified internal relations. It may even lie within a space of several dimensions in order to represent information about the perceived shape of the corresponding object. This richness is obtained by the use of various representational devices foreign to formal model structures.

V: THE PROBLEM OF PROPOSITIONAL ATTITUDES

Formal Semantics and the Problems of Referential Opacity

Sentences that express propositional attitudes such as beliefs, wants, and desires, are extremely problematical for any semantic theory. They give rise to a number of related referential difficulties. First, they do not allow different expressions that refer to the same entity to be freely substituted *salva veritate*. One cannot assert, as I remarked earlier, that Mr. Buckley wants to meet Mrs. Thatcher from the fact that he wants to meet the leader of the Conservative Party. Quine (1953, 1960) called such contexts, where identicals cannot be substituted with impunity, *referentially opaque*. Second, sentences that express propositional attitudes do not necessarily permit inferences to be made that depend on existential generalization:

> Arthur believes that Henry Higgins invented the phonetic alphabet.
> Therefore, there is someone whom Arthur believes invented the phonetic alphabet.

Arthur may truly hold his belief even though Henry Higgins does not actually exist. Third, the way in which a particular individual is designated may materially affect the truth of a propositional attitude. It may be true that:

> James believes that the president of the company is a paragon of sobriety

but false that:

> James believe that the man in the gutter is a paragon of sobriety

even though the two descriptions happen (unknown to James) to designate the same individual. Fourth, there is a problem of interpretation when a quantifier occurs in the context of a propositional attitude. A sentence such as:

> The king believes that someone has betrayed him

may be construed to mean either:

> There is some person whom the king believes has betrayed him:
> $(\exists x)$ (Person(x) & the king believes that x has betrayed him)

or, alternatively:

> The king believes that there is some person who has betrayed him:
> The king believes $(\exists x)$ (Person(x) & x has betrayed him).

In the first sentence, the quantifier is outside the context created by the verb, but the variable that it binds is within that context; but, as Quine emphasized, there is a grave difficulty in quantifying into contexts that are referentially opaque, because it is unclear what exactly the variables within them range over.

Quine has long maintained a scepticism about modal logic because operators such as *necessarily* create opaque contexts but since he regards belief as less dispensable than modality, he has been driven to attempt an account of propositional attitudes that relies solely on the extensions of expressions. The first step in his procedure (see Quine, 1960) is to set up a precise method for handling the referential ambiguities that they create. Each potentially identifying expression in the complement of a verb such as *believe* may, or may not, be treated as identifying, and there is a similar ambiguity with potentially referring expressions such as definite noun phrases. As a transitory analytic device, Quine accordingly treats belief as a relation between a believer and an intension; or a relation between a believer, an individual, and an intension; or a relation between a believer, several individuals, and an intension; the choice depends upon how many arguments are taken to refer. Thus each parenthesized portion in the following analyses names an intension:

(1) The chief believes that there are some people who hijacked planes:
The chief believes $[(\exists x)\ (\exists y)$ (Person(x) & Plane(y) & hijacked $(x, y))]$

(2) There is a certain person that the chief believes has hijacked a plane:
$(\exists x)$ (Person(x) & The chief believes w $[(\exists y)$ (Plane(y) & hijacked$(w, y))]$ of x

(3) There is a certain plane that the chief believes has been hijacked by someone:
$(\exists y)$ (Plane(y) & The chief believes z $[(\exists x)$ (Person(x) & hijacked $(x, z))]$ of y)

(4) There is a certain person and a certain plane such that the chief believes that the person has hijacked the plane:
$(\exists x)$ $(\exists y)$ (Person(x) & Plane(y) & The chief believes w z [hijacked (w, z)] of x and y).

Quine's next step is to rid himself of his intensional "creatures of darkness". He replaces them with the sentences themselves, which he names by using quotation marks. Thus, instead of:

The chief believes that there are some people who hijack planes.

he introduces:

The chief believes-true "There are some people who hijack planes".

Unfortunately, this step introduces some oddities and puzzles. One may truthfully say, "The Martian believes we are friendly," without in any way wishing to assert, "The Martian believes-true 'We are friendly' " (See Church, 1950). Quine, however, points out that it is not necessary for the subject of a belief-sentence to speak the language used in the object of the sentence. But he admits that there is a difficulty with language. His final alternative is accordingly to eliminate the objects of propositional attitudes: he retains the intensional notation for convenience but no longer regards it as referring to anything. He treats the opacity-producing verb and its sentential object as a one-place predicate, e.g. "x believes-that-humans-are-friendly", that may be true or false of any individual. This treatment has the desirable consequence for Quine that it inhibits inference from within opaque contexts. But it also, as his fellow extensionalist, Davidson (1969) has emphasized, renders natural language beyond the pale of a Tarskian definition of truth. There would be an infinite number of one-place predicates based on opaque constructions, and no way of specifying their truth conditions.

May one then reject an extensional treatment of opacity? It would seem so, though the reader should be warned that some proponents of "possible worlds" semantics sometimes write as though the distinction between extensions and intensions can be abolished (see Montague's, 1974, remarks in 'English as a formal language', and his subsequent withdrawal of them in 'Universal grammar').

The paradigm of an "intensional" solution to opacity is provided by Frege's (1892) account. He argued that when an expression occurs in an opaque context (Frege called such contexts, "oblique") it ceases to name an individual or whatever extensional category is relevant, but rather names an "individual concept" or whatever intensional category is relevant. Thus, when a sentence occurs within an opaque context, one can no longer treat of its truth value but rather must treat of its meaning, i.e. the proposition that it expresses. This line of thought, subsequently developed by Church (1951), led Carnap (1956) to stipulate that an inference from one opaque sentence to another is valid on condition that the conclusion is "intensionally isomorphic" with the premise. This stratagem lies at the heart of a whole series of attempted solutions to the problem of propositional attitudes. What has to be elucidated, however, is the nature of the intensions, or meanings, that occur in the context created by such verbs as *believe, want*, and *desire*.

Hintikka (1969) proposed an early and representative approach based on a "possible worlds" semantics. His starting point was direct failures of reference within opaque contexts. Even if there is no such person as Kilroy, it may still be true that an individual believes, say, that Kilroy was here. The predicate calculus in its orthodox form is ill-suited to languages in which names and other singular terms fail to refer. Hintikka accordingly suggested that allowance is made for referential failure by adopting a so-called "free" logic in which terms only refer if it is established that something exists for them to refer to. The fact that the singular term, a, refers to something is established by demonstrating the truth of an assertion of the following form:

$$(\exists x)\,(x = a).$$

In this way, existence is treated as a predicate, and the natural way of expressing the formula above is: *a exists*.

Hintikka formulated a model-theoretic interpretation for his "free" logic, making use of his model-set version of formal semantics. The key to his handling of quantification in modal contexts is to give formulae of the form:

$$(\exists x) \text{ such that necessarily } (x = a)$$

a role similar to that played by the formula that establishes that a exists. Why is it that given that 9 is necessarily greater than 7, and the number of planets equals 9, one cannot infer that the number of planets is necessarily greater than 7? Hintikka's solution to this celebrated problem posed by Quine (1953) is simply that it is not a necessary truth that the number of planets equals 9. There is no premise of the form:

$$(\exists x) \text{ such that necessarily (the number of planets} = x)$$

and therefore in some possible states of affairs the number of planets does not equal nine. Only when you can be sure that a singular term – here a definite description – refers to the same individual in all accessible possible worlds, can you quantify into a modal context, or substitute identicals within it. In the formal semantics, the structural rules for quantifiers must be formulated in the following way: if there is someone who possibly (or necessarily) has a certain property, then there is at least one nameable individual, referred to by the same name in all accessible worlds, who possibly (or necessarily) has that property; and if everyone possibly (or necessarily) has a certain property, then every nameable individual who has the same name in all accessible worlds also has that property.

One of the strong arguments adduced by Frege (1892) for the need to recognize intensions was the obvious difference between the following two identities:

The Morning star = The Morning star
The Morning star = The Evening star.

It is natural to account for them, as Frege did, by pointing out that two expressions with different intensions may have the same extension. Hintikka's analysis shows that the first identity is a necessary truth because in all possible worlds whatever is denoted by the lefthand side of the identity is also denoted by the righthand side. But the second identity is not a necessary truth because in some possible world what is denoted by "the Morning star" may not be the same as what is denoted by "the Evening star".

Hintikka has extended his approach to deal with propositional attitudes in a fairly direct way. The assertion that "John believes that S" amounts to making a division in the relevant set of possible worlds into two classes: those that are compatible with John's belief in S, and those that are not compatible with John's belief in S. Hence, we can analyze the meanings of such sentences according to the schemata:

$$x \left\{\begin{array}{l}\text{believes}\\ \text{hopes}\\ \text{remembers}\\ \text{perceives}\\ \text{desires}\\ \text{etc.}\end{array}\right\} \begin{array}{r}\text{that } p = p \text{ is the case in all accessible possible}\\ \text{worlds compatible with what } x\end{array} \left\{\begin{array}{l}\text{believes}\\ \text{hopes}\\ \text{remembers}\\ \text{perceives}\\ \text{desires}\\ \text{etc.}\end{array}\right.$$

The appropriate formal semantics for such sentences, according to Hintikka, requires a set of possible worlds and a set of individuals that exist in each possible world. The statement of the semantic rules for propositional attitudes may be made in the following way:

> '*a* believes that *p*' is true in a possible world *w* if and only if *p* is true in all the accessible possible worlds to *w*, i.e. in the set of worlds compatible with *a* believing *p* in *w*.

Obviously, different propositional attitudes may require different "accessibility" relations.

Hintikka's procedures for handling quantification in the context of a propositional attitude are analogous to his procedures for modal contexts. In order for existential generalization to apply in a context such as, "*a* believes that *b* is a spy," "*b*" must refer to the same individual in all the accessible possible worlds compatible with what *a* believes. Where this set includes the actual world, this condition can be formulated as follows:

$$(\exists x)\ (x = b)\ \&\ a \text{ believes } (x = b))$$

Granted that this condition is true, then clearly one may argue validly from "*a* believes that *b* is a spy" to "there is someone whom *a* believes to be a spy."

An individual constant within the scope of a verb like "believes" does not necessarily specify a unique individual – indeed, as we have seen, it may fail to refer to anyone at all. One can have beliefs both about individuals who happen to satisfy particular definite descriptions – whoever they are, and about specific individuals. This contrast is exactly the distinction between Donnellan's (1966) attributive and referential use of definite descriptions. Suppose, for example, that the following statement is true:

> John believes that the thirteenth President was a Whig.

The underlying logic of such a statement can be represented as:

> John believes (*Wb*).

Such an analysis corresponds to the case where John's belief is about the thirteenth President whoever he may have been, and it is of course quite consistent in "free" logic with the non-existence of such an individual. However, since there was a thirteenth President, the analysis can be refined according to Hintikka's provision:

$$(\exists x)\ (x = b)\ \&\ \text{John believes } (Wb)))$$

On the other hand, the sentence might be taken to mean that John believes that the individual who happens to have been the thirteenth President (though John doesn't know it) was a Whig. According to Hintikka, this interpretation is analyzed as:

$$(\exists x)\ (x = b)\ \&\ \text{John believes}\ (Wx))).$$

Finally, one might wish to allow that John has a belief about a specific individual, to whom he could refer in a number of ways:

$$(\exists x)\ (x = b)\ \&\ (\text{John believes}\ ((x = b)\ \&\ Wx))).$$

The condition on the substitution of identicals is still simpler. If John believes that the thirteenth President was Millard Fillmore, then one may readily make the inference:

> John believes that the thirteenth President was a Whig.
> Therefore, John believes that Millard Fillmore was a Whig.

In general, a substitution of identicals in the context of a propositional attitude like "belief" requires that the identity is also subsumed under the same attitude, or one that implies it, for the same person.

There are two major problems with any such analysis of propositional attitudes based on 'possible' worlds: one concerns the concept of a 'possible' individual, and the other concerns the notion of intensions as functions from 'possible' worlds. I will discuss these two problems separately.

The Problem of 'Possible' Individuals

A formal semantics for propositional attitudes depends on the postulation of possible worlds and possible individuls to inhabit them. Certain philosophers, notably Quine (see his reply to Kaplan, in Davidson and Hintikka, 1969) have considerable reservations about the notion of a 'possible' individual. The question arises as to how the same individual is to be identified from one possible world to another – the problem of Trans-World Heir Lines, as Kaplan has dubbed it; and the answer to such a question is easily tainted with the flavor of essential and inessential attributes – a flavor that is too much for Quine's metaphysical scruples. Other philosophers such as Lewis (1968) have tried to solve the problem of identity by abolishing it and arguing instead that an individual has only a counterpart in a possible world. Perhaps a more crucial question, however, is whether to postulate (1) that the same set of individuals is to be found in all possible worlds (differing merely in their properties and relations), or (2) that in each world accessible to a given world there may be a more extensive domain containing new individuals not existing in the given world – an arrangement that is appropriate for coping with historical development, with each future generation bringing with it new individuals, or (3) that different possible worlds may vary freely in the sets of individuals that they contain – some may have the same domain of individuals, others may have different domains. This decision is intimately related to whether or not a particular formula in modal logic, the so-called "Barcan" formula (named for Ruth Barcan-Marcus) is taken to be valid (see Hughes and Cresswell, 1968). A specific instance of the formula is:

> If everyone is necessarily mortal, then necessarily everyone is mortal.

Such a statement can be true only on the assumption that the *same* domain of individuals is contained in all possible worlds, otherwise even if everyone who actually exists is mortal there may be individuals – Gods, perhaps – in other possible worlds who are immortal. If you reject the notion that the same set of individuals is to be found in all worlds, then you are rejecting the validity of the Barcan formula.

The Barcan formula also relates to the issue of quantifying into opaque contexts, as can be brought out by considering the following inference:

> It is possible that someone is a traitor.
> ∴ There is someone who is possibly a traitor.

The inference seems distinctly implausible since it moves from an assertion of the possible truth of a statement (modality *de dicto*) to the possible possession of a property by an actual individual (modality *de re*). Yet, the Barcan formula is equivalent to an assertion that the first sentence strictly implies the second.

If the Barcan formula is accepted, then the only way to give a coherent account of validity is by assuming that possibility concerns the properties of a fixed set of (actual) individuals. But, if the relation of identity is introduced into the logic, then, as Quine (1953) has demonstrated, all sorts of difficulties arise. Even in the weakest of modal systems (T), the Barcan formula together with identity enables one to derive the generalization that every statement of a true identity is a necessary truth, i.e. there are no contingently true statements of identity. The earlier discussion of Hintikka's theory shows why it must be so in such a logic: *the only way one can substitute identicals with impunity in a modal context is if the statement of their identity is a necessary truth*. It is indeed a common practice in formal semantics to argue that proper names are *rigid* designators, that is, they pick out the same individual in all possible worlds in which they pick out any individual (see Kripke, 1971, 1972; Montague, 1974). Hence, any statement of identity such as:

George Orwell = Eric Blair

is a necessary truth. Yet, it strikes a psychologist as decidedly odd to say that the statement of such an identity is necessarily true; as Frege (1892) remarked about another example, it was a considerable astronomical achievement to determine the identity of the Morning star and the Evening star.

From the 'constructive' standpoint of mental models, the issue of what 'possible' individuals to postulate and the problem of identifying them from one world to another hardly arise. If you ask me whether Hitler might have been a successful minor artist in 1940 rather than the leader of the Third Reich, then I use my knowledge of him, and his early *mileu*, to try to construct a scenario in which this possible individual exists. There is no problem about identifying the person I am imagining: I am constructing him to be Hitler even though he may lack many of the properties of the actual man. Likewise, I can readily imagine that Hitler was really two separate individuals – one, a lover of dogs, children, and Wagner, the other, a despotic anti-semite; and if I was as lucky as George Lakoff, I might even be able to dream that I was Brigitte Bardot and that I kissed me. A listener similarly seems to be invited to construct a designation violating rigidity when he is addressed thus: "If Stalin had been Genghis Khan, then there wouldn't even have been show trials," or "If Lenin had not been Lenin, then the revolution would have failed." The claim that identities are necessary truths fails to explain why the assertion:

If Eric Blair hadn't existed, then George Orwell would not have, either.

does not seem to be equivalent to:

If George Orwell hadn't existed, then Eric Blair wouldn't have, either.

The first sentence is undoubtedly true, but the second sentence seems false – George Orwell might not have existed if Eric Blair had not been educated at a 'prep' school and Eton. Likewise, the question:

Which was named first, Phosphorus or Hesperus?

is perfectly sensible even though we now know that both expressions refer to the planet, Venus. But, if the identity is a necessary one, as Kripke claims, the question ought to be equivalent to:

Which was named first, Phosphorus or Phosphorus?

The Problem of an Intensional Analysis of Propositional Attitudes

Orthodox intensional analysis of propositional attitudes assumes that intensions can be analyzed within a 'possible worlds' semantics. We have seen that this assumption leads to some fairly intractable problems about the identity of individuals, but it also runs into trouble of a different sort with some observations originally pointed out by Mates (1952). Suppose that the following two sentences are synonymous:

John is a bachelor
John is an adult human male who is not married.

It is obvious that whoever believes that John is a bachelor, believes that John is a bachelor. Hence, it ought to be obvious that whoever believes that John is a bachelor, believes that John is an adult human male who is not married. Yet this conclusion seems very much less obvious, and Mates claims that if anyone should doubt it, then an intensional explication of propositional attitudes is incorrect. One rejoinder is that if you believe that John is a bachelor, but not that he is an adult human male who is unmarried, then you simply do not understand the two sentences (see Church, 1954; Katz, 1972). However, Mates's argument can be raised about propositions as a whole.

If a proposition is a function from possible worlds to a truth value, then any contradiction expresses the same proposition as any other contradiction, and any necessary truth expresses the same preposition as any other necessary truth. Nevertheless, it may not be feasible to interchange such propositions *salva veritate* within a propositional attitude context. For example, John may believe that $2 + 2 = 5$, but it does not thereby fellow that he believes, say, that there are more integers than primes.

If one propositions cannot be substituted for another *salva veritate*, then the two must somehow differ in meaning. Hence, one contradiction (or necessary truth) is not synonymous with another, and what is needed is a semantic theory that will distinguish them. The orthodox analysis of intensions as functions from possible worlds to truth values will not do.

One proposed refinement rests on the old adage: "Why be difficult when with a little more effort you can be impossible". It depends on the introduction of *impossible* worlds (cf. Hintikka, 1975). The intension of a sentence is accordingly a function from a set of possible worlds and a set of impossible worlds. It follows that the contradiction "2 + 2 = 5" is not identical to the contradiction "There are more integers than primes", since they will be true in different impossible worlds, and the substitution of one for another is no longer required to maintain the same truth value in the context of a propositional attitude. However, the problem with impossible worlds – apart from the fact that they are impossible – is that once they are admitted into semantic theory even the definition of simple operations becomes extremely cumbersome. Hence, a second method of developing a more refined semantics has been advocated by Bigelow (1978) and Cresswell (this volume). It takes into account the *way* in which the intension of a sentence is derived from the intensions of its parts (what Lewis, 1972, called the 'meaning' of a sentence), and accordingly can distinguish between two sentences with the same intension.

A third approach rests on an influential analysis of the pragmatics of context that has been proposed by Kaplan (1977). As he points out, it is necessary to distinguish the context of an utterance from the circumstances of its evaluation. A simple way to grasp the nature of this distinction is to consider the sentence:

I am speaking now.

It is true in any context in which it is uttered, but it is not thereby logically true – the speaker does not necessarily have to be speaking. There are accordingly some possible worlds and times in which the sentence is false. One must accordingly distinguish between the context of a sentence and the circumstances of its evaluation. The machinery for making the distinction can be based on "possible worlds", and was originally provided by Hans Kamp (1971) in his analysis of the indexical expression, "now". Both Stalnaker (1978) and Klein (1979) have adopted this more refined semantical analysis that depends on a system of double indexing in which a set of possible worlds is used twice, once for context and once for circumstances of evaluation.[10] Since a proposition is a function from possible worlds to a truth value, the *propositional concept* expressed by a specific utterance is accordingly a function from pairs of possible worlds – one member of the pair corresponding to a context, and the other to a circumstance of evaluation – to a truth value. In other words, a propositional concept or 'meaning' is a function from contexts to an intension, and an intension is a function from worlds to a truth value. In order to handle propositional attitudes, it is necessary to look, not at intensions, but the finer grained notion of a propositional concept.

One drawback with all of these sorts of solution is that they lead to over refinement in semantic theory. There is nothing wrong in principle with the semantic mill grinding ever finer grains of meaning, but its work is otiose except in the case of modal expressions and propositional attitudes: elsewhere the ordinary notion of an intension suffices for analytical purposes. Moreover, even the very finest of semantic discriminations still runs into problems.

One difficulty has been pointed out by Bas van Fraassen (in a talk at a workshop on semantics at the University of Texas, Austin, 1978). He illustrates it with the following anecdote: The king's son is thrown into prison as a result of the misdeeds of his wicked uncle, and is forced to wear an iron mask. His fellow prisoners suggest that he appeals directly to the king. "It's no use," he replies, "the king believes that I am dead". Subsequently, the king visits the prison, and his son appears before him wearing the iron mask. When he is returned to his cell, the inmates ask what happened. "The king believes that I am a common criminal", he replies.

The problem is to account for the interpretation of the two utterances made by the king's son, and, in particular, for the two uses of, "I". According to Kaplan's (1977) theory, such indexical expressions refer directly: it is as though the relevant individual becomes a part of the proposition expressed. But this hypothesis clearly breaks down in the context of a propositional attitude. The king hardly believes of his son both that he is dead and that he stands before him as a common criminal.

Some authors have suggested that the phenomena of propositional attitudes reflect a fundamental shortcoming in model-theoretic semantics (Katz and Katz, 1977); others argue that they reflect a fundamental shortcoming in human nature (Partee, 1979). The point is, Partee claims, that the performance limitations of speakers using the mundane extensional language must be reflected in the competence of speakers talking about that usage (see Linsky, 1977). People may hold mistaken beliefs or succumb to fallacies, and these limitations must be taken into account in characterizing their propositional attitudes. The idealizations of formal semantics must give way to the quirks of individual psychology when discourse is explicitly addressed to that topic. Indeed, it is time to consider the whole issue of propositional attitudes from a psychological standpoint.

The Mental Representation of Propositional Attitudes

Since even little children can understand assertions about propositional attitudes, the analysis in terms of possible worlds may be misleading. The infant on the Clapham omnibus chats about who still believes in fairies perhaps without even a tacit knowledge of scope and opacity, just as his elders, as I have argued, may reason from quantified assertions without even a tacit knowledge of the relevant rules of inference. The relation between formal semantics and psychological semantics may be analogous to an example drawn by Seymour Papert. You might suppose that your nervous system has to carry out some complex computations in order to enable you to catch a ball. In fact, as Papert points out, there is a very much simpler procedure: look at the ball, and if it appears to move downwards with respect to your field of view, run forwards, if it appears to move upwards with respect to your field of view run backwards, and if it appears stationary with respect to your field of view, don't move – it will hit you in the eye. A logician trying to develop a formal semantics for natural language is somewhat like a mathematician trying to work out the differential equations that ought to be solved to catch the ball. What is needed to make psychological sense of propositional attitudes is, in my view, an extension of the notion of a mental model, a study of the semantics of such verbs as *believe*, and an analysis of certain aspects of referring expressions.

Alan Garnham and I have recently argued that:

> ... the real context of an utterance consists of the *models* of the current conversation that the speaker and the listener create and maintain. These models represent the universe of discourse – its individuals, events, relations, and so on – and, most importantly, they incorporate what is known about the knowledge of other participants. A speaker structures his remarks partly on the basis of what he knows about the listener's discourse model; a listener interprets utterances partly on the basis of what he knows about the speaker's discourse model. (Johnson-Laird and Garnham, 1979).

What we had in mind was a generalization of the mental models used to represent quantified assertions; and we attempted to show that this idea could illuminate a number of phenomena concerning definite and indefinite descriptions. It is, for instance, uniqueness within a model rather than in reality that is crucial for the use of definite descriptions. If a speaker remarks:

The man who lives next door drives to work

then his referential usage neither entails nor presupposes that there is only one man living next door to him. His description designates the only neighbour who is relevant in the context. We were also concerned with Donnellan's (1966) distinction between referential and attributive uses of definite descriptions, and since this distinction has been claimed to solve the problems of opacity (Cole, 1978), or to be elucidated by propositional attitudes (as in Hintikka's analysis above), it is worth analyzing it in more detail.

Suppose a speaker claims:

> The murderer of Smith is insane

then his definite description is used attributively, according to Donnellan, if he is concerned solely with the murderer of Smith whoever he may be; it is used referentially if he intends to pick out a particular individual, whom he might have designated in some other way. An attributive usage makes an essential use of the definite description and, Donnellan claims, it is crucial that there is some entity that matches the description or else the speech act is abortive. A referential usage, however, makes an inessential use of the description – some other designation would do, and, moreover, if the actual description fails to match any entity, the consequences may not be disastrous. If a speaker asserts:

> The woman drinking the martini is a publisher

then he may designate a particular individual, and be understood correctly, even if it turns out that the lady in question is drinking gin.

Garnham and I argue that Donnellan's analysis is flawed. There are cases where even though there is no entity corresponding to an attributive use of a definite description, communication succeeds perfectly. Consider the following scenario. John has told everyone that he is going to see *The Sound of Music*. He does indeed see it, but he also makes a clandestine visit to another cinema. You believe that unbeknownst to him his wife, Mary, has found out he has seen another film. Even though neither she nor you know what the second film was, you might ask her:

> How do you think John enjoyed the film that he doesn't know that you know he saw last night?

Your attributive designation will be perfectly intelligible. Moreover, it will be perfectly intelligible if, unbeknownst to *you*, Mary has discovered that her husband has found out that she knows about his visit to another film. In this case, of course, there is nothing that matches your attributive description – he knows she knows – but no harm is done. Mary realizes that there is no film corresponding to your description, but she also knows of her husband's deception and that he has found out about her finding out: your supposition is entirely compatible with an earlier stage in the history of events.

We go on to argue that the referential-attributive distinction is based on a speaker's intentions, but it must be made twice over: once in terms of whether the speaker intends to designate an entity referentially or attributively, and once in terms of whether he intends the listener to interpret his designation referentially or attributively. There *are* asymmetries. If you have reason to believe that John went to the cinema, then you might inquire:

What was the movie John saw last night?

Your definite description is attributive for you, but you intend it to be referential for your listener. The view that we take is that the two-fold referential-attributive distinction applies to both definite and indefinite descriptions, and that it may also be made in opaque contexts.[11] The distinction depends on the knowledge that the speaker intends to be relevant to the interpretation of his utterance. In an attributive use, no other unique descriptions which fit the designation are intended to be relevant to its interpretation, even if they are known to the speaker or listener. In order to use a description referentially, a speaker must have a certain minimal knowledge about what it designates (see Johnson-Laird and Garnham, 1979, for the details), and he is committed to the substitution *salva veritate* of other of its designations in his assertion.

An individual's beliefs, wants, hopes, and other such propositional attitudes can be represented in a mental model. Part of such a model will, of course, be beliefs about the beliefs of other people, and in general propositional attitudes about their propositional attitudes. Let us take belief as a paradigmatic example of a propositional attitude in order to simplify the discussion. Person *A* may have beliefs about person *B*, including beliefs about *B*'s beliefs about *A*, beliefs about *B*'s beliefs about *A*'s beliefs about *B*, and so on *ad infinitum*. Philip Cohen (1978) has devized a computer program that uses semantic networks nested in this way. He prevents the potentially embarrassing infinite regression by adopting an idea from David Lewis's (1969) analysis of conventions: as soon as there is no difference between an adjacent odd numbered (or even numbered) pair of nested beliefs, they can simply be identified and the regress stops there. For example, if there is no difference between John's beliefs about Mary and what he believes she believes he believes about her, then the latter can be identified with the former. In this way a *mutual belief* can be represented (see Schiffer, 1972).

The essential phenomenon about (other) people's beliefs is that they may be mistaken. They may believe that Sherlock Holmes exists or that Bianca

Jagger is a figment of a press agent's imagination. They may believe that Euthanasia is a country somewhere in South-East Asia, or that insecticide is a lemming-like collective suicide by a colony of social insects. They may believe that $\sqrt{2}$ is a rational number, or that a quantity of liquid is increased by pouring it from a broad beaker into a narrow one. When you mentally represent someone else's beliefs, then you may insulate them totally from your own. But usually, of course, there is some communality, which will in turn be represented in your mental model. If, for instance, you believe that all the linguistis at a certain university are Montague grammarians, and I believe that at least some of them are, then the relevant part of your model of the world will correspond to the following sort of state of affairs:

$$\begin{array}{l} l = m \\ l = m \\ l = m \\ \quad (m) \end{array}$$

where '*l*' denotes a linguist at the university and '*m*' denotes a Montague grammarian, and my model will correspond to this sort of state of affairs:

$$\begin{array}{l} l = m \\ l = m \\ (l)\ (m) \end{array}$$

In your representation of my beliefs, you may well establish that there are certain individuals whom we agree about, as is illustrated in Table 2.

The so-called problems of opacity confound two distinct matters: the referential-attributive distinction and failures of reference. If I think that a certain linguist has become a Montague grammarian, then I may express this belief to you, depending on the circumstances, in a variety of ways, such as:

> A well known linguist has become a Montague grammarian.
> The chairman of Euphoric State University's linguistics department has become a Montague grammarian.
> Arthur Ortcutt has become a Montague grammarian.

My intention may be to designate an individual referentially or attributively, and there may be an asymmetry between my intentions as far as I am concerned and as far as you are concerned (see Johnson-Laird and Garnham, 1979, for the arguments showing how indefinites and proper names may be used in either way). If, as a consequence of hearing my remark, you report my belief, then, in principle, there are different ways in which you can designate

TABLE 2
An example of a nested set of beliefs within a mental model

Your belief: (All the linguists are Montague grammarians)		Your belief about my belief: (At least some of the linguists are are Montague grammarians)
$l = m = p$	=	$l = m$
$l = m$		$l = m$
$l = m$		$(l)\ (m)$
$(m)\ (p)$		

Note. A token '*l*' represents a linguist at a certain university, a token '*m*' represents a Montague grammarian at the university, and parentheses indicate that the individual may or may not exist. Uniqueness within a mental model of this sort can be directly represented. Thus, if '*p*' represent a member of the class of pilots, then you believe that the only linguist who is a pilot is a Montague grammarian and that I, too, believe this individual to be a Montague grammarian, though you do not know whether I know that this person is a pilot. There are, of course, many other alternative methods for representing co-reference. My only empirical claim is that people often represent classes by thinking of an arbitrary number of members of them, and hence, I postulate this format for beliefs rather than the descriptive format of a semantic network used by Cohen (1978) and others.

the relevant linguist. If my intention was that the designation should be attributive for you, and it was not thwarted, then you may say:

Phil believes that $\ulcorner x \urcorner$ has become a Montague grammarian

where $\ulcorner x \urcorner$ stands for the same designation as I used. Your usage will be attributive and normally intended to be taken by your listener as attributive, since you will not be committed to the substitution of other designations of the individual in your assertion.

Let us suppose, alternatively, that my original utterance was intended to be referential for you, that this intention was not thwarted, and moreover, that you believe that Arthur Ortcutt, a well known linguist, is the chairman of ESU's linguistics department. You may use any of the same designations as those above in order to report my belief, but now there is a problem. My usage though intended to be referential for you, may not have been for me. If I had said:

Arthur Ortcutt, whoever he may be – you'll know him, has become a Montague grammarian then you should use my designation in order to make a faithful report of my belief, or alternatively, quality some other designation:

> Phil believes that the chairman of the ESU Linguistics department, he knows him only as Arthur Ortcutt, has become a Montague grammarian.

Where, however, my usage is both referential for you and me, then you may exercise considerably more freedom in your choice of designation in describing my belief. Nevertheless, the general principle appears to be *not* to use designations that might implicate that I have some knowledge that, in fact, I do not possess. You should not use the designation, "the leader of the Europhic Elks," for example, if I do not know that it also designates the relevant individual.

What propositional attitudes add that complicates this analysis is *failure* of reference in true assertions. Regardless of whether I originally designated an individual referentially or attributively, you may have good reasons for supposing that there is no such person. This possibility is obvious in the case of an attributive designation. For example, I remark:

> I'd like to meet the man who lives at 221b Baker Street, whoever he may be.

You, who know perfectly well that there is no one who lives at that address, can report my views:

> Phil would like to meet the man who lives at 221b Baker Street.

without being committed to the existence of such an individual, except in your model of my beliefs. What is less obvious, however, is that even when referential designations are used in the context of a propositional attitude, there may be a failure of reference that does not affect the truth of the assertion. If, for instance, I share the allegedly common delusion of believing that Sherlock Holmes is a real person, who lives at 221b Baker Street and who is the greatest detective in the world, then you, who know all these facts about my beliefs, may instead report my remarks in the following words:

> Phil would like to meet Sherlock Holmes.

Your designation can be referential by the usual criteria, except that you do not intend it to designate an actual person: in particular, you will be committed to the substitution *salva veritate* of other designations that also pick out the same individual in your model of my beliefs, e.g.

> Phil would like to meet (the person whom he thinks) the greatest detective in the world.

The question of existence is indeed independent of the referential-attributive distinction.

Existence is the critical factor for such inferences as:

> The king believes that someone has betrayed him.
> Therefore, there is someone whom the king believes has betrayed him.

or:

> The king believes that Arthur Ortcutt has betrayed him.
> Therefore, there is someone whom the king believes has betrayed him.

An inference that leads to a conclusion in which there is quantifying into the context of a propositional verb is warranted provided the originally designated individual exists. Contrary to what has been assumed by some theorists (e.g. Kaplan, 1969), the designation may well be attributive rather than referential. The king and I may believe that he has been betrayed by the man in the iron mask, but we may know nothing else about this individual. I might accordingly assert:

> The king believes that the man in the iron mask, whoever he may be, has betrayed him.

and thereby intend to be committed to the inference:

> There is someone whom the king believes has betrayed him.

If the king merely believes that someone or other is a traitor, then the validity of 'exporting' the quantifier from the context of belief again depends solely on the question of existence.

Granted that the referential-attributive distinction is independent of propositional attitudes, then it follows of course that any attempt to explain that distinction by reference to particular propositional attitudes is unworkable (*pace* Hintikka, 1969), and likewise that the converse attempt to elucidate opacity in terms of the referential-attributive distinction is equally erroneous (*pace* Cole, 1978).[12]

The analysis of propositional attitudes in terms of mental models can accommodate cases that cause difficulties for a 'possible worlds' semantics.

It is necessary to assume that one person can possess a mental model of another person's beliefs, and that among the representation of another's beliefs can be information about their misconceptions. The substitution of one necessary truth or contradiction for another is warranted only when the model of an individual's relevant system of thought enables the inference to be drawn. The assertion:

Albert thinks that $2 + 2 = 5$

warrants the conclusion:

Albert thinks that $2 + 3 = 6$

only if Albert's system of arithmetic, taken together with the first assertion, allows one to infer the second assertion. In practice, the conclusion has to be *constructed* on the basis of such knowledge.

The contrasting uses of indexicals within expressions of propositional attitudes can be accommodated in a similar way. In van Fraassen's example, listeners must take the indexical in:

The king believes that I am dead

to pick out an individual who claims to be the king's son. In this way, they can take the remark to mean that the king believes of his son that he is dead. The designation, "his son", would be referential for all concerned: the king, his son, and the listeners. Listeners must take the indexical in:

The king believes that I am a common criminal

to pick out the man in the iron mask, and they must infer from the context that the king has failed to identify him as his son. In this way, they can take the remark to mean that the king believes of the man in the iron mask that he is a common criminal. The designation, "the man in the iron mask", may be attributive for the king or erroneously referential where he is under a definite misapprehension about the identity of the man.

One unexpected advantage of an analysis in terms of mental models is that it brings to light a new problem associated with propositional attitudes. Suppose you discover that a friend has an erroneous belief: he thinks, for example, that men who dress up in women's clothes are members of some religious order – they have unusual habits, perhaps. You might describe your friend's idiosyncratic views to a third party:

My friend thinks that transvestites are monks.

This remark, however, is open to an entirely different interpretation. Suppose, on the other hand, that you have another friend, who is in error, not on a factual matter, but on questions of lexical meaning: he believes that the word *transvestite* means a member of a religious order. You must represent this error in your model of his lexicon – you may have to bear it in mind in talking to him. It will certainly cause you to interpret a remark such as:

> St. Francis was a transvestite

rather differently if it happens to be made by your friend. You might explain this assertion to a third party:

> My friend thinks that transvestites are monks.

This statement clearly does not imply:

> My friend thinks that men who dress up in women's clothing are monks.

However, precisely this inference *is* warranted in the case of the factual error of your first friend.

What such examples establish is that a semantic theory formulated for a language can never be rich enough to cope with propositional attitudes. This idealization must be abandoned: speakers often have only an imperfect grasp of their language and this fact must be allowed for in the analysis of discourse about their ignorance. In general, assertions about an individual's language warrant those inferences that can be constructed from them, based on a model of that person's knowledge of the language. Hence, the theory of mental models emphasizes the communicative aspects of language, and the constructive manner in which propositional attitudes are considered – not *simpliciter*, but as remarks founded on a mental representation of another person's mental world.

One final question: which verbs characterize propositional attitudes? The answer tends to take the form of an *ad hoc* list. However, one advantage of pursuing a decompositional semantics is that a case can be made to show how the phenomena of opacity are inherited by all verbs that contain a particular sort of primitive that gives rise to it, namely, the primitive that corresponds to the construction of a mental model. Miller and Johnson-Laird (1976, Sec. 7.3) argue, for example, that verbs of vision derive from two primitives: one of them, which underlies the verb *to see*, is the process involved when an internal model of the external world is constructed out of information from the receptors; and the other, which underlies the verb *to look at*, depends essentially only on the alignment of the eyes. The verb *to see* expresses a propositional attitude, as in the following sentence:

> Picasso saw a bull's head where I saw just a bicycle seat and a pair of handlebars.

The verb *to look at* does not express a propositional attitude. Hence, only those verbs that can be based upon seeing are potentially opaque, e.g. *sight, glimpse, spy, regard, view, behold, watch, search, seek*. Verbs that are based on *look at* remain transparent, e.g. *glance, stare, peer, peep, peek.*

VI: CONCLUSIONS

Critics of *applied* formal semantics often point out that there is more to the meaning of ordinary discourse than truth conditions and extensions. They argue that such matters as questions and requests and promises, illocutionary and perlocutionary force, and conventional and conversational implicature, lie outside what can be reasonably treated by model-theoretic analyses. There is no doubt that many semanticists have deliberately chosen to ignore such matters; there is no doubt that the effects of language cannot be entirely a matter of intensions or extensions. Paraphrase is not poetry. However, I have not discussed these problems, because there are increasing signs that formal methods may be used to deal with many of them equally as well as any other methods that are available.

The problem that lexical semantics is unknowable, I have argued, turns out to be solvable, but at a price. Suppose as a matter of fact that no intensions – either mental or abstract – could be specified for words, then formal semantics would have been based on the existence of functions which, by assumption, cannot be formulated. In reality, it seems that these functions are often partial ones, and that a semantics of prototypes, or default values, is needed for natural language. Assignments are therefore inevitably incomplete, since model structures must in effect by constrained by special sorts of meaning postulate, e.g. *if x is a lemon, then x is yellow unless the context implies otherwise*, which are intended to capture a relation that is weaker than entailment but stronger than a mere induction to which a probability is attached. However, the only certain way to ensure that the assumptions of formal semantics are warranted for natural language is to attempt to specify such postulates, or alternatively, some species of decompositional analyses.

The same argument may be made, of course, about the functions employed in the structural rules of formal semantics. How, for example, does the intension of an adverb operate on that of a verb to create a new intension? Miller and Johnson-Laird (1976, p. 537) explored this issue in relation to an adverbial modification of verbs of motion:

> We may assume that the complex procedure UPWARD operates in the following way. A subprocedure, which can be thought of as the -WARD component, locates in the procedure to be modified the two locative components defining the process – in the present case the arguments [that specify an earlier and a later location]. If there is no such pair of arguments, the computation fails: the procedure to be modified violates the selectional restrictions on -WARD. A further subprocedure, which can be thought of as the UP-component, then inserts into the procedure to be modifed a new component specifying that the later location is OVER the earlier one.

However, a more comprehensive analysis of the specific details of all the different sorts of structural rules is required.

Montague evidently believed that syntactic research should not be pursued far in advance of its corresponding semantics, or else, as the linguistic literature illustrates, the postulated syntactic rules would be likely to be erroneous. Perhaps this principle should be extended to the semantics of basic lexical items. A cognitive science of meaning ought to be concerned with specifying the nature of basic intensions, rather than merely assuming that such specifications are feasible in principle.

The difficulty of propositional attitudes for formal semantics is, in part, a legacy of a metaphysical assumption that can be traced back to Frege – a bias against psychologism. A strong version of psychologism is that words themselves refer to mental processes. Frege, however, cautioned us not to confuse a proposition with the mental processes through which we become aware of it. He argued that propositions are neither in the world nor in our minds, but in some "third realm" of Platonic entities. Thus, the theorem of Pythagoras is timelessly true – true independently of whether anyone considers it to be true. This sort of reaction to the earlier views of Mill and his Empiricist predecessors has largely permeated formal semantics. Yet, I believe that it is a reaction to a particular brand of psychologism – that variety which identifies meanings with images. As Dummett (1967) remarks, in characterizing Frege's views: "The mental images which a word may arouse in the mind of speaker or hearer are irrelevant to its meaning, which consists, rather, in the part played by the word in determining the truth-conditions of sentences in which it occurs." Images often seem, of course, to be a wholly subjective epiphenomenon.

The fruits of extreme anti-psychologism are an exaggerated Realism, the doctrine that the meaning of a proposition is its truth conditions, which are independent of how anyone may come to know them. A Realist semantics, however, must take pains to avoid dealing with the meanings of basic lexical items and of sentences expressing propositional attitudes. With the former, it is forced to postulate that meanings are not mental entities; with the latter, it must either ignore human failings or else itself fail to do justice to ordinary discourse.

A very much more appropriate philosophy of language is to be found in the 'constructivism' of Wittgenstein's later works (see, e.g. Hacker, 1972, for this interpretation), but it is marred for our purposes by Wittgenstein's anti-mentalistic conception of meaning. Yet, his idea of a criterion can be explicated in terms of the notion of a default value.[8] The status of a default value is a matter of convention, but a convention that reflects those aspects of the world that become – by interaction with our cognitive apparatus – embodied in the semantics of our language. To some extent a human society imposes its conceptions upon the world; but to some extent the world imposes its nature upon the conceptions of society. The traffic in both directions is constrained by our biological endowment as reflected in our conceptual and perceptual processes. How the world is, and can be, are matters that we apprehend only through the machinery of our cognitive abilities, either by direct perception or by indirect acts of constructive thought, acts which ultimately underlie science. The spontaneous interpretation of ordinary discourse depends largely on our tacit skills, most of which are exercised outside conscious awareness. They provide us with our basic categorizing principles – a predilection for conceiving objects in terms of prototypes rather than as sets of necessary and sufficient properties – with which to organize our experience. Just as we shall never know that we know the 'true' extension of a natural kind term, so we will never know that we know the 'true' nature of reality. For this reason, it is more instructive to concentrate upon the communication of concepts and to approach language as a systematic device for conveying a mental model from one mind to another.

In place of such one-sided philosophies as Realism, Idealism, and Empiricism, I propose a 'constructivism' based upon a mentalistic analysis of meaning, that is, a weak version of 'psychologism' in which an account of the meanings of words is necessarily an account of the tacit mental processes that relate them to their extensions. Language relates to reality through the medium of the mind, and in particular through the human ability to construct models of actual and possible worlds.

Linguists of diverse persuasions have recently begun to be concerned with psychologically plausible accounts of syntax. The methods of formal semantics are likewise sufficiently powerful to be usefully employed in formulating a psychological theory of meaning. However, as we have seen, there remain some obstacles to be overcome. I have concentrated on lexical semantics because it is fundamental but presents no obviously insurmountable barriers, and on propositional attitudes because they seem to require a radical but feasible re-orientation in applied formal semantics in order to cope with incomplete intensions and model structures.

The major difference between formal and psychological semantics is that model structures provide extensions for expressions in the language, with the work of evaluation being done by the assignment function and the structural rules, whereas mental models are actively constructed, modified, and manipulated, in order to serve many other functions apart from providing a basis against which to evaluate assertions. Moreover, the idea that reasoning often consists in constructing and testing models is quite alien to the 'syntactic' tradition of logic, where uninterpreted formulae are manipulated according to formal rules of inference. Yet, the psychological thesis has some empirical support, and the additional advantage of making the problem of how children learn to reason rather more tractable than it has seemed in the past.

There is one outstanding obstacle to the ultimate reconciliation of formal and psychological semantics. Although it is natural to think of the end product of comprehension as the meaning of a sentence, this entity is unlikely to be a simple mental object that rolls off the end of a cognitive conveyor belt. If a listener constructs a model of discourse, or an integrated propositional representation of it, then the process of interpretation will often consist of merely adding some element, corresponding to part of the utterance, to the existing model. There may be no moment in time when the listener may be said to have the whole of the meaning of the sentence in mind. Moreover, speakers can exploit this 'real time' aspect of their utterances deictically, as, for example, when commentators or instructors time their remarks to coincide informatively with the events that they are describing. It is unclear how this aspect of performance can be accommodated within a formal theory. Indeed, one of the major appeals of developing a 'procedural semantics' of the sort advocated by Woods (1967, 1969) and Davies and Isard (1972) is that it forces the theorist to consider processes. "This is a signal virtue in comparison to model-theoretic and linguistic approaches that tend naturally to emphasize structure at the expense of process. Psychological processes take place in time, and so, too, do the operations of computers" (Johnson-Laird, 1977).

Processing is similarly singularly sensitive to context. Hence, a remark such as:

Mary is at the table

will elicit one chain of processes if it is a response to a question about Mary's whereabouts – finding the table and then checking for Mary, but a very different chain if it is an identification of a particular table – finding Mary and then checking for a table. An utterance can 'control' such temporal aspects of comprehension, and a speaker may likewise interrupt one process with another, changing clauses midstream.

The pioneers of the logical analysis of natural language maintained that it did not wear its true semantics on its sleeve. They revized its underlying structure so as to cast it into a shape that would fit the formal dress of the predicate calculus. This procrustean tailoring was always implausible from the standpoint of psychology. Hence, it is greatly to Montague's credit that he developed a richer conception of formal languages, which could be used in the analysis of natural language without reducing the number of its syntactic categories and without postulating a radically different 'hidden' logical structure for its sentences. Montague evidently cared not a jot for psychological reality: he conceived his work as a branch of mathematics or logic. But is the study of the syntax and semantics of a natural language a part of mathematics or a part of psychology? One may as well ask whether the study of mental arithmetic, or of mathematical prodigies, is a matter for mathematics or psychology. There is every reason to suppose that such phenomena can be investigated by both disciplines. The free communication of ideas between them has yet to be achieved: there is no tunnel between them, but we are beginning to see how the land lies.

Laboratory of Experimental Psychology,
University of Sussex

ACKNOWLEDGMENTS

This paper owes much to the three Workshops on Semantics held in 1979 at the University of Texas, Austin. I am very grateful to Stan Peters and Phil Gough for the opportunity to attend them, and to the Sloan Foundation for making my attendance possible. Colleagues, collaborators and fellow participants have all given me the benefit of their advice and ideas. I want particularly to thank Kate Ehrlich, Alan Garnham, Steve Isard, Ewan Klein, George Miller, and Stan Peters, for allowing me to appropriate some of their wisdom. My research is supported by the Social Science Research Council (G.B.).

NOTES

[1] The domain of the function should contain other arguments such as time (see Montague, 1974). Context can also be treated by introducing still further indexes (see Lewis, 1972) or in a rather different way (see Section V).

[2] Semantic networks, of course, also utilize non-linear representations. Assertions about the same entity are gathered together at the node representing that entity. This network structure facilitates the process of search. It does not have any essential semantic function: the same information could be represented in an unordered list of assertions in which co-reference is established in some other way.

[3] Hintikka (1974) argues that a sentence such as, "Some relative of each villager and some relative of each townsman hate each other," is synonymous with the sentence obtained by switching round the two noun phrases, "Some relative of each townsman and some relative of each villager hate each other." He concludes that it is accordingly necessary to abandon a strictly linear order of quantifiers: they must be 'branching' in order to allow that neither of the formulae corresponding to the two noun phrases is necessarily within the scope of the other. Whether Hintikka's arguments are sound is a matter of controversy; my own predilection is to follow Barwise's (1978) exegesis in which it turns out that the examples above can be represented in the first order predicate calculus by a formula corresponding to, "For every villager and every townsman there is a relative of one and a relative of the other that hate each other." However, Barwise introduces further examples that may require branching quantifiers, e.g. "The richer the country, the more powerful one of its officials."

[4] I am grateful to Alan Garnham for drawing my attention to Hacker's revealing study of Wittgenstein's philosophy.

[5] Stalnaker (in a workshop on semantics, University of Texas, Austin, 1978) has argued cogently that the objects of thought and speech are one and the same. However, as he points out, there is a tension between this view and Putnam's thesis that meanings are not in the mind. It would follow that beliefs are not in the mind, either. This conclusion may be acceptable to philosophers – Stalnaker does not find it implausible – but I think that psychologists are liable to take it as a *reductio ad absurdum*.

[6] Putnam's (1970) arguments were originally directed against Katz's theory of semantics. However, it should be noted that they apply equally to those psychological theories of meaning based on meaning postulates. If there are no analytic truths of the form *every lemon has P*, then the meaning of *lemon* cannot be captured in meaning postulates of an orthodox sort.

[7] Partee (1979) has slightly shifted her ground and argued that if semantics is to be treated as a branch of psychology, then it is necessary to give up some of the idealizations of 'possible worlds' semantics in order to cope with propositional attitudes.

[8] The idea that criteria can be treated as default values arose in conversation with Alan Garnham (see also his unpublished paper, 'Constructivism as a unifying thesis in semantics').

[9] Lawyers, of course, are often concerned to close the lexicon, and to replace a prototype with a set of necessary and sufficient conditions. To take a typical example, the London Building Acts define a warehouse class of building as (and I quote from memory) a warehouse, manufactory, brewery, distillery or any other building exceeding 150 thousand foot square which is neither a public nor a domestic building. The quantity of

litigation on matters not pertaining to case law reflects, I imagine, an inability and a disinclination to close it completely.

[10] Here, as elsewhere, I ignore the fact that times and perhaps other indexes are required in addition to worlds.

[11] Partee (1972) has suggested that the (orthodox) referential-attributive distinction also applies to indefinite descriptions, and that it is independent of questions of scope.

[12] Cole's theory is also rejected by Klein (1979), who advocates a scope interpretation along the lines laid down by Montague's (1974) proper theory of quantification.

REFERENCES

Anderson, J. R.: (1976) *Language, Memory, and Thought*, Erlbaum, Hillsdale, N. J.

Anderson, J. R.: (1978) 'Arguments concerning representations for mental imagery,' *Psychological Review* 85, 249–277.

Asher, R.: (1972) *Talking Sense*, Pitman, London.

Baker, G. P.: (1974) 'Criteria: a new foundation for semantics,' *Ratio* 16, 156–189.

Barwise, J.: (1978) 'On branching quantifiers in English,' *Journal of Philosophical Logic* 8, 47–80.

Berlin, B. and Kay, P.: (1969) *Basic Color Terms: Their Universality and Evolution*, University of California Press, Berkeley.

Bigelow, J. G.: (1978) 'Believing in semantics,' *Linguistics and Philosophy* 2, 101–144.

Bruner, J. S., J. J. Goodnow, and G. A. Austin: (1956) *A Study of Thinking*, Wiley, New York.

Carey, S.: (1978) 'The child as word learner,' in M. Halle, J. Bresnan, and G. A. Miller (eds.) *Linguistic Theory and Psychology Reality*, MIT Press, Cambridge, Mass.

Carnap, R.: (1956) *Meaning and Necessity: A Study in Semantics and Modal Logic*, second edition, Chicago University Press, Chicago.

Chomsky, N.: (1965) *Aspect of the Theory of Syntax*, MIT Press, Cambridge, Mass.

Church, A.: (1950) 'On Carnap's analysis of statements of assertion and belief,' *Analysis* 10, 97–99.

Church, A.: (1951) 'The need for abstract entities in semantic analysis,' *Contributions to the Analysis and Synthesis of Knowledge. Proceedings of the American Academy of Arts and Sciences* 80, 100–112.

Church, A.: (1954) 'Intensional isomorphism and identity of belief,' *Philosophical Studies* 5, 65–73.

Clark, H. H. and E. V. Clark: (1977) *Psychology and Language: an Introduction to Psycholinguistics*, Harcourt Brace Jovanovich, New York.

Cohen, P.: (1978) 'On knowing what to say: planning speech acts,' Ph.D. dissertation, Technical Report No. 118, Dept. of Computer Science, University of Toronto.

Cole, P.: (1978) 'On the origins of referential opacity,' in P. Cole (ed.), *Syntax and Semantics, Vol. 9: Pragmatics*, Academic Press, New York.

Collins, A. M. and M. R. Quillian: (1972) 'Experiments on semantic memory and language comprehension,' in L. W. Gregg (ed.), *Cognition in Learning and Memory*, Wiley, New York.

Davidson, D.: (1969) On saying that,' in D. Davidson and J. Hintikka (eds.), *Words and Objections: Essays on the Work of W. V. Quine*, Humanities Press, New York.

Davidson, D. and J. Hintikka (eds.): (1969) *Words and Objections: Essays on the Work of W. V. Quine*, Humanities Press, New York.

Davies, D. J. M.: (1974) 'Representing negation in a Planner system,' Proceedings of Artificial Intelligence and Simulation of Behaviour (AISB) Society, Summer Conference, Sussex University.

Davies, D. J. M. and S. Isard (1972) 'Utterances as programs,' in D. Michie (ed.), *Machine Intelligence* 7, Edinburgh University Press, Edinburgh.

Donnellan, K. S.: (1966) 'Reference and definite descriptions,' *Philosophical Review* 75, 281–304.

Dummett, M.: (1967) 'Frege,' in P. Edwards (ed.), *Encyclopedia of Philosophy*, Collier Macmillan, New York.

Ehrlich, K., K. Mani and P. N. Johnson-Laird: (1979) 'Mental models of spatial relations,' mimeo, Centre for Research on Perception and Cognition, Laboratory of Experimental Psychology, Sussex University.

Fisher, S. C.: (1916) 'The process of generalizing abstraction; and its product, the general concept,' *Psychological Monographs* 21, No. 2 (whole No. 90).

Fodor, J. D., J. A. Fodor and M. F. Garrett: (1975) 'The psychological unreality of semantic representations,' *Linguistic Inquiry* 4, 515–531.

Frege, G.: (1892) 'On sense and reference,' in P. T. Geach and M. Black (eds.), *Translations from the Philosophical Writings of Gottlob Frege*, Blackwell, Oxford, 1952.

Gruber, J. S.: (1965) 'Studies in lexical relations,' Ph.D. dissertation, MIT.

Hacker, P. M. S.: (1972) *Insight and Illusion: Wittgenstein on Philosophy and the Metaphysics of Experience*, Oxford University Press, London.

Halff, H. M., A. Ortony and R. C. Anderson: (1976) 'A context-sensitive representation of word meanings,' *Memory and Cognition* 4, 378–383.

Hewitt, C.: (1971) 'Description and theoretical analysis (using schemas) of PLANNER: a language for proving theorems and manipulating models in a robot,' Ph.D. dissertation, MIT.

Hintikka, J.: (1962) *Knowledge and Belief: An Introduction to the Logic of the Two Notions*, Cornell University Press, Ithaca, N. Y.

Hintikka, J.: (1963) 'The modes of modality,' *Acta Philosophica Fennica* 16, 65–82.

Hintikka, J.: (1969) *Models for Modalities: Selected Essays*, D. Reidel, Dordrecht.

Hintikka, J.: (1974) 'Quantifiers vs. quantification theory,' *Linguistic Inquiry* 5, 153–177.

Hintikka, J.: (1975) 'Impossible possible worlds vindicated,' *Journal of Philosophical Logic* 4, 475–484.

Hughes, G. E. and M. J. Cresswell: (1968) *An Introduction to Modal Logic*, Methuen, London.

Isard, S.: (1978) 'Models,' mimeo, Centre for Research on Perception and Cognition, Laboratory of Experimental Psychology, University of Sussex.

Jackendoff, R.: (1972) *Semantic Interpretation in Generative Grammar*, MIT Press, Cambridge, Mass.

Johnson-Laird, P. N.: (1975a) 'Models of deduction,' in R. J. Falmagne (ed.), *Reasoning: Representation and Process in Children and Adults*, Erlbaum, Hillsdale, N. J.

Johnson-Laird, P. N.: (1975b) 'Meaning and the mental lexicon,' in A. Kennedy and A. Wilkes (eds.), *Studies in Long Term Memory*, Wiley, London.

Johnson-Laird, P. N.: (1977) 'Procedural semantics,' *Cognition* 5, 189–214.

Johnson-Laird, P. N.: (1978) 'The meaning of modality,' *Cognitive Science* 2, 17–26.

Johnson-Laird, P. N.: (1979a) 'Mental models of meaning,' in A. K. Joshi, I. Sag, and B. L. Webber (eds.), Proceedings of the Workshop on Computational Aspects of Linguistic Structure and Discourse Setting, University of Pennsylvania, May, 1977, Cambridge University Press, Cambridge, in press.

Johnson-Laird, P. N.: (1979b) 'Images, models, and propositions,' mimeo, Centre for Research on Perception and Cognition, Laboratory of Experimental Psychology, University of Sussex.

Johnson-Laird, P. N. and A. Garnham: (1979) 'Descriptions and discourse models,' mimeo, Centre for Research on Perception and Cognition, Laboratory of Experimental Psychology, University of Sussex.

Johnson-Laird, P. N. and J. G. Quinn: (1976) 'To define true meaning,' *Nature* 264, 635–636.

Johnson-Laird, P. N. and M. J. Steedman: (1978) 'The psychology of syllogisms,' *Cognitive Psychology* 10, 64–99.

Johnson-Laird, P. N. and P. C. Wason (eds.): (1977) *Thinking: Readings in Cognitive Science*, Cambridge University Press, Cambridge.

Kamp, H.: (1971) 'Formal properties of "Now",' *Theoria* 37, 227–273.

Kaplan, D.: (1969) 'Quantifying in,' in D. Davidson and J. Hintikka (1969), Ibid. Reprinted in L. Linsky, 1971, Ibid.).

Kaplan, D.: (1977) 'Demonstratives: an essay on the semantics, logic, metaphysics and epistemology of demonstratives and other indexicals,' Paper read to March 1977 meeting of the Pacific division of the American Philosophical Association.

Karttunen, L.: (1973) 'Possible and must,' in J. P. Kimball (ed.), *Syntax and Semantics*, Vol. I, Academic Press, New York.

Katz, J. J.: (1972) *Semantic Theory*, Harper and Row, New York.

Katz, J. J. and J. A. Fodor: (1963) 'The structure of a semantic theory,' *Language* 39, 170–210.

Katz, F. M. and J. J. Katz: (1977) 'Is necessity the mother of intension?' *Philosophical Review* 86, 70–95.

Kintsch, W.: (1974) *The Representation of Meaning in Memory*, Erlbaum, Hillsdale, N. J.

Klein, E.: (1979) On sentences which report beliefs, desires and other mental attitudes,' Ph.D. dissertation, University of Cambridge.

Kratzer, A.: (1977) 'What 'must' and 'can' must and can mean,' *Linguistics and Philosophy* 1, 337–355.

Kripke, S.: (1963a) 'Semantical analysis of modal logic: I, normal propositional calculi,' *Zeitschrift für mathematische Logik und Grundlagen der Mathematik* 9, 67–96.

Kripke, S.: (1963b) 'Semantical considerations on modal logics,' *Acta Philosophica Fennica* 16, 83–94. (Reprinted in L. Linsky, Ibid.).

Kripke, S.: (1971) 'Identity and necessity,' in M. K. Munitz (ed.), *Identity and Individuation*, New York University Press, New York.

Kripke, S.: (1972) 'Naming and necessity,' in D. Davidson and G. Harman (eds.), *Semantics of Natural Language*, D. Reidel, Dordrecht.

Lakoff, G.: (1971) 'On generative semantics,' in D. D. Steinberg and L. A. Jakobovits (eds.), *Semantics: An Interdisciplinary Reader in Philosophy, Linguistics and Psychology*, Cambridge University Press, Cambridge.

Lakoff, G.: (1972) 'Hedges: a study of meaning criteria and the logic of fuzzy concepts,' in *Papers from the Eighth Regional Meeting of the Chicago Linguistic Society*, Chicago Linguistic Society, Chicago.

Lewis, D.: (1968) 'Counterpart theory and quantified modal logic,' *Journal of Philosophy* 65, 113–126.

Lewis, D.: (1969) *Convention: A Philosophical Study*, Harvard University Press, Cambridge, Mass.

Lewis, D.: (1972) 'General semantics,' in D. Davidson and G. Harman (eds.), *Semantics of Natural Language*, D. Reidel, Dordrecht.

Linsky, L. (ed.): (1971) *Reference and Modality*, Oxford University Press, London.

Linsky, L.: (1977) 'Believing and necessity,' *Proceedings and Addresses of the American Philosophical Association* 50, 526–530.

McCawley, J. D.: (1968) 'The role of semantics in a grammar,' in E. Bach and R. T. Harms (eds.), *Universals in Linguistic Theory*, Holt, Rinehart and Winston, New York.

Martin, E.: (in press) 'The psychological unreality of quantificational semantics,' in W. Savage (ed.), *Minnesota Studies in Philosophy of Science, Vol. 9*, University of Minnesota Press, Minneapolis.

Mates, B.: (1952) 'Synonymity,' in L. Linsky (ed.), *Semantics and the Philosophy of Language: A Collection of Readings*, University of Illinois Press, Urbana.

Miller, G. A.: (1972) 'English verbs of motion: a case study in semantics and lexical memory,' in A. W. Melton and E. Martin (eds.) *Coding Processes in Human Memory*, Winston, Washington, D. C.

Miller, G. A.: (1977a) *Spontaneous Apprentices: Children and Language*, Seaburg Press, New York.

Miller, G. A.: (1977b) 'Images and models, similes and metaphors,' mimeo, Rockefeller University.

Miller, G. A. and N. Chomsky: (1963) 'Finitary models of language users,' in R. D. Luce, R. R. Bush, and E. Galanter (eds.), *Handbook of Mathematical Psychology, Vol. II*, Wiley, New York.

Miller, G. A. and P. N. Johnson-Laird: (1976) *Language and Perception*, Harvard University Press, Harvard. Cambridge University Press, Cambridge.

Minsky, M.: (1975) 'Frame-system theory,' in R. C. Schank and B. L. Nash-Webber (eds.), *Theoretical Issues in Natural Language Processing*, Preprints of a conference at MIT. (Reprinted in Johnson-Laird and Wason, 1977).

Montague, R.: (1974) *Formal Philosophy*, edited by R. H. Thomason, Yale University Press, New Haven.

Norman, D. A. and D. E. Rumelhart: (1975) 'Memory and knowledge,' in D. A. Norman, D. E. Rumelhart, and the LNR Research Group, *Explorations in Cognition*, Freeman, San Francisco.

Osgood, C. E.: (1970) 'Interpersonal verbs and interpersonal behavior,' in J. L. Cowan (ed.), *Studies in Thought and Language*, University of Arizona Press, Tucson.

Palmer, S. E.: (1975) 'Visual perception and world knowledge: notes on a model of sensory-cognitive interaction,' in D. A. Norman, D. E. Rumelhart, and the LNR Research Group, *Explorations in Cognition*, Freeman, San Francisco.

Parsons, T.: (1972) *A Semantics for English*, 17th Draft of a projected book.

Partee, B. H.: (1972) 'Opacity, coreference, and pronouns,' in D. Davidson and G. Harman (eds.), *Semantics of Natural Language*, D. Reidel, Dordrecht.

Partee, B. H.: (1979) 'Semantics – mathematics or psychology?' in R. Bauerle, U. Egli and A. von Stechow (eds.), *Semantics from Different Points of View*, Springer-Verlag, Berlin.

Partee, B. H.: (1981) 'Montague grammar, mental representation, and reality,' in S. Kanger and S. Ohman (eds.), *Philosophy and Grammar*, D. Reidel, Dordrecht.

Prior, A.: (1957) *Time and Modality*, Clarendon Press, Oxford.

Putnam, H.: (1970) 'Is semantics possible?' in H. Kiefer and M. Munitz (eds.), *Languages, Belief and Metaphysics, Vol. 1* of *Contemporary Philosophic Thought: The International Philosophy Year Conferences at Brackport*, State University of New York Press, New York.

Putnam, H.: (1973) 'Explanation and reference,' in G. Pearce and P. Maynard (eds.), *Conceptual Change*, D. Reidel, Dordrecht.

Putnam, H.: (1975) 'The meaning of "meaning",' in K. Gunderson (ed.), *Language, Mind and Knowledge: Minnesota Studies in the Philosophy of Science, VII*. University of Minnesota Press, Minneapolis.

Putnam, H.: (1978) *Meaning and the Moral Sciences*, Routledge and Kegan Paul, London.

Pylyshyn, Z. W.: (1973) 'What the mind's eye tells the mind's brain: a critique of mental imagery,' *Psychological Bulletin* 80, 1–24.

Quine, W. V. O.: (1953) *From a Logical Point of View*, Harvard University Press, Cambridge, Mass.

Quine, W. V. O.: (1960) *Word and Object*, MIT Press, Cambridge, Mass.

Rosch, E.: (1973) 'On the internal structure of perceptual and semantic categories,' in T. M. Moore (ed.), *Cognitive Development and the Acquisition of Language*, Academic Press, New York.

Rosch, E.: (1976) 'Classification of real-world objects: Origins and representations in cognition,' in S. Ehrlich and E. Tulving (eds.), *La memoire semantique*, Bulletin de psychologie, Paris. (Reprinted in Johnson-Laird and Wason, 1977, Ibid.).

Russell, B. A. W.: (1936) 'On order in time,' in R. C. Marsh (ed.), *Logic and Knowledge: Russell's Essays 1901–1950*, Allen and Unwin, London, 1956.

Schiffer, S. R.: (1972) *Meaning*, Oxford University Press, London.

Shepard, R. N. and J. Metzler: (1971) 'Mental rotation of three-dimensional objects,' *Science* 171, 701–703. (Reprinted in Johnson-Laird and Wason, 1977, Ibid.).

Smith, E. E., E. J. Shoben and L. J. Rips: (1974) 'Structure and process in semantic memory: A feature model for semantic decisions,' *Psychological Review* 81, 214–241.

Stalnaker, R. C.: (1972) 'Pragmatics,' in D. Davidson and G. Harman (eds.), *Semantics of Natural Language*, D. Reidel, Dordrecht.

Stalnaker, R. C.: (1978) 'Assertion,' in P. Cole (ed.), *Syntax and Semantics, Vol. 9: Pragmatics*, Academic Press, New York.

Steedman, M. J.: (1977) 'Verbs, time, and modality,' *Cognitive Science* 1, 216–234.

Tarski, A.: (1956) *Logic, Semantics, Metamathematics: Papers from 1923 to 1938*, Oxford University Press, Oxford.

Templin, M.: (1957) *Certain Language Skills in Children: Their Development and Interrelationship*, University of Minnesota Press, Minneapolis.

Ullmann, S.: (1962) *Semantics: An Introduction to the Science of Meaning*, Blackwell and Mott, Oxford.

Wason, P. C. and P. N. Johnson-Laird: (1972) *Psychology of Reasoning: Structure and Content*, Batsford, London. Harvard University Press, Cambridge, Mass.

Wertheimer, R.: (1972) *The Significance of Sense: Meaning, Modality, and Morality*, Cornell University Press, Ithaca, New York.

Winograd, T.: (1972) *Understanding Natural Language*, Academic Press, New York.

Wittgenstein, L.: (1922) *Tractatus Logico-Philosophicus*, Routledge and Kegan Paul, London.

Wittgenstein, L.: (1953) *Philosophical Investigations*, Blackwell, Oxford.

Woods, W. A.: (1967) 'Semantics for a question-answering system,' Mathematical Linguistics and Automatic Translation Report NSF–19, Harvard Computational Laboratory.

Woods, W. A.: (1979) 'Procedural semantics,' in A. K. Joshi, I. Sag, and B. L. Webber (eds.), Proceedings of the Workshop on Computational Aspects of Linguistic Structure and Discourse Setting, University of Pennsylvania, May 1977. Cambridge University Press, Cambridge, in press.

Woodworth, R. S.: (1938) *Experimental Psychology*, Holt, New York.

Wykes, T. and P. N. Johnson-Laird: (1977) 'How do children learn the meanings of verbs?' *Nature* 268, 326–327.

M. J. CRESSWELL

THE AUTONOMY OF SEMANTICS [1]

I'm going to begin by telling you what I think is the most certain thing I know about meaning. Perhaps it's the only certain thing. It is this. If we have two sentences *A* and *B*, and *A* is true and *B* is false, then *A* and *B* do not mean the same.

I have said "sentences", but perhaps that's not quite right because somebody might bring up the following sort of objection. If *A* is

A: Yesterday I visited my oculist

and *B* is

B: Yesterday I visited my eye doctor,

and we grant John Searle's assumption that "oculist" and "eye doctor" are synonymous then one might try to refute my "most certain principle" (should I keep referring to it as the MCP?) by imagining *A* said on Wednesday and, say, being true, and *B* said on Thursday. Then *A* and *B* would differ in truth value but would still be synonymous. But this is no objection because in this situation *A itself* would have changed truth value. And whatever refinements are needed to get *A* having the same truth value as itself will get *A* to have the same truth value as *B*.

The Most Certain Principle does not claim that all sentences do have truth values. The supposition that they do is certainly not a most certain one, even for those of us who think that far more sentences have truth values than a lot of people think. Nor does the principle claim that there are only two truth values. Nor does the principle say what exactly are the bearers of truth and falsity, nor what truth and falsity are. And still less of course is the principle committed to anything like possible worlds.

But it is not the truth of the principle which makes it important for me, but the fact that it is the most certain fact I know in semantics. I am deliberately hammering this point because I want to use it methodologically. I want to use the fact that this principle *is* the most certain thing in semantics, to insist that any adequate semantics must make the concept of truth one of its central concepts. I have heard a linguist say to me: "What has semantics to do with truth?" If my Most Certain Principle really is the most certain

S. Peters and E. Saarinen (eds.), Processes, Beliefs, and Questions, 69–86.

principle about meaning then any account of meaning which does not give truth the central position is trying to explain something which is the most certain in terms of something which is less certain. And while one cannot perhaps *prove* that this is bad methodology, it's at least a good enough reason for me to try to base semantics on the notion of truth.

So I'm going to tell a little story about the essential nature of language. It's a story that ended a paper I wrote four and a half years ago called 'Semantic Competence'. It goes like this, that the crucial feature of language is its use to communicate from one person (or, if you like, from one language-user, where this is meant to be completely neutral about the nature of the language-user) to another a representation of how the world is.

The question of *why* the person is so communicating, or of what kind of purpose is to be achieved, seems to me, and I argued this in 'Semantic Competence' better seen as a question of what I called in that paper *semantic performance*. A representation of a way the world is of course entails the possibility of representing ways the world isn't but might be. And these ways the world might be are called *possible worlds*. So what goes on in linguistic communication is that the speaker (or more neutrally the message source) has in mind a representation of a set of possible worlds and the result of the communication is that the hearer (message target?) forms a representation of the same set of possible worlds.

In my paper on semantic competence I argued that the basic semantic ability is the ability to tell, in any situation, whether a sentence is, in that situation true, or false. This view of course is much more contentious than the Most Certain Principle. Yet I still believe it is a plausible one, and one which grows naturally out of the most certain principle, and which does justice to it in a way in which I at least don't see that any other approach to semantics does.

The question that I want to discuss in this paper arises because of the connection between the set of possible worlds which is the meaning of a sentence in truth conditional semantics and the representation of this set of worlds in the minds of the language users. In particular the question I want to raise is whether the nature of this representation is relevant for semantics. Jerry Fodor has argued that there is an internal representation, which he calls a language of thought, which plays a crucial role in psycholinguistics. My concern is whether there is an autonomous discipline of semantics, and I am assuming it is truth-conditional semantics, which either does not involve a language of thought, or perhaps is at least not committed to discovering its exact nature.

I shall first argue for the following thesis:

If it were not for the problem of propositional attitudes, then possible-worlds semantics (in which the meaning of sentences, in context,[2] are propositions, *viz.* sets of possible worlds) would have the status of a special science standing to psychology in the way Fodor claims psychology stands to physics.

I shall then note that the problem of propositional attitudes upsets this rather comfortable picture, and will consider various solutions to the problem. Finally I will sketch one possible solution, based on structured meanings, which tries to keep semantics as close as possible to the ideal situation which would obtain if all language users were logically perfect, and which would allow an autonomous semantics based on possible worlds.

So let's look at the first thesis. Suppose that we ignore the problem of propositional attitudes. Suppose that we are prepared to say that propositions are sets of worlds and that it really is the case that when we believe a proposition (or stand in any other relation to it) we really do believe all propositions logically equivalent to it. Stalnaker has championed this position in [28]. Very briefly and very roughly he argues that the best theory of rational behaviour is one in which we imagine an agent's beliefs and desires, which result in his action, as being defined by the possible worlds in which they are realized. "To explain why a person did something, we show that by doing it, he could satisfy his desires in a world in which his beliefs are true" ([28], p. 81). Fodor, also, seems to think that rational action is best understood in terms of surveying possibilities, and makes the representation of "real and possible states of affairs" a precondition of his language of thought ([16], p. 32).

Fodor is specifically concerned to combat the view that what he calls a special science like psychology can only be made respectable if it is reduced to physics. Fodor distinguishes between "token physicalism" and "type physicalism" ([16], p. 13). Token physicalism applied to psychology is simply the view that each particular psychological event is a physical event. Type physicalism is much stronger, and, in Fodor's opinion much less plausible. It supposes that the theoretical entities and laws needed in a special science must be neatly reducible to the laws of physics. He uses the concept of money as an illustration. No doubt every particular monetary transaction involves a physical event; but the different physical events which constitute a particular kind of monetary transaction may be so different (banknotes, cheques, computers etc.) that no economic law could or should be stated in physical terms. I know that the details of Fodor's claims are argued over but the general idea seems surely plausible enough to justify the existence of the special sciences with their own theoretical entities and their own (not necessarily exceptionless) laws and regularities.

Now it seems to me that possible-worlds semantics as I (and Stalnaker) have described it could be seen to be related to psychology in much the same way as Fodor thinks that psychology is related to physics. This means that although a set of possible worlds will, presumably, have *some* psychological representation, say in Fodor's language of thought, it will not be a matter for semantics to say which, for the simple reason that just which representation is involved may have as little intrinsic connection with the proposition as Fodor thinks a particular neural configuration has with the psychological representation.

The next thing to get out of the way is an objection that this procedure is circular. For it may be said that the notion of the epistemic status of a possible world is just what is itself in doubt and so we cannot expect to give an account of this knowledge is we have to assume possible worlds in the first place. My reply to this is roughly along the lines of a reply Quine makes to a very similar suggestion. In his essay 'Epistemology Naturalized' he defends, from an exactly analogous objection, the study of epistemology as a natural science. In Quine's account we postulate the physical world and regard knowledge in terms of the interaction of the physical world with its environment. But of course this presupposes the very things we are trying to explain, *viz.* the physical world of which we are trying to get knowledge. Now I have myself raised some doubts [12] about the metaphysical presuppositions of this procedure but it does seem to me that Quine's approach is quite justified as far as epistemology is concerned. For the same reason then, provided one accepts Fodor's view about the status of a special science, there is no circularity in trying to understand the notion of a possible world by postulating a possible world.

Of course I want to concede that for many other purposes than truth-conditional semantics one may wish to consider either how this knowledge of truth conditions affects behaviour (see for instance Jonathan Bennett's discussion of tribal in [2], pp. 211–241) or how this knowledge may be represented in terms of routines for linguistic behaviour (see for instance Miller and Johnson-Laird's discussion of "Did Lucy bring the dessert?" [22, pp. 170–197]). Nothing that I have said about the autonomy of semantics is intended to cast doubt on the validity for certain other purposes of studying things which are not needed in semantics itself.

So much then for the thesis that if it were not for the problem of propositional attitudes semantics could be seen as a special science based on possible worlds.

The problem is that if two propositions are logically equivalent then they are the same set of worlds and so are only one proposition. But, notoriously, we get, apparently, cases where people take different propositional attitudes to distinct but logically equivalent propositions.[3]

I first want to say something about the connection between propositional attitudes and the internal representation of a proposition. For it might seem that believing a proposition is simply standing in a relation to a representation of that proposition.

Now it is probably true that what makes someone believe something is indeed standing in a certain relation to an internal representation of a proposition; just as it is true that saying that *p* is standing in a certain relation (say of uttering) to an *external* representation of a proposition. But this doesn't really help. For if my believing that *p* is made so by my standing in a relation to my representation of *p* and your believing that *q* is made so by your standing in a relation to your representation of *q* then no amount of discrimination among the representations will help in an analysis of what the *p* and *q* are of which they are representations. For suppose that *p* is a set of possible worlds. Suppose then that *q* is the same set of possible worlds (i.e. *q* is logically equivalent to *p*). Then, by Leibniz' law, any representation of *p* is also a representation of *q*. In other words the problem is not how to distinguish representations but how to distinguish what they are representations of.

The first solution I want to discuss is really a non-solution. This is a solution which takes propositions as primitive entities in their own right. Although every proposition may have with it a set of worlds in which it is true, yet the proposition itself is not to be analysed as a set of worlds. Some such view as this seems espoused by Richmond Thomason [30], and I myself many years ago [4] treated propositions in this way. I have since brought a number of objections against this approach. My main objection is that the connection between propositions and truth is now lost. One can of course simply postulate a set of worlds *in addition* to the set of propositions and stipulate which worlds the proposition is true in, but truth and falsity in a world do not seem to emerge as essential to the nature of the proposition itself. This may seem a relatively minor criticism except that if we take seriously my most certain principle as insisting that semantics be truth-based then it really does cut into the whole basis of semantics.[4]

One kind of analysis of propositions which tries to preserve a distinction between propositional identity and logical equivalence divides the worlds into the possible and the impossible and claims that two propositions are logically equivalent iff they are true in the same possible worlds, but can still be distinct should they differ on the impossible ones.[5]

Before I consider the disadvantages of this line of approach, I'd like to consider its appeal. This is because one of the problems about propositional attitudes is that there really are too many apparently incompatible solutions and that each solution lacks precisely one of the advantages of other solutions. The advantage of the impossible worlds solution is that it enables us to talk about what happens in impossible worlds as if they were real worlds.

Consider for instance the sentence

(1) If the predicate calculus were decidable, logic would be a lot less interesting.

It is very tempting to suppose that this sentence is true iff in the nearest world to ours in which the antecedent is true so is the consequent. (Well it's as tempting as the Stalnaker/Lewis semantics is in any case.)

But in fact it's this very attractiveness which is its downfall. Look at it this way. If we call a proposition logically necessary iff it contains all the possible worlds, and logically possible iff it contains at least one possible world then indeed one can have many distinct logically necessary propositions (and many distinct logically impossible propositions) because no constraints are imposed on their truth in impossible worlds. And as a consequence two distinct propositions can be logically equivalent by being true in the same possible worlds, but not in the same impossible worlds. But suppose then that we decide to call a proposition *strongly* logically necessary only if it is true in *all* worlds. In *this* sense of logical necessity there cannot be distinct but logically equivalent propositions. Now I was brought up to suppose that logical necessity is the strongest kind of necessity that there is, and so the problem of propositional attitudes appeared to be solved only because we were using a kind of necessity which was too weak.

A similar situation applies in regard to the truth functors. If $\sim$ is a functor which changes the truth value in *all* worlds then $\sim\sim p$ could never be a different proposition from p. We would have to say that it changes the truth value only in the possible ones; but it seems hard to say why it should be any feature of a *world* which should prevent $\sim$ changing the truth value of a proposition. It is surely rather a feature of the meaning of $\sim$. So it is only if $\sim$ is not a *real* negation that $\sim\sim p$ could be different from p. And even if we do allow the intensional functors to misbehave in some worlds, we still seem to be left with no way of telling from the truth conditions, just which functions the operators are. If ~ can misbehave in impossible worlds who is to say which kind of misbehaviour represents the real negation.[6]

A quite different approach is the quotational approach. Some philosophers would no doubt want to analyse away all non-extensional operators as metalinguistic predicates[7] but I am here only concerned with this approach as applied to propositional attitudes. I have in [14] discussed this solution at some length so that all I want to say now is that even if a propositional attitude statement can be construed as a relation between a person and a sentence yet this relation will only hold because the sentence has the meaning it does, and therefore the hard work of the analysis must consist in specifying the notion of meaning on which the relation depends. And of course it is just such work which is being done by the various suggestions we are examining in this paper.

A theory which looks like a quotational theory but isn't really is Stalnaker's. In normal situations Stalnaker wants to say that the objects of belief are propositions, and that propositions are sets of worlds. However Stalnaker concedes that mathematical beliefs produce a difficulty.[8] His solution is to suggest that in the case of logic and mathematics the objects of belief are propositions about the meanings of expressions. It is the fact that the words used to formulate the truths of mathematics might not have meant what they do which enables distinct sets of worlds to be assigned to different sentences of mathematics.

Stalnaker concedes that a fully worked out theory of exactly how this can be so does not yet exist and indeed there are *prima facie* difficulties. Actually, since the solution I'm going to propose later for consideration will share some features of Stalnaker's, I'll say a little about its implications.

Stalnaker, as far as I can tell, wants to hold that *that*-clauses, as a rule, denote propositions, and that propositions are sets of possible worlds. I too want to make this to be so as far as possible, and the solution I'm going to advocate is going to suppose that it is only in certain cases that propositional attitude sentences are construed hyperintensionally.[9] Consider the sentence

(2) Belinda believes that the set of stars is finite.

Construed intensionally this will assert a relation between Belinda and a set of worlds. But mathematically there are at least two ways of defining what it is for a set to be finite. Let us call a set 'finite' iff it cannot be put into a 1-1 correspondence with a proper subset of itself, and let us call a set 'inductive' iff it can be put into a 1-1 correspondence with a proper initial segment of the natural numbers. Then, on the intensional account, (2) is equivalent to

(3) Belinda believes that the set of stars is inductive

(because it is a mathematical truth that all and only finite sets are inductive). Presumably, on Stalnaker's view, and I think I agree with him here, there is a sense of (2) and (3) in which they are equivalent. But I think that there also has to be a sense of these sentences in which they are not equivalent, for certainly it seems possible that the following sentence is false

(4) Belinda believes that all and only finite sets are inductive.

What this means then is that on Stalnaker's view we would have to postulate an ambiguity in (2).[10] At first sight this seems implausible, and indeed I think that 'ambiguity' is not the appropriate word. Perhaps one should call it a 'level of construal', and I want to go on now to consider a theory of propositional attitudes which will indeed propose various levels of construal for sentences with *that*-clauses. Actually this view has a more respectable ancestry than one might think; after all Frege's theory of sense and reference could be seen as the view that a word has different meanings depending on the context in which it occurs.

I mentioned a little while ago that although some kind of internal representation is almost certainly used when a proposition is believed yet the semantics of belief is concerned not so much with the representation itself but rather of what it is a representation of. One might compare it to the distinction between an arithmetical function and a Turing machine which computes that function. Many different Turing machines can compute the same function and so, even if we can only understand the function via a Turing machine which computes it, yet the function itself cannot be identified with any one of these machines.

The object of the representation must be a public entity because reference to it is used in reporting the beliefs of others. It is therefore natural to suppose that if might have an intimate connection with the public entity used to report the belief, *viz*. the sentence. For reasons hinted at it seems that the entity cannot be the sentence itself since the sentence itself need not have meant what it does. One candidate is that it is the structure obtained from the sentence by replacing each separate symbol with its meaning.

The view of structured meanings which fits best with possible-worlds semantics is the one worked out by David Lewis [21, pp. 182–186]. Lewis's account of meanings can be illustrated by a simple sentence.

(5) Cicero sings.

On the simplest possible worlds semantics for this sentence (not necessarily the correct one) *Cicero* will be a name whose semantic value is Cicero and *sings* will have as its value the function ω such that for any object a, $\omega(a)$ is the set of worlds in which a sings (complications like tense and the like are here ignored). The *intension* of (5) will be produced by the general rule that the value of the sentence will be the set of worlds which is the value of the function which is the meaning of the verb for the argument which is the meaning of the name. In this case it will be the set of worlds in which Cicero sings. The meaning however is different. For that would be something like the ordered pair $\langle$Cicero, $\omega\rangle$.

It may be that single symbols themselves may have to have structured meanings also. The advantages of this approach, if it can be made to work, are several. In the first place the new entities are, in a sense, things that we already need anyway. For in working out the semantic value of a sentence in a possible-worlds semantics we do need to have, on the way, intensions for all the symbols of the sentence. In the second place the fact that their structure follows the structure of the sentence means that they are in a sense 'public' entities whose structure is available to all speakers of the language irrespective of the nature of their private internal representations of meaning. In the third place the meanings are completely determined by the intensions (in conjunction with the structure of the sentence). In other words this account of meanings really does arise naturally out of the attempt to articulate the truth-conditional view of semantics that I began with.

The problem however is that Lewis' system of meanings does not, as it stands, solve the problem of propositional attitudes.

Let us take an example sentence

(6) Veronica believes that Yvonne sings.

The precise difficulty is with the intension of *believes*. For on a Lewis account the intension of a sentence like (6) is obtained by the intension of *believes* operating on the intension of *Veronica* and the intension of *Yvonne sings.*[11] But the *intension* of *Yvonne sings* is just a set of possible worlds so that any logically equivalent sentence may replace it without changing the truth conditions of (6).

The obvious way to solve the problem is to suppose that the *intension* of *believes* operates not on the intension of the embedded sentence but on the structured entity which is its meaning. Basically this is what I am going to propose, but only when necessary. The problem about this solution arises because of the possibility of iteration. If I say

(7) Stephen believes that Veronica believes that Yvonne sings

then it seems that the intension of *believe* must be defined for arguments which involve itself and this of course is set-theoretically impossible.[12] In fact an adaptation by Richmond Thomason of an argument of Richard Montague's has shown that many intensional operators which seem to be needed in formalizing ordinary language cannot have the properties they are supposed to have if they operate on structured meanings. Thomason presumably considers this as a reason for preferring his own theory of taking propositions as primitive entities (a theory we have already discussed) but there is another way of going. That is to say that the propositional-attitude operators are mostly purely intensional, in that they operate on sets of possible worlds, but that occasionally they operate on structured meanings. Recall the example

(2) Belinda believes that the set of stars is finite.

We suggested there that this sentence has several levels of construal, first what we might call the 'ordinary' or perhaps the zero level at which *believes* is an ordinary intensional operator. The next level is one in which the embedded sentence has as its intension not its intension but rather its (structured) meaning. This paper is being non-committal on the precise structure of the underlying base language and there are many ways to indicate hyperintensionality. One might for instance adapt the symbol θ as used in [9]. The 'hyperintensional' level of construal would then be

(8) Belinda believes θ (that the set of stars is finite).

(Note that in this example the symbol *finite* will also have to be decomposed into a structured meaning.[13])

However we cannot stop there because the symbol *believes* in (2) will only be defined for sets of worlds. What we need is a new symbol,[14] say *believes*$_1$ whose *intension* takes as arguments not just sets of worlds but rather structured meanings. The intension of *believes*$_1$ would be connected with that of *believes*$_0$ (we shall use the 0 subscript to indicate the lowest, purely intensional level) but obviously not determined by it. I shall say something about this in a moment. One might wonder now why we need *believes*$_0$ at all. Why can't we use *believes* in (2) under the assumption that in this sentence the meaning has only the very simplest structure of a set of worlds. There are two answers. To cope with a sentence like

(9) Stephen believes$_2$ θ (that Veronica believes$_1$ (θ that Yvonne sings))

we need to go up to another *believes* [15] and Thomason's argument will show that we cannot identify them all. But there is another answer which links with the claim of this paper that the internal aim of semantics itself is to avoid hyperintensionality as much as it can. (I put it this way to show that I don't regard it as merely a methodological policy, but something inherent in the nature of language itself.) This means that the hyperintensional belief operators will have a semantics parasitic on the central meaning of the purely intensional operator *believes*$_0$.

This dependence can be made even stronger if we impose a constraint which I'll call Stalnaker's constraint. It is this, whenever the meaning of α is an argument of the value of *believes*$_1$ (or *believes*$_{n>1}$) then there is a set of worlds which is an argument of the intension of *believes*$_0$ and for which *believes*$_0$ has the same value for that set of worlds. I call it Stalnaker's constraint because it embodies the principle that what appears to be a relation of belief and a proposition which is the intension of the sentence is *really* a relation between a person and *another* proposition. Of course the detailed work here would require that we say something about how to get to this set of worlds.

In order to test the Stalnaker constraint one would have to look in detail at the semantics of words like *believe* and *know*. One possible suggestion is to suppose, as e.g. Miller and Johnson-Laird [22] have done, as well as Fodor [16], that meanings are represented internally as some sort of computational routines. I have already said why I do not believe that one can actually identify the meanings themselves with the routines, since the meanings themselves have to be a specification of what the routines are routines for. But one can perhaps use the notion of a structured meaning for this purpose. For it is not hard I think to imagine an agent using the inner representations of the nodes of the intension tree which is a meaning under our present supposition, to compute a representation of the set of worlds in which that meaning is true. A word like *prove* would presumably be true of a θ expression just in case the agent had actually carried out such a construction. *prove* then would seem not to have to satisfy Stalnaker's constraint. Of course there would be an intensional *prove* whose semantics would be something like that the agent had computed *some* representation of that intension. So the intensional *prove* would be parasitic on the hyperintensional *prove* (other words like this would be *say*, which sometimes even has a quotational element).[16]

believe however perhaps does satisfy Stalnaker's constraint, for when one believes that p, in a hyperintensional case, certainly I think in a mathematical situation, it might be argued that one believes that someone has run through the computation and arrived at the truth of p,[17] and of course that set of worlds need not be the set of worlds in which p is true. This as a matter of fact may explain the plausibility of mathematical intuitionism, for while, in this semantics, the *truth* of a mathematical proposition cannot be analysed as the existence of a proof of it yet the belief in the proposition has to be analysed as just that. Unfortunately it is not quite as simple as that. For consider a false mathematical belief. In this case no one could have performed a correct computation of it. Yet in the world as the believer holds it to be someone has done just that. I have to confess that I have no real solution to this problem. Perhaps one is here thinking of a possible world as near as it can possibly be to ours but in which there is such a computation. I.e. a world in which the calculator makes only a few mistakes. It's not an entirely happy solution and I'd like to think something more plausible could be said.[18]

To fill this account out of course one would need to say something about the structure of the computational routines involved. Some would be mathematical, others perceptual. This would be the point at which the kind of research done say, by Miller and Johnson-Laird, *would* become relevant.[19]

So far we have considered different levels of construal only for propositional attitude verbs. There will of course have to be corresponding levels for modifiers of these verbs.[20] And there seem to be a few cases in which a hyperintensional interpretation seems to be required for an operator which is normally purely intensional. Consider again a sentence cited earlier:

(1) If the lower predicate calculus were decidable, logic would be a lot less interesting.

One of the advantages of the impossible worlds approach was that it enabled the same semantics to be used for impossible antecedents as for possible antecedents (though of course it gave no account of what an impossible world was and how there could be a nearness relation defined over them). If we stick to possible worlds of course (1) is trivially true, and true for any consequent. And indeed I believe that there is one interpretation of (1) for which this is exactly right. That is the interpretation in which the counterfactual operator $\Box\!\!\rightarrow$ is the ordinary intensional counterfactual operator. But sometimes in a sentence like (1) we really do seem to be treating the antecedent seriously. In this case the antecedent would be a θ expression and $\Box\!\!\rightarrow$ would become $\Box\!\!\rightarrow_1$. In some way its interpretation would be parasitic on the intensional case. There is no nearest world in which the predicate calculus is decidable. But perhaps there is a world in which the nearest thing to the predicate calculus is the nearest thing to decidable. Or perhaps there is a nearest world in which someone made a mistake in the decidability proof. The point about using $\Box\!\!\rightarrow_1$ is simply that we don't have to dabble around with the literal possible worlds meaning for the intensional case.

Well so much then for my current suggestion for solving the problem of propositional attitudes. It is not, one has to admit, a very neat solution with its ambiguities and its levels of representation. It might be thought far simpler, if we are interested in the autonomy of semantics, just to take propositions as basic values for sentences and live with the difficulties I alluded to earlier. As a partial answer to this feeling I would like to go back now to some of the solutions I discussed earlier and see how a levels-of-meaning view is involved even here, or at least that some sort of levels-of-meaning view is needed to make these solutions plausible.

For a start it should be clear that something like a hierarchy seems involved in Stalnaker's version of the quotational approach.

It is perhaps less obvious how a hierarchical view is involved in the impossible worlds solution, but it goes like this. We first imagine a set of possible worlds and necessity is truth in all of these; but, perhaps as a result of thinking about these worlds (or as a result of new perceptions) the mind is introduced to new worlds.[21] Of course a new necessity operator then becomes definable but this is no longer an objection because this operator in turn can be displaced by the creation of even newer worlds. There is of course a cost in this way of salvaging the impossible worlds solution, for we now need an analysis of the process whereby new worlds are created. (Still this may be one of the respects in which the solution will have to take account of psychological factors.)

Even the treatment of propositions as primitive entities does not escape the demand for hierarchical treatment. For Kaplan has mounted an argument intended to show that there can be no such thing as the set of all propositions.

In its barest details Kaplan's argument is simply this: (A) There must be at least as many worlds as there are propositions because for any proposition there must be a possible world in which it is the only proposition believed. (B) There must be at least as many propositions as there are sets of worlds because there must, for any world, be two propositions which differ only in truth value at that world. But (A) and (B) are incompatible and so Kaplan is led to conclude that there is no set of all propositions, and to develop a type theory of propositions. Gettier has taken up the idea of world types.[22] I do not myself feel that Kaplan's argument is conclusive, in particular I'm not sure of (A), particularly if one thinks that not all propositions can be represented, and so it may not be even logically possible to distinguish them. Nevertheless the argument can be used as a softening up device for at least some hierarchical features in an analysis of propositional attitudes.

I can't pretend in this paper to have gone through all the solutions to the problem of propositional attitudes, though I have tried to mention a wide range of them. One way in which I have certainly restricted myself is by assuming that semantics is to be done within a possible-worlds framework. I tried at the beginning of the paper to make plausible the adoption of such a framework. I also think that that framework is supported by the large amount of particular semantic work done within it. (Indeed I would feel very unhappy in attempting to justify any semantic framework in advance of its application to particular problems.) But the main argument of the paper has been to show simply some of the implications for a possible worlds semantics of the necessity to provide for the truth conditions of sentences about propositional attitudes.

Victoria University of Wellington

NOTES

[1] This paper has benefited considerably from some long discussions with Angelika Kratzer in January and February of 1979.

[2] Throughout this paper I am for simplicity going to ignore the fact that the meanings of most sentences of natural language are context-dependent and cannot easily be thought of simply as sets of possible worlds. Some useful remarks on this point are made by Stalnaker in [27]. Of course formal semantics based on possible worlds takes context-dependence into account in a variety of ways.

[3] Surprisingly, good examples are hard to come by outside mathematics and logic (there are nice ones by Barbara Partee in [24, p. 317f] and John Bigelow in [3, p. 103]). This fact would seem to support one of the claims of this paper that hyperintensionality (i.e. operators used in such a way as not always to licence replacement of logical equivalents within their scope) is avoided as far as possible. It is often used as an objection to possible worlds semantics [19, p. 230f] that the problem of propositional attitudes arises so easily. To those of us who think it a problem for *any* semantics this is actually a virtue.

[4] One can get possible-worlds directly from propositions by having a function I such that where p is a proposition then $I(p)$ (the *intension* of p) is a set of worlds. Alternatively, we can manufacture possible worlds if we have a notion of logical consequence $\models$

between a set of propositions and a proposition. Provided we have a designated logically impossible proposition f we can define a set A of propositions as consistent iff $A \dashv f$ ($\dashv$ means 'not $\models$') and as maximal iff, for any p, if $A \cup \{p\}$ is consistent then $p \in A$. We can then identify a world as a maximal consistent set of propositions and define a proposition as true in a world iff it is a member of that set. My trouble here is that I don't understand the notion of consistency involved unless it is explicated in terms of possible worlds in the first place. (I have elaborated this point in [13].)

Basing worlds on maximal consistent sets has seemed popular however [17, p. 154] as also has the idea of basing worlds on properties [26].

5 In [5] and [6] I called these non-classical worlds. Montague in [23, p. 231] called them designated points of reference.

6 This point is elaborated in [9, p. 25f] where it is called the indeterminacy problem (*vide* also Bigelow [3, p. 105]). It even holds of the elaborate construction in terms of heavens set out in [7, p. 42f], though in that work I did make some attempt to analyse the notion of a possible world.

7 But *vide* Thomason [29] and Montague [23, Chapter Ten] for problems about carrying this through. (I discuss some of these problems later.)

8 Assuming that mathematical propositions if true are true in all worlds and if false are true in none. Stalnaker accepts this [28, p. 88] and so do I.

9 As remarked in Note 3 a *hyperintensional* operator is one which does not even respect logical equivalence. An *intensional* operator respects logical equivalence but not necessarily material equivalence. An *extensional* operator respects material equivalence.

10 Not the ambiguity between 'finite' and 'inductive' (which only arises when (2) and (3) are both construed hyperintensionally) but the ambiguity between the case in which 'finite' is construed intensionally and the case in which it is construed hyperintensionally.

11 I regard the function of the 'that' to be simply to convert the sentence into a syntactically appropriate argument for a transitive verb. But I don't think the points I am trying to make turn on that.

12 This is set out more fully in [9, p. 33f]. Bigelow [3, p. 115] has avoided this consequence by having surrogates for the intensions as parts of the meanings, but he still cannot avoid self-reference paradoxes.

13 In my opinion this is the biggest difficulty about the theory of structured meanings. For, unless we count the evidence of the generative semanticists [20], there seems no grammatical indication of the structure of a lexical item. What would be nice would be if cases like (8) only occurred with words introduced by some sort of fairly explicit definition. (This would explain why this sort of hyperintensionality typically seems to occur only in technical disciplines like mathematics.)

14 I see no need for *believes*$_1$ to be in a different *syntactic* category from *believes*$_0$. All that would happen was that in certain cases the expression would be semantically uninterpretable.

15 Notice that this is only if *all* the believings are construed hyperintensionally. It is possible at any time to revert to an intensional operator by dropping the θ. Indeed it seems to me that this is what usually happens. All of the following are interpretable.

Stephen believes$_0$ that Veronica believes$_0$ that Yvonne sings
Stephen believes$_0$ that Veronica believes$_1$ (θ, that Yvonne sings)
Stephen believes$_1$ (θ, that Veronica believes$_0$ that Yvonne sings).

[16] Some nice examples are discussed by Partee [24]. Bigelow [3] has shown how to incorporate reference to quotation. Bigelow also has shown how to quantify into hyperintensional contexts (p. 118f) and I would follow his solution here.

Partee also instances cases of indirect speech in which it seems not easy to recover the original sentence from the reporting sentence. This kind of case often involves quantification into comparative sentences. In a sentence like

(i) She told us that she was older than she was

the actual sentence used might

(ii) I am thirty.

I would suspect that cases of this kind are very rarely hyperintensional. One would not expect the same problem to arise with

(iii) She giggled that she was older than she was.

If the occurrence of *tell* in (i) is intensional rather than hyperintensional then it can be dealt with in a manner analogous to that used in counter-factual cases in [8, p. 284].

[17] Or perhaps better that if someone *were* to go through such a computation then they would arrive at the truth of *p*.

[18] Perhaps it could be made more plausible if we understood 'correct' not strictly in terms of getting the right answer but rather in terms of making no mistakes, and we construed making no mistakes in an almost psychological way. I.e. in our belief world we are satisfied at each stage no mistake is recognised and that the calculation does end with a result which yet turns out to be wrong. Maybe the work done here by Dunn [15] and Belnap [1] on reasoning from inconsistent premises can help. Or yet again maybe a "disposition to respond affirmatively" might be involved in an analysis of belief.

[19] For instance a computational routine involving a memory search would be one way of getting perceptional information into the process [22].

[20] E.g. in the phrase 'firmly believes' the meaning of firmly will have to differ according as 'believes' is the intensional or one of the hyperintensional believes. Stalnaker's constraint could be very helpful here because it would avoid having to find a new meaning for the modifier.

[21] Hintikka in various places (e.g. [18]) seems to have something a bit like this in mind, though as far as I can tell he has not actually introduced propositional attitude operators into his language in this article.

[22] Neither of these suggestions is published though both Kaplan and Gettier have prepared some class notes on the topic. I heard Kaplan's argument at a talk he gave to a semantics conference in Vancouver in October 1975, and heard about Gettier's work when I visited Amberst in October 1977.

REFERENCES

[1] Belnap, N. D., 'How a computer should think,' in G. Ryle (ed.), *Contemporary Aspects of Philosophy*, Oriel Press, 1977, pp. 30–56.

[2] Bennett, J. F., *Linguistic Behaviour*, Cambridge, Cambridge University Press, 1976.
[3] Bigelow, J. C., 'Believing in semantics,' *Linguistics and Philosophy* 2 (1978), pp. 101–144.
[4] Cresswell, M. J., 'Functions of propositions,' *The Journal of Symbolic Logic* 31 (1966), pp. 545–560.
[5] Cresswell, M. J., 'Classical intensional logics,' *Theoria* 36 (1970), pp. 347–372.
[6] Cresswell, M. J., 'Intensional logics and logical truth,' *Journal of Philosophical Logic* 1 (1972), pp. 2–15.
[7] Cresswell, M. J., *Logics and Languages*, London, Methuen, 1973.
[8] Cresswell, M. J., 'The semantics of degree,' in B. H. Partee, ed., *Montague Grammar*, New York, Academic Press, 1976, pp. 261–292.
[9] Cresswell, M. J., 'Hyperintensional logic,' *Studia Logica* 34 (1975), pp. 25–38.
[10] Cresswell, M. J., 'Categorical languages,' *Studia Logica* 36 (1977), pp. 257–269.
[11] Cresswell, M. J., 'Semantic competence,' in F. Guenthner and M. Guenthner-Reutter, eds., *Meaning and Translation*, London, Duckworth, 1978, pp. 9–27.
[12] Cresswell, M. J., 'Can Epistemology be naturalized,' *Southwestern Journal of Philosophy* 9 (1979), pp. 19–30.
[13] Cresswell, M. J., 'Semantics and logic,' *Theoretical Linguistics* 5 (1978) pp. 19–30.
[14] Cresswell, M. J., 'Quotational theories of propositional attitudes' *Journal of Philosophical Logic* 9 (1980), pp. 17–40.
[15] Dunn, J. M., 'Intuitive semantics for first-degree entailments and "coupled trees",' *Philosophical Studies* 29 (1976), pp. 149–168.
[16] Fodor, J. A., *The Language of Thought*, New York, Thomas Y. Crowell, 1975.
[17] Hintikka, K. J. J., 'On the logic of perception,' *Models for Modalities*, Dordrecht, Reidel, 1969, pp. 151–183.
[18] Hintikka, K. J. J., 'On depth semantics: definition and its motivation,' in H. Leblanc, ed., *Truth, Syntax and Modality*, Amsterdam, North Holland, 1973.
[19] Katz, J. J., 'Effability and translation,' in F. Guenthner and M. Guenthner-Reutter, eds., *Meaning and Translation*, London, Duckworth, pp. 191–234.
[20] Lakoff, G. 'On generative semantics,' in D. D. Steinberg and L. A. Jakobovits, eds., *Semantics: An Interdisciplinary Reader in Philosophy, Linguistics and Psychology*, Cambridge, Cambridge University Press, 1971, pp. 232–296.
[21] Lewis, D. K., 'General semantics,' in D. Davidson and G. Harman, eds., *Semantics of Natural Language*, Dordrecht, Reidel, 1972, pp. 169–218.
[22] Miller, G. A., and P. N. Johnson-Laird, *Language and Perception*, Cambridge, Mass., Belknap Press, Harvard, 1976.
[23] Montague, R. M., *Formal Philosophy* (ed. R. H. Thomason), New Haven, Yale University Press, 1974.
[24] Partee, B. H., 'The semantics of belief sentences,' in K. J. J. Hintikka, J. M. E. Moravcsik and P. Suppes, eds., *Approaches to Natural Language*, Dordrecht, Reidel, 1973, pp. 309–336.
[25] Quine, W. V., 'Epistemology Naturalized,' *Ontological Relativity and Other Essays*, New York, Columbia University Press, pp. 69–90.
[26] Rescher, N., *A Theory of Possibility*, Pittsburgh, University of Pittsburgh Press, 1975.

[27] Stalnaker, R. C., 'Pragmatics,' in D. Davidson and G. Harman, eds., *Semantics of Natural Language*, Dordrecht, Reidel, 1972, pp. 380–397.

[28] Stalnaker, R. C., 'Propositions,' in A. F. Mackay and D. D. Merrill, eds., *Issues in the Philosophy of Language*, New Haven, Yale University Press, 1976, pp. 79–91.

[29] Thomason, R. H., 'Indirect discourse is not quotational,' *The Monist* 60 (1977), pp. 340–354.

[30] Thomason, R. H., 'A model theory of propositional attitudes' *Linguistics and Philosophy* 4 (1980), pp. 47–70.

BARBARA HALL PARTEE

BELIEF-SENTENCES AND THE LIMITS OF SEMANTICS

I. INTRODUCTION

One of the goals of the conference of which this paper is a part is to compare the enterprise of formal semantics with that of procedure-oriented psychological semantics. The former has traditionally been the domain of logicians and philosophers, the latter the domain of psychologists and computer scientists, with some linguists on each side. The problem that is evident at the outset is that semantics is treated very differently within these two enterprises, each side seemingly committed to assumptions that lead to inadequacies by the other's criteria. A fruitful comparison could lead to either of two outcomes, which we might characterize roughly as the "Separatist" position and the "Common Goals" position.

We might arrive at the Separatist position by elucidating how the different goals of the two enterprises lead to different assumptions and different criteria of adequacy. If each enterprise is internally consistent, we might be able to conclude that the apparent conflicts between them are not genuine but are simply the result of the different goals and assumptions of the two enterprises. David Dowty (1980) and Hilary Putnam (1978) take such a view; I think perhaps Max Cresswell (this volume) is advocating it as well.

Alternatively, we might arrive at the Common Goals position if we can discover a potential common enterprise with goals and assumptions that are agreeable to both sides. Partee (1979) takes a step in this direction starting from the premise that formal semantics has some internal inadequacies, especially with regard to the semantics of propositional attitudes, and might be improved by modifying it in the direction of psychological theories of semantics.

It seems to me remarkably difficult to decide between these two positions. This is undoubtedly due in part to the fact that neither enterprise is monolithic, and disagreements within each side are probably as great as any differences between them. But I think there are some major conceptual issues involved that are very much worth exploring, centering particularly on questions about knowledge (such as whether and how the competence/performance distinction can be drawn in semantics). I will argue in the end that the Common Goals

S. Peters and E. Saarinen (eds.), Processes, Beliefs, and Questions, 87–106.

position is tenable, but only if we recognize that a complete semantics for a human language is in a certain sense impossible. Along the way, I will try to show how the problem of giving an adequate account of the semantics of belief-sentences presents fundamental difficulties for either approach, how these difficulties are related to the difficulty of characterizing semantic competence and to the inextricable interdependence of language and conceptual framework, and how the limits on human knowledge lead naturally (and in fact desirably) to the impossibility of a complete, finitely statable semantics for a human language.

The paper is organized as follows. Part II is a summary of the arguments in Partee (1979) designed show that formal semantics has internal problems which might be solved by making it more psychologistic. Part III is a discussion of the various criteria that a semantic account of belief-sentences might be required to meet, noting that most of the "direct" evidence is in a sense negative, and most of the positive criteria are highly theory-bound. Part IV argues that any humanly attainable form of "semantic competence" requires a careful distinction between what is "known" and what is "determined by what is known", and that the biggest apparent gulf between formal and psychological semantics comes from failure to make that distinction. A resolution to the problem of how we can know a language including undecidable statements is offered. Part V deals with the problem of distinguishing differences in belief from differences in language, particularly with respect to theory-laden terms, and draws the conclusion that it is this problem that makes it impossible in a certain sense to give a complete, finitely representable semantics for a single idiolect. In Part VI I indicate why I believe that the foregoing conclusion is a welcome one, suggesting that the "open-endedness" of human-language semantics provides us with a good way to cope with our awareness of the limitations of our own knowledge, and hence that an appreciation of the limits of semantics may provide an opening wedge into more general inquiries about the properties of (what we hope is) "higher intelligence", particularly knowledge about our own knowledge.

II. THE PROBLEM OF BELIEF-SENTENCES IN FORMAL SEMANTICS AND THE SUGGESTION THAT MORE PSYCHOLOGISM MIGHT HELP [1]

Belief-sentences pose well-known semantic problems for just about any semantic theory; but the problems are of particular concern for the enterprise of Montague grammar, since they appear to threaten its very foundation.

In Partee (1979), I argued that there is no semantic type within Montague's intensional logic of the right sort to serve for the objects of the propositional attitude verbs, since substitution of intensionally equivalent expressions is a valid operation for any type in the intensional logic, but is not always valid in propositional attitude contexts. The problematical cases were of two sorts: (a) logical equivalence, as illustrated by the argument from (1) to (2),

(1) Irene believes that *P*.
(2) ∴ Irene believes that *Q*.

where *P* and *Q* are any two logically equivalent sentences; and (b) lexical items with the same intension, such as proper names, as in (3)–(4) or natural kind terms, as in (5)–(6).

(3) The ancients did not know that Hesperus was Phosphorus.
(4) ∴ The ancients did not know that Hesperus was Hesperus.
(5) John wonders whether woodchucks are groundhogs.
(6) ∴ John wonders whether woodchucks are woodchucks.

Almost everyone agrees that these three arguments are invalid,[2] though Montague's system treats them as valid. In the earlier paper it was argued that what makes those arguments invalid are facts about human (or machine) psychology which are correlated with the impossibility of a finite being "knowing" a Montague grammar.

In the case of the logical equivalence problem, the connection with "knowing the grammar" can be made as follows: (i) Propositions are analyzed as functions from possible worlds to truth values. (ii) Two sentences which are logically equivalent will be true in exactly the same possible worlds, hence will express the same proposition. (iii) Since logical equivalence is in general undecidable, finite beings (e.g. people or computers) cannot always know whether two sentences are logically equivalent and therefore express the same proposition. (iv) Since the semantics of the language (e.g. the fragment in Montague (1973), hereafter PTQ) assigns the same proposition to every pair of logically equivalent sentences, and must do so to meet the logicians' primary criteria of adequacy, then there is a clear sense in which no finite being can know the language.[3] (v) The reason we are inclined to regard inferences such as that from (1) to (2) as invalid is that we know that the subject of the sentence, if a finite being, may not recognize the logical equivalence of the two embedded sentences. This point is complicated by the fact that we may not mean to attribute any direct relation between the holder of the propositional attribute and the particular form of words we use in the embedded sentence; I do not mean to be advocating a quotational theory of propositional attitude sentences.[4] But we do assume that people cannot have attitudes to sets of possible worlds directly, invariant under all the different ways of finitely representing them (e.g. by sentences which pick out the proposition which is true at just that set of worlds). (What would this require? It would require a finite scheme for representing as many distinct sets of possible worlds as there are distinct propositions expressible in the language in which we are making belief attributions, together with a decision procedure for telling whether two such representations are representations of the same set of possible worlds. But as long as the language has at least the expressive power of first-order logic, there can't be such a decision procedure. Caveat: I don't know how to prove this; but I think it must be true.) (vi) The impossibility of logical omniscience for finite beings thus seems to be the reason *both* for the limits on our knowledge of the semantics of our language and for the failure of substitutivity of logically equivalent sentences in propositional attitude sentences.

Another way of putting the point is to view Montague's semantics as a super-competence model, e.g. a semantics for English as spoken by God. Such a view of the semantics seems to work perfectly well for the subparts of the language which contain no propositional attitude expressions, and also for propositional attitude sentences with "God" as their subject (assuming that God could be acquainted with propositions as sets of possible worlds directly), but it still fails for propositional attitude sentences with humans or other finite beings as subjects, since God would *not* make the inference from (1) to (2).[5] God would not have the problem with knowing the semantics discussed in (iv) above, but would recognize that the ordinary holders of propositional attitudes have the analogous problem discussed in (v). Hence for the propositional attitudes, Montague's semantics fails even as a super-competence model.

In the case of lexical items with the same intension, exemplified by (3)–(4) and (5)–(6) above, the problem is of a different sort, and hinges crucially on the idea that proper names and certain natural kind terms act as *rigid designators*, i.e., have intensions which pick out the same extension in every possible world (see Kripke, 1972 and Putnam, 1975). Here the problem is not one of lack of logical omniscience, but rather that a speaker of a language can very well fail to know that two terms in it have the same intension and yet be a competent speaker by all criteria accessible to the language community. The *Hesperus–Phosphorus* case is one in which for a very long period *none* of the speakers of the language knew that the two names had the same intension. Whether two names have the same intension or not can depend in part on facts about the actual world that obtained in the context in which the names were introduced into the language; it is the lack of factual omniscience that leads to cases of speakers' ignorance of whether two names have the same intention, and it is awareness of such possible ignorance that makes us unwilling to consider such inferences as (3)–(4) and (5)–(6) valid. Again there is a close connection between limits on our semantic competence and limits on the inferences that can be validly drawn from propositional attitude sentences.

In the remainder of the paper I will be focusing more on the first type of problem, the logical equivalence problem, than on the second (although a distinct problem concerning lexical items will be raised in the later sections.) One reason is that the second problem is less general: one could readily imagine languages in which there were no pairs of lexical items with the same intension, so that the second problem would not arise, but any language with at least the expressive power of first-order predicate logic (hence, presumably, any natural language) will have the first problem. Another reason is that some promising lines of attack have been suggested for the second problem,[6] which do not however seem to bear on the first problem.

Because of the connections between the problem of "knowing" a Montague semantics and the claimed failure of the Montague semantics to make the correct predictions about propositional attitude sentences, it was suggested in Partee (1979) that we try to change the underlying basis of the semantics of Montague grammar to make it more "psychologistic", in hopes of simultaneously making the semantics more epistemologically accessible and making possible a more adequate account of the semantics of propositional attitude expressions. Replacing Montague's Platonistic conception of intensions with the more epistemologically accessible notion of procedures or algorithms was suggested as one part of such a change, although no specific proposals were made.[7]

What follows will be focused primarily on obstacles that confront such a "Common Goals" position.

III. WHAT SHOULD AN ADEQUATE ACCOUNT OF BELIEF-SENTENCES DO?

Perhaps one of the reasons that belief-sentences remain a perennial problem is that in quite a variety of approaches to semantics, the standard criteria of adequacy fail to give clear guidelines for what an adequate analysis of belief-sentences should accomplish.

A. *Synonymy judgments*

Linguists, for example, have often taken synonymy judgments as crucial data for a semantic analysis to capture. But it is debatable whether any two belief-sentences whose embedded clauses differ are ever synonymous (Mates, 1950; Putnam, 1954; Sellars, 1955). So for example, it is debated whether (7) and (8) are synonymous, assuming that the words *Greek* and *Hellene* are themselves synonymous.

(7) John believes that all Greeks are Greeks.
(8) John believes that all Greeks are Hellenes.

So the criterion of capturing synonymy does not seem to give any clear positive evidence about how to semantically analyze the content of the belief-clause. It provides some negative evidence, however: neither truth-values nor truth-conditions make fine enough discriminations.

B. *Procedural semantics*

How about procedural semantics? I am not entirely clear about what the central adequacy criteria are taken to be in this approach, and my relative lack of familiarity with it may be evident, but it seems from the discussion in Johnson-Laird (1977) that the central aim is to model psychological processes that occur when a sentence is produced or understood. This approach has certain attractions, but it seems to me that it, too, fails to provide clear adequacy criteria for the analysis of belief-sentences.

The attractive cases are those of logically equivalent sentences built up in dissimilar ways. For example, a procedural semantics would surely give quite different analyses for the embedded sentences of (9) and (10) (taken from Bigelow, 1978b), thus correctly predicting that (9) and (10) can have different truth values.

(9) Marian believes that Robin will win.
(10) Marian believes that everyone who does not compete, or loses, will have done something which Robin will not have done.

But again this is negative evidence only. I know of no evidence that any two belief-sentences whose embedded clauses differ are ever associated with the *same* procedure.

Miller and Johnson-Laird (1976) suggest that capturing valid entailments fits within the enterprise of procedural semantics (p. 333). But the fact that there cannot be any finite procedure for determining the validity of entailments in general should suggest that procedural semantics cannot accept that goal without radically altering the conception of "procedure" that lies at its foundation. Johnson-Laird (this volume) seems clearly committed to considering procedures speakers can actually use, and his remarks indicate a greater concern for the inferences people actually or warrantedly draw rather than for an account of logical entailment *per se*. Although he does not explicitly say so, I gather that he would agree to the following: if formal semantics, i.e., a theory of truth conditions and entailment relations for natural language sentences, is possible but requires theoretical constructs which are not realizable as humanly usable procedures, then psychological semantics will disavow the goal of characterizing entailment relations and the two enterprises will definitely not be directly comparable.

Woods (1979) seems readier to extend the notion of procedure to infinite procedures, procedures that require time travel, and other sorts of procedures beyond the capacities of humans or any other finite actual beings, so that it seems that his notion of procedure cannot be meant to be psychologically grounded in the way that Johnson-Laird's is.

If procedural (or more generally, psychological) semantics does take on the goal of characterizing valid entailments, the remarks of section C below apply; if it does not, what sorts of criteria might it offer for judging the adequacy of a semantic account of belief-sentences? Johnson-Laird (this volume), like many formal semanticists, lays more stress on the need for a rich enough theory to prevent unwanted inferences than on positive criteria. But the beginnings of some positive criteria on his view can be found in the following statements.

Even little children can understand assertions about propositional attitudes. (p. [48]).

An individual's beliefs, wants, hopes, and other such propositional attitudes can be represented in a mental model. Parts of such a model will, of course, be beliefs about the beliefs of other people . . . Person *A* may have . . . beliefs about *B's* beliefs about *A's* beliefs about *B*, and so on *ad infinitum* . . . As soon as there is no difference between an adjacent odd numbered (or even numbered) pair of nested beliefs, they can simply be identified and the regress stops there. (p. [50]).

The theory of mental models emphasizes the communicative aspects of language, and the constructive manner in which propositional attitudes are considered – not *simpliciter*, but as remarks founded on a mental representation of another person's mental world. (p. [56]).

... the phenomena of opacity are inherited by all verbs that contain a particular sort of primitive that gives rise to it, namely, the primitive that corresponds to the construction of a mental model. (p. [56]).

The criteria that seem to emerge here include the following: (i) the semantic account of belief-sentences should not require conceptual apparatus beyond the powers of a child; (ii) it must be finitely representable (hence the concern to block a potentially infinite sequence in constructing mental models of other people's mental models); (iii) the constructs needed for the interpretation of the objects of propositional attitudes should be closely related to the constructs used in explicating what goes on in the understanding of simple sentences (the candidate proposed for both being the construction of a mental model). All of these criteria concern the psychological plausibility of accounts of the semantics of belief sentences.

C. *Entailment*

Within the tradition of formal semantics, the primary criteria of adequacy for the semantics of any construction are that it get the truth conditions and entailment relations right. In the case of the propositional attitude sentences, part of the problem is to try to determine just what the truth conditions *are*, and since we have no independent way of stating them, (without bringing in equally problematical notions like propositions or meanings or synonymy), we have to go at the problem obliquely through consideration of entailment relations.

But then we run immediately into the problem that there seem to be almost no valid entailments at all involving belief-sentences which differ just in the contents of their that-clauses. There do seem to be a few, in cases involving constructional (not lexical) synonymy;[8] e.g. (11) and (12) entail each other (assuming the sentences are constructed identically except for their one obvious difference).

(11) Mary believes that for John to leave now would be a mistake.
(12) Mary believes that it would be a mistake for John to leave now.

These cases are of general interest in considering the relation between syntax and semantics, but they do not provide a very broad range of positive evidence.[9]

It might seem tempting to suggest that one belief-sentence entails another when their embedded clauses are related by a very simple logical equivalence; but since entailment is transitive, we could not admit any two equivalence rules which could iterate with each other without predicting entailment between belief-sentences whose embedded clauses differed by a long chain of simple equivalences, a prediction we are assuming to be false.[10]

In general, the evidence from entailment is almost entirely negative; as Mates's (1950) argument showed, almost *any* difference in the embedded clauses of belief-sentences leads to non-entailment. Thus the primary criterion of adequacy associated with formal semantics provides plenty of evidence *against* proposals for the semantics of propositional attitudes (e.g., against Montague's in PTQ), but no evidence *for* any analyses except the extremely weak sort of evidence associated with correctly failing to predict non-occurring events.

D. *Auxiliary hypotheses*

If all we wanted to do was to block invalid inferences, the simplest way would be to adopt the suggestion of Quine (1960) to treat each distinct combination of "believes that" with a following clause as a semantically unanalyzed primitive. The principal argument against that approach, due originally to Davidson (1970), comes not from adequacy criteria for the "output" of a semantic theory, but from consideration of properties we want the theory itself to have. In this case, the relevant desideratum is that the theory be compatible with evidence about the learnability of a language, and although we have indicated above that there may be a sense in which English isn't learnable, it would be giving up on semantics completely to countenance a theory in which an infinite number of syntactically complex expressions of a language were each treated as separate semantic primitives.

In fact I believe that most of the positive evidence for what an adequate semantics of belief-sentences should do is of two sorts: (a) assumptions about the general form of a semantic theory, and (b) judgments about inferences which include belief-sentences together with other premises. The previous paragraph illustrated an argument of the first type; the common assumptions most generally relevant here are (i) that the syntax be finitely statable, (ii) that the semantics be finitely statable and assign a semantic value to each syntactically well-formed expression.

As anyone who is not too myopically immersed in formal semantics is undoubtedly aware,[11] there are a great many intuitively valid inferences which include belief-sentences together with additional auxiliary premises. The required auxiliary premises often involve other propositional attitudes and/or metalinguistic predicates, e.g. that the subject knows that woodchucks are groundhogs or recognizes the relevant logical equivalence.[12] (They are generally left unexpressed in normal circumstances, but the previously discussed invalid inferences show that they are nevertheless crucial.) Since these sentences are as hard to analyze as the originals, they don't provide much *direct* help. But indirectly they help provide a good general test of the adequacy of an account of belief-sentences. Whereas we have argued that a semantics which requires assumptions of logical omniscience and assumptions of uniform knowledge of the intensions of lexical items has to be wrong (as part of a theory of human language), it is perfectly reasonable to try to construct the semantics in such a way that the semantic interpretation of a belief-sentence taken together with added premises about the subject's language and reasoning can support the validity of a given inference. (There is of course room for widely differing opinions about how much of the burden will fall on semantics proper within a larger theory of language use and reasoning. I sometimes think that all the semantics alone should tell us about sentence of the form "John believes that . . . " is, in effect, "There is something (some proposition?) that John believes". But that would probably predict too many such sentences to come out true.)

In the long run, I believe that most of the evidence that will help us decide between any two competing accounts of belief-sentences that manage to survive the negative tests of the entailment criteria will come from these two larger domains – the overall adequacy of the theories of syntax and semantics in which they are embedded, and their compatibility with accounts of inferences in which belief-sentences play a part. I agree with Brian Loar: "The upshot will be that semantics is part of propositional-attitude psychology, and stands or falls with it" (1976, p. 138).

IV. WHAT IS SEMANTIC COMPETENCE?

Some of the most fundamental difficulties in trying to reconcile the goals of formal semantics and psychological or procedural semantics arise when we try to characterize a notion of semantic competence compatible with both. (I intend the term "competence" in the sense of Chomsky, 1965.) As a starting point, let us review some of the common assumptions about competence in syntax.

If we view the primary task of syntax as the characterization of the set of all and only the well-formed expressions of a language,[13] then a theory of syntactic competence is (at least in part) a theory of what underlies the ability of a native speaker to distinguish well- from ill-formed expressions.

The assumption that speakers have such an ability derives its plausibility from two kinds of factors: (i) associated theories of "performance" factors which (it is hoped) can explain mismatches between the posited ability and observed data, and (ii) the absence of any reason to believe that the posited ability is in principle unattainable.[14] The basic assumptions that are crucial for the latter are that the well-formed expressions of a natural language constitute an at most denumerably infinite set, and furthermore a set which is recursive. (If we weaken this assumption to "recursively enumerable", we must change the characterization of competence to the ability to generate only and any well-formed expressions, or to the ability to recognize well-formed expressions as such but without being able to recognize all ill-formed expressions as ill-formed.) Therefore the language can be characterized by a finite set of primitives and a finite set of rules, and there is no problem in principle in attributing some form of knowledge of (or more cautiously, ability characterizable by) these primitives and rules to native speakers. Finite representability is crucial; the principal argument that there must be a grammar "in the head" (and not just a list of all the expressions) rests on the claim that there are infinitely many expressions in any natural language together with the fact that the brain is finite.

Now if we turn to the problem of characterizing semantic competence from the perspective of formal semantics, the difficulty is in maintaining finite representability while taking the recognition of valid entailments to be the semantic counterpart of the recognition of well-formed expressions.

At first it seems that undecidability makes such competence impossible.[15] But if we make a more careful distinction between "what the speaker knows" and "what properties of the language are determined by what the speaker knows", then undecidability of entailment does not by itself make semantic competence impossible. If one knows, for instance, a complete set of axioms and rules of inference for first-order logic, then what one knows uniquely determines the set of logically true sentences of first-order logic, even though the set is undecidable.[16] (A very suggestive account of how we might come to learn an undecidable language is found in Loar, 1976, who combines Lewis's theory of conventions with the notion of an "effective sublanguage" and something like a notion of simplicity for internal representations.)

So undecidability by itself does not create any insurmountable obstacle to a "common goals" merger of formal and psychological semantics. It does show that we must not try to take the ability to make entailment judments, or the ability to decide, "given all the facts", whether a sentence is true (Cresswell, 1978) as the thing a theory of semantic competence is about, or it does follow that semantic competence will not be attainable by finite creatures. We can consistently maintain the possibility of a competence theory for semantics only by keeping "competence" free of any kind of process notions such as judging or understanding. In syntax, assuming the language is recursive, we can perfectly well have competence theories of sentence generation and of parsing, or of the making of grammaticality judgments; all of these can in principle be done perfectly by a finite device (if it does not have a fixed bound on how much time or auxiliary computing space it can use). In semantics, on the other hand, the only kind of competence theory that can possibly be compatible with the goal of characterizing valid entailments is the kind analogous to "knowledge of the grammar" in syntax. A competence theory can't be a theory of understanding. But psychological semantics doesn't *have* to be a theory of understanding either; it can certainly include the theory of the nature of our knowledge of the semantics of our language. But this leads to a sharp break between "psychological semantics" as including such studies and "procedural semantics" as characterized by a primary concern for the processes involved in using that knowledge in the production and comprehension of sentences, or the making of validity judgments. The claim that our knowledge of the semantics of the language simply *consists in* (the knowledge of) the procedures we use in such processes (which I believe to be both Johnson-Laird's and Woods' position) is thus incompatible with the claim that a natural language can be correctly characterized by a semantics according to which some sentences are determinately true but undecidable.

This is not to say that we know that a natural language can be so characterized, or if it can be, that such a semantics can be finitely representable. For example, much work in formal semantics is based on logics like Montague's which can be model-theoretically interpreted but are not finitely axiomatizable. It is not known, however, that the "best" semantic theory will require a non-finitely-axiomatizable logic, or a non-finitely-characterizable model structure, so how big a problem this is still an open question.[17]

The biggest problem, I think, is that a finitely and completely statable semantics for a natural language (even for a single speaker) may not be possible at all. If that is the case, the notion of semantic competence will need serious rethinking. But to get to that problem, we need to return to some problems about belief-sentences.

V. DIFFERENCES IN BELIEFS AND DIFFERENCES IN LANGUAGE

Sometimes we perceive a clear ambiguity in a belief-sentence between a reading which is clearly "metalinguistic" and one which is not, as in Johnson-Laird's example:

(13) My friend thinks that transvestites are monks.

On one reading, the friend has a straighforward misapprehension about the meaning of "transvestite"; on the other, he simply has a false belief about, for example, why certain men dress in women's clothing.

Sgall et al. (1977) suggest that there is a sharp distinction between metalinguistic contexts and other non-extensional contexts, such that if the metalinguistic contexts are factored out, substitution under some version of intensional isomorphism in belief-contexts will be valid. This idea is perhaps related to Montague's (1970) suggestion that there is an additional "quotational" sense of belief in addition to a purely intensional one, and even more closely to the suggestion of Bigelow (1978b), that the arguments of propositional attitude verbs should be taken to be "semantic structures" which contain, in effect, both a quotation of the embedded sentence and a representation of its meaning. Bigelow's proposal seems better suited than a simple ambiguity approach for handling cases where we seem to need sensitivity simultaneously to the words and their meanings, as in (14).

(14) Thomason believes that semantics is a branch of mathematics.

But I believe that cases of this sort involve more than just words and their fixed meanings; to sharpen our intuitions, let's focus on the word "semantics" and contrast (14) with (15).

(15) Loar believes that semantics is a branch of psychology.

Assume for the sake of argument that we, Thomason, and Loar are all in agreement about what "mathematics" and "psychology" mean and that they are non-overlapping in extension. Now it does seem as though the sentences describe some differences about what the term "semantics" denotes, and yet it would certainly seem inappropriate to accuse either of them of ignorance about the meaning of the lexical item. (Certainly (14) is not likely to be construed as suggesting that Thomason has gotten "semantics" confused with "statistics", for instance.) In fact, it looks as though we can't hold on to the assumption of a fixed meaning for "mathematics" and "psychology", since it seems that psychology covers more enterprises on Loar's view than on Thomason's, and conversely for mathematics.

In fact I believe these cases, like many cases involving theory-laden vocabulary, show the impossibility of separating meanings from beliefs sufficiently to give a single semantics for the language.[18] Putnam's analysis of the natural-kind terms, if he is right, shows that intensions can depend in part on how the world is; Lewis's arguments (mentioned in footnote 16) show that those examples don't necessarily stand in the way of a psychological competence theory compatible with the words having fixed intensions. But in cases like (14) and (15), there is no hope of appealing to an eventual "correct theory" of scientific disciplines to fix the intensions of the three terms "semantics", "mathematics", and "psychology". The debate alluded to in (14) and (15) is much more a debate about what semantics *is* than about what "semantics" means. It is in part a debate about how to carve up our conceptual space – what questions should be grouped together for common investigation, what the appropriate sort of primitive notions are for laying the foundations of a theory many of whose particulars we are all in agreement on. The domain from which the value of the word "semantics" is to be selected is very much a domain of mental constructs; the issue is not so much which possible worlds are compatible with Loar's or Thomason's belief but of what sort of structure they want to impose on the world they're both in. I can't assume that the word "semantics" has a fixed meaning or a fixed intension in even my own idiolect of English and still make proper sense of (14) and (15); if I try to operate with a fixed meaning, I think I will have to misunderstand at least one of those sentences.

Johnson-Laird in fact reaches a similar conclusion. He would say that to understand (14), I have to construct a mental model of Thomason's mental model (at least of the part of it that concerns semantics); I have to iterate the construction to understand (16):

(16) Loar believes that semantics is a branch of psychology and that Thomason believes that semantics is a branch of mathematics.

(Note that there is no upper bound on the number of distinct representations of "semantics" that would be required if we continued to iterate.) According to Johnson-Laird, even the *transvestite* examples "establish . . . that a semantic theory formulated for a language can never be rich enough to cope with propositional attitudes." I'm not convinced by the *transvestite* example nor by the old *woodchuck–groundhog* problems; but I am convinced by the general problem of words whose meanings are fixed primarily by their place within large sets of beliefs. (The problem of theoretical terms is an old one in philosophy of science and has certainly played a large role in Quine's writings; I don't know why its implications for the possibility of fixing an interpretation for a language have been so generally ignored within the formal semantics tradition.)

Another perspective on the problem comes from considering language acquisition and concept development, which generally go hand in hand. Thinking in terms of model theoretic semantics, the domains one has available as possible interpretations for new lexical items continually become richer, and it is most noticeable in the acquisition of theoretical terms that considerable enrichment of the conceptual domain-space generally takes place *after* some of the new terms are to some extent acquired. In learning a word like "semantics", one is not just learning a mapping from a lexical item to an already "known" model-theoretic entity – the appropriate entity has to be "constructed" as well. (This point was emphasized in Harman, 1973.)

The technical side of the problem appears in various attempts to implement the proposal of Lewis (1970) that structured meanings might the appropriate interpretations of objects of propositional attitudes. Cresswell's work on the problem made it clear that the iteration of belief-contexts was one of the central difficulties. Bigelow (1978a) presented a treatment which had many nice properties but required for every *m* and *n* a distinct primitive lexical item, $believes^{m}_{\langle\sigma_1, \sigma_2, \ldots, \sigma_n\rangle}$; the upper subscript provided ramifications to prevent functions from applying to themselves, while the lower one provided for positions to be quantified into. This would clearly prevent the language from being finitely representable. In his later article (Bigelow, 1978b) he avoids the need for either kind of unbounded indexing by taking the object of belief to be a "semantic structure" of an expression rather than a meaning. Although there are only finitely many primitive constants in his language, the system has some very puzzling features, notably the requirement that for every object *d* in any domain, the ordered pair $\langle \theta, d \rangle$ is an *expression* in the corresponding syntactic category. It also includes the requirement that the domain D_1 of things must be very large relative to all other domains, since D_1 must include "a semantic marker" for every member of every domain, and D_1 must include every sequence of elements of D_1. The system has a great many nice properties, avoids all the unwanted inferences, and looks as though it could permit appropriate inferences in conjunction with auxiliary hypotheses. (The discussion of the Liar Paradox at the end of the article suggests that the system is not known to be consistent.) Whether the system in some sense requires infinitely many primitives, I'm not sure; I think that it does, by requiring a distinct semantic marker (an element of D_1) for every element of every domain. If the arguments of this section are correct, then either there must be infinitely many primitives somewhere in the theory, or the theory must be inadequate for handling iterated belief contexts involving theoretical terms in their complements.

VI. THE LIMITS OF SEMANTICS

I argued above that a fairly completely statable semantics for a natural language is impossible, even for a single speaker. I should qualify that and exempt any speaker who is willing to be sufficiently closed-minded, since the assumptions I required for the argument included the following: (i) the language contains some words with theory-dependent meanings; (ii) the speaker believes that it is possible that the "right" theory, if there is one, has not yet been thought of by anyone. If a speaker were to "close off" his semantics, fixing on a particular model structure or conceptual structure (adopting a fixed metaphysics), and fixing on a finite set of interpretations for each lexical item, then it would probably be possible to give a finitely specifiable semantics for that speaker's language.

But the negative characterization of what it would take to be such a speaker clearly indicate that we are better off if a complete semantics for our language is impossible. It seems to me that what we have here is a remarkable adaption for coping with our limitations to finiteness and with the awareness of the necessary incompleteness of our knowledge. I don't think it matters in this respect whether one believes in objective truth or not; if there is such a thing, we suppose that we can never know all of it. Given that we have no way of arriving at an optimal state of knowledge, we are clearly better off if we do not at any point assume a rigid conception of what alternative states of affairs there may be or what the total stock of possible individuals might be. Our conceptions of alternative possibilities are limited by the constraint of finite representability, but we can always alter them. We can even consider alternative logics, or the possibility that there is no such thing as objective truth.

We can only work with fragments; we cannot guarantee our own consistency; we can't be sure we understand each other. To idealize away from the factors which make a completely specified semantics impossible, via simplifying assumptions ("closed world" and/or "closed language" assumptions), may be expedient or even essential for particular real-life communication situations or for studying parts of the language in detail, just as one may believe the arguments of the skeptic and yet continue to take knowledge for granted for all practical purposes.[19]

But if we were to idealize away these factors for good in trying to construct a theory of human language (as Montague seems to have done in his theory of universal grammar, and as everyone does who starts from the assumption of a fixed universal set of semantic primitives or primitive concepts), we would be limiting ourselves to the description of the language of creatures or machines whose minds are much more narrowly and rigidly circumscribed than those of humans. We cannot change the fact of our limitations of finiteness, but we are blessed with the awareness of our ignorance and the ability to decrease it.

I now believe that there is no incompatibility in the enterprises of formal semantics and psychological semantics; the apparent conflicts may well have resulted from the false assumption on both sides that a human language must have a finitely representable semantics. Abandoning that assumption opens up interesting new possibilities for trying to understand more about how our minds work by studying how our language works, and suggests a new dimension for the concept of language creativity.

University of Massachusetts, Amherst

ACKNOWLEDGEMENTS

This paper was not completed until more than a year after the conference at which a (very different) early version of it was presented, and I am indebted to more people than I can name for ideas and for support that were crucial in its development and eventual completion. Besides those mentioned in the text and the footnotes, I particularly want to thank Emmon Bach, Ed Gettier, Elliot Soloway, Douglas Moran, Gennaro Chierchia, Brian White, Richard Larson, Joyce Friedman, Elisabet Engdahl, Stephen Isard, Ed Zalta, Jonathan Mitchell, James Munz, and Hans Kamp. Only Emmon Bach read the manuscript; he suggested a number of improvements, but I take responsibility for the results.

NOTES

[1] This section is a revised and condensed version of parts of Partee (1979).

[2] I will not have any more to say here about the view, espoused by Montague and by David Kaplan among others, that the inferences in question *are* valid, although I believe that that view is not as implausible as it appears at first sight.

[3] This is not to deny that there may be other perfectly good senses in which we want to say that speakers *do* know their language; see section IV. Also see Barwise and Perry (1980) for a fundamentally different approach which would avoid such a conclusion.

[4] See Partee (1979a) for some discussion of the difficulties of quotational theories; these have also been discussed widely in the philosophical literature. See especially Bigelow (1978b).

[5] See Linsky (1977).
[6] See Stalnaker (1978) and discussion of his and related suggestions by Kaplan and van Fraassen in Partee (1979).
[7] But see Siegel (1979) for an interesting proposal along these lines.
[8] Such cases were pointed out by Carnap (1947) and have been discussed at least by Katz (1972), Partee (1973), and Sgall et al (1977).
[9] One might be tempted to go farther and include cases of one-way "constructional entailment" (i.e. entailment based on compositional semantic rules) since it would appear that (a) entails (b) (again holding everything equal except the obvious difference).

(a) Mary believes that a poet who lives in Boston will visit us.
(b) Mary believes that a poet will visit us.

However, such one-way entailments yield invalid inferences with other propositional attitude verbs (e.g. *doubt that, wonder whether, wish that*). This can't be taken care of with simple meaning postulates specifying particular such verbs as upward-entailing, downward-entailing, or neither (see Ladusaw, 1979, and Linebarger, 1980), unless a way could be found to make meaning postulates sensitive to the differences between "constructional entailment" and logical entailment in general. (This cannot be done with meaning postulates of the sort used by Montague in PTQ, for instance, since they simply constrain the possible interpretations of the intensional logic and are not sensitive to syntactic distinctions among different logically equivalent sentences.) This is probably another aspect of the original problem.
[10] Katz at one time proposed "one-step entailment" as a condition for synonymy; the resulting problems about transitivity were among the reasons for general non-acceptance of such a proposal.
[11] I am grateful to Tyler Burge (personal communication) for helping me out of an earlier very pessimistic state of mind by emphasizing this point.
[12] Hintikka, in Hintikka (1962) and elsewhere, has emphasized this point.
[13] This was Chomsky's early view and it is still current in most approaches involving formal semantics, but Chomsky and other generative grammarians now characterize syntax in part or whole as a system for mapping between variously postulated levels of representation. The characterization of competence changes accordingly, but I don't believe the differences affect the main points here.
[14] The possibility of syntactic competence has not gone entirely unchallenged, but since I am discussing an unproblematic view of syntactic competence only to highlight the problematic status of semantic competence, arguments that syntactic competence is not so simple don't hurt my main point.
[15] I have claimed as much in print, but David Lewis and Jerry Fodor have convinced me (in discussion at this conference and elsewhere) that I was assuming an unnecessarily demanding view of competence.
[16] David Lewis has similarly convinced me that my earlier worries about not knowing the intensions of lexical items can be allayed by a similar distinction: insofar as a lexical item has a determinate intension at all, it has it by virtue of what is in at least some speakers' heads together with facts about the way the world is, including in some cases facts about the history of the use of the word. We can then identify lexical semantic competence with whatever it is in speakers' heads that determines a function from such external factors to intensions.

17 See for instance the very different approach taken in Barwise (1981) and Barwise and Perry (1981), which departs from possible-worlds semantics in significant ways and in which the logical equivalence problem disappears.

18 Harman (1973) used similar arguments to argue against the possibility of universal semantic representations.

19 It is for these reasons that I believe that the conclusions of this paper are fully compatible with the enterprise of constructing explicit syntactic and semantic rules for fragments of natural language (as in Montague grammar and related theories of formal syntax and semantics), an enterprise which had had marked success in illuminating a wide variety of semantic phenomena. The only thing ruled out by the conclusions here, if they are correct, is the possibility of viewing the grammars of fragments as steps toward the eventual construction of a single complete finite syntax and semantics for an entire language. (Kripke and Stalnaker have both expressed (personal communication) similar views about the utility of using "possible worlds" constructions to explain various intensional phenomena while doubting the coherence of positing a single set of "*all* possible worlds" to cover *all* intensional phenomena.)

BIBLIOGRAPHY

Barwise, Jon: (1981) 'Scenes and other situations', *Journal of Philosophy* 78.7, 369–397.

Barwise, Jon: (1981) 'Semantic innocence and uncompromising situations', in P. A. French, T. E. Uehling and H. K. Wettstein, eds., *Midwest Studies in Philosophy VI*, Univ. of Minnesota Press, Minneapolis, pp. 387–404.

Bigelow, John: (1978a) 'Semantics of thinking, speaking, and translation', in F. Guenthner and M. Guenthner-Reutter, eds., *Meaning and Translation*, New York University Press, New York, pp. 109–135.

Bigelow, John: (1978b) 'Believing in semantics', *Linguistics and Philosophy* 2, 101–144.

Carnap, Rudolf (1947) *Meaning and Necessity: A Study in Semantics and Modal Logic*, Univ. of Chicago Press, (enlarged ed. 1956).

Chomsky, Noam: (1965) *Aspects of the Theory of Syntax*, MIT Press, Cambridge, Mass.

Cresswell, M. J.: (1978) 'Semantic competence', in F. Guenthner and M. Guenthner-Reutter, eds., *Meaning and Translation*, New York University Press, New York.

Cresswell, M. J.: (1982) 'The autonomy of semantics', this volume, pp. 69–86.

Davidson, Donald and Gilbert Harman, eds.: (1975), *The Logic of Grammar*, Dickinson Pub. Co., Encino, Calif.

Davidson, Donald: (1970) 'Semantics for natural languages', in *Linguaggi nella società e nella tecnica*, Edizioni di Comunità, Milano, pp. 177–188. Reprinted in Davidson and Harman, 1975.

Dowty, David: (1980), *Word Meaning and Montague Grammar*, Synthese Language Library, D. Reidel Publishing Co., Dordrecht.

Harman, Gilbert: (1973) 'Against universal semantic representation', unpublished manuscript (?), Princeton University.

Hintikka, Jaakko: (1962) *Knowledge and Belief*, Cornell Univ. Press, Ithaca, NY.

Johnson-Laird, Philip: (1977) 'Procedural semantics', *Cognition* 5, 189–214.

Johnson-Laird, Philip: (1982) 'Formal semantics and the psychology of meaning', this volume, pp. 1–68.

Katz, Jerrold J.: 1972) *Semantic Theory*, Harper & Row, New York.

Kripke, Saul: (1972) 'Naming and necessity' in D. Davidson and G. Harman, eds., *Semantics of Natural Language*, D. Reidel, Dordrecht.

Ladusaw, William: (1979) *Polarity Sensitivity as Inherent Scope Relations*, unpublished doctoral dissertation, University of Texas, Austin.

Lewis, David: (1970) 'General semantics', *Synthese* 2, 18–67.

Linebarger, Marcia: (1980) *The Grammar of Negative Polarity Items*, unpublished doctoral dissertation, MIT, Cambridge, Mass.

Linsky, L.: (1977) 'Believing and necessity', *Proceedings and Addresses of the American Philosophical Association* 50, 526–538.

Loar, Brian: (1976) 'Two theories of meaning', in G. Evans and J. McDowell, eds., *Truth and Meaning: Essays in Semantics*, Oxford Univ. Press, 138–161.

Mates, Benson: (1950) 'Synonymity', in *Meaning and Interpretation*, Univ. of Calif. Publications in Philosophy 25, 201–226. Also in L. Linsky, *Semantics and the Philosophy of Language*, Urbana, 1952.

Miller, George A. and Philip N. Johnson-Laird: (1976) *Language and Perception*, The Belknap Press of Harvard Univ. Press, Cambridge, MA.

Montague, Richard: (1970) 'Universal grammar', reprinted in Montague (1974), pp. 222–246.

Montague, Richard: (1973) 'The proper treatment of quantification in ordinary English', reprinted in Montague (1974), pp. 247–270.

Montague, Richard: (1974) *Formal Philosophy: Selected Papers of Richard Montague*, edited and with an introduction by Richmond Thomason, Yale Univ. Press, New Haven.

Partee, Barbara: (1972) 'The semantics of belief-sentences', in J. Hintikka, J. Moravcsik, and P. Suppes, eds., *Approaches to Natural Language*, D. Reidel, Dordrecht.

Partee, Barbara: (1979) 'Semantics–mathematics or psychology?', in R. Bäuerle, U. Egli, and A. von Stechow (eds.), *Semantics from Different Points of View*, Springer-Verlag, Berlin, pp. 1–14.

Putnam, Hilary: (1954) 'Synonymity and the analysis of belief-sentences', *Analysis* 14, 114–22.

Putnam, Hilary: (1975) 'The meaning of "meaning"', in K. Gunderson, ed., *Language, Mind and Knowledge*, Minnesota Studies in the Philosophy of Science VII, Univ. of Minnesota Press, Minneapolis.

Putnam, Hilary: (1978) 'Reference and understanding', in *Meaning and the Moral Sciences*, Routledge and Kegan Paul, London.

Quine, W. V. O.: (1960) *Word and Object*, MIT Press, Cambridge.

Sellars, Wilfrid: (1955) 'Putnam on Synonymity and Belief', *Analysis* 15, 117–20.

Sgall, P., E. Hajičová, and O. Prochazka: (1977) 'On the role of linguistic semantics', *Theoretical Linguistics* 4, 31–59.

Siegel, Muffy: (1979) 'Some thoughts on propositional attitudes, psychological meanings, and intensions in Montague Grammar', unpublished manuscript, Temple University.

Stalnaker, Robert: (1978) 'Assertion', in Peter Cole, ed., *Syntax and Semantics, Vol. 9: Pragmatics*, Academic Press, N.Y. (315–332).

Woods, William: (1979) 'Procedural semantics and a theory of meaning', paper presented at the University of Texas Conference on semantics of natural language and natural language processing.

ROBERT C. MOORE AND GARY G. HENDRIX

COMPUTATIONAL MODELS OF BELIEF AND THE SEMANTICS OF BELIEF SENTENCES

I. COMPUTATIONAL THEORIES AND COMPUTATIONAL MODELS

Over the years the psychology of belief and the semantics of belief sentences have provided a seemingly endless series of fascinating problems for linguists, psychologists, and philosophers. Despite all the attention that has been paid to these problems, however, there is little agreement on proposed solutions, or even on what form solutions should take. We believe that a great deal of light can be shed on the problems of belief by studying them from the viewpoint of computational models of the psychological processes and states associated with belief. The role of computational theories and computational models in the cognitive sciences always seems to be a matter of controversy. When such theories and models are discussed by non-computer scientists, they are frequently presented in a rather apologetic tone, with assurances and caveats that, of course, this is all oversimplified and things couldn't really be like this, *but* . . .

This may be the result of an unwarranted inference that anyone who takes a computational approach in one of these disciplines thereby endorses what is sometimes called the thesis of "mechanism" (Lucas, 1961): that minds can be completely explained in terms of machines, which in contemporary discussions are usually taken to be computers. When the metaphysical doctrine of dualism was more widely held, the mechanism thesis could be rejected on the grounds that minds were nonphysical. It appears to be more fashionable to adhere to a materialistic metaphysics nowadays, but to hold that the way minds are embodied in brains is so complex as to be beyond all human understanding, or at least too complex to be represented by Turing machines or computer programs. On the basis of current knowledge, these questions appear to us to be completely open. The existing evidence may well have as little relevance to future discoveries as the arguments of the Greek philosophers about atomism have to modern atomic theory.

Work reported in this paper was supported by the National Science Foundation under Grant No. MCS76–22004, and by the Defense Advanced Research Projects Agency under Contract N00039–79–C–0118 with the Naval Electronic Systems Command.

S. Peters and E. Saarinen (eds.), Processes, Beliefs, and Questions, 107–127.

We wish to argue, however, that the usefulness of computational approaches in the cognitive sciences does not depend on how (or even whether) these questions are eventually answered. In elaborating this view, it will be helpful to make a distinction between computational theories and computational models. We will say that a theory of a cognitive process is a computational theory if it claims that the process is a computational process. The mechanism thesis can be viewed as the claim that *every* cognitive process is a computational process. Obviously, one can hold that certain cognitive processes are computational without claiming that all are, so having a particular computational theory of some cognitive process still leaves the mechanism thesis an open question.

The construction of computational theories is the most obvious use of computational ideas in the cognitive sciences. However, even without computational theories, computational models can be extremely useful. By a computational model of a cognitive process we mean a computational system whose behavior is similar to the behavior of the process in some interesting way. The important point is that one can make use of computational models without making any claims about the nature of the process being modeled. For example, the use of computational models in weather forecasting does not commit one to the claim that meteorological processes are computational.

What makes computational models in meteorology interesting is the fact that they can make useful predictions about the behavior of the system being modeled. In the cognitive sciences few models, computational or otherwise, have such predictive power, and we are hard pressed to think of any cases in which the predictions that are made can be considered useful. Thus at our current level of understanding, prediction of behavior does not appear to be the most productive role for computational models of cognitive processes.

What computational models do seem to be good for is clarification of conceptual problems. Many of the most vexing problems in the cognitive sciences are questions as to how any physical system could have the properties that cognitive systems apparently possess. Computational models can often supply answers to questions of this kind independently of empirical considerations regarding the way human (or other) cognitive systems actually function. The point is that conceptual arguments often proceed from general observations about some cognitive process to specific conclusions as to what the process must be like. One way of testing such an argument is to construct a computational model that satisfies the premises of the argument and then to see whether the conclusions apply to the model. When used in this way, a computational model may be best thought of not so much as a model of a process, but rather as a model (in the sense of "model theory" in formal logic) of the theory in which the argument is made. That is, a conceptual argument ought to be valid for all possible models that satisfy its premises, so it had better be valid for a particular computational model, independently of how closely that model resembles the cognitive process that is the "intended model."

In the remainder of this paper we will try to apply computational models in this way to investigate some of the problems about belief and the semantics of belief sentences. First we will present a model of belief that seems to satisfy most of our pretheoretical notions. Then we will ask what implications it would have for the semantics of belief sentences, if human belief were analogous to our model. As will be seen below, this leads us to some conclusions quite different from those drawn by other authors.

II. INTERNAL LANGUAGES

Before going into the details of what a computational model of belief might look like, we need to deal with a set of objections that have been raised to one of the basic assumptions we will make. The assumption is that beliefs are to be explained in terms of expressions in some sort of internal language that is not the language used externally – a "language of thought" to use Fodor's (1975) term. To possess a particular belief is to bear a certain computational relation to the appropriate expression in this internal language. This sort of explanation has frequently been attacked by philosophers, particularly Ryle (1949) and Wittgenstein (1953), as incomprehensible, but this is surely a case of a conceptual argument that fails when applied to computational models. Many computer systems have been built that have internal languages in this sense, and we are unable to find appeals to any features of human cognition in the usual arguments against internal languages that would make these arguments inapplicable to those systems. In particular, the internal language used in one of these computer systems always has a well-defined syntax, and usually a clear notion of inference defined in terms of manipulations of the formulas of the language. Whether these languages have truth-conditional semantics is more problematical, but for purposes of psychological explanation this may well be unnecessary. After all, if truth-conditional semantics cannot be given for the internal language the machine uses, although we know how to explain the behavior of the machine (since it was specifically designed to have that behavior), then such semantics cannot be required for the explanation. But if truth-conditional semantics is not required to perform "psychological explanation" for machines, why should it be required for humans?

Even if we accept the existence of computer systems that use such an internal language as a "model-theoretic" demonstration that the arguments against internal languages are misguided, just where they go wrong remains an interesting question. It would clearly be impossible to examine all such arguments in this brief paper, (and we confess that we are not scholars of that literature,) but it may be instructive to look at at least one example. One familiar type of argument used by behaviorists against any number of concepts in cognitive psychology runs something like this:

> The only evidence admissible in psychology is behavioral evidence. There will always be many hypotheses, equally compatible with any possible behavioral evidence, about what *X* an organism has. Therefore, there is no empirical content to the claim that an organism has one *X* rather than another. Therefore the notion of *X* is unintelligible.

Quine has used this type of argument repeatedly in his discussions of the indeterminacy of translation (1960), ontological relativity (1971), and knowledge of grammatical rules (1972). "Set of expressions in an internal language" is one of the concepts frequently substituted for "*X*" in this schema. The argument has some plausibility when applied to the human mind, where we have very little idea of how expresssions in an internal language might be physically represented. It loses that plausibility when applied to computational models. If we recast the argument we can see why:

> The only evidence admissible for analyzing computer systems is behavioral evidence. There will always be many hypotheses, equally compatible with any possible behavioral evidence, about what set of expressions in an internal language from the basis of a computer system's "beliefs." Therefore, there is no empirical content to the claim that a computer system has one set of expressions rather than another. Therefore the notion of a set of expressions in an internal language in a computer system is unintelligible.

Where this argument breaks down depends on what is taken to be behavioral evidence. If we take behavioral evidence to be simply the input/output behavior of the system when it is running normally, then there is certainly more than behavioral evidence to draw upon. With a computer system we can do the equivalent of mapping out the entire "nervous system," and so understand its internal operations as well. On the other hand, if behavioral evidence includes internal behavior, it becomes much less plausible to say that there will be no way to tell which set of expressions the system possesses.

At this point, a computer scientist might be tempted to shout, "Of course! To find out what internal expressions the systems has, all you have to do is to print them out and look at them!" – but there is more to be said for the Quinean argument than this. What are directly observable, after all, are the physical states of the machine and their causal connections. There are many levels of interpretation between them and the print-out containing the set of expressions we wish to attribute to the machine. A Quinean might argue that there will be other interpretations that will lead to a different set of expressions, perhaps in a different internal language. With computer systems, however, the fact that they are designed to be interpreted in a certain way makes it extremely likely that any alternative interpretation would be far less natural, and so could be rejected on general grounds of simplicity and elegance. If this were not the case, it would be like discovering that the score of Beethoven's Ninth is actually the score of Bach's Mass in B Minor under a different, but no more complex, interpretation of the usual system of musical notation.

The Quinean argument fares somewhat better when applied to humans because there is no *a priori* reason to assume that human brains are designed to be interpreted in any particular way. Thus it is more plausible that there might be multiple descriptions of the operation of the brain in terms of internal languages, and that these descriptions, while incompatible with one another, are nevertheless equally compatible with all the evidence, including neurological evidence. But as the example of the computer system shows, and contrary to the Quinean argument, there is also no *a priori* reason to assume that this must be the case. It is, as the saying goes, an empirical question. It should be clear that one of the empirical commitments of any theory in cognitive psychology is that there be a preferred interpretation of the physical system in terms of the entities postulated by the theory. If this commitment is recognized, then failure to find a preferred interpretation makes the theory not incoherent or unintelligible, but simply false.

In view of all this, the best that can be said for the Quinean argument is that it points out the possibility that there will be more than one theory compatible with any evidence that can be obtained. But this is always the case in science. Surely no one would suggest that atomic theory is incoherent because there might be some as yet undiscovered alternative that is equally compatible with the evidence. Thus our consideration of computational models leads us to agree with Chomsky (1975, p. 182) that Quine's indeterminacy doctrine comes to no more than the observation that nontrivial empirical theories are underdetermined by evidence.

III. A COMPUTATIONAL MODEL OF BELIEF

The basic outlines of the computational model of belief presented below should be familiar to anyone acquainted with developments in artificial intelligence or cognitive simulation over the past few years. In calling this a model of belief, however, we must be careful to distinguish between psychology and semantics. Our model is intended to be a psychologically plausible account of what might be going on in an organism or system that could usefully be said to have beliefs. Even if we assume that the model does describe what is going on, the semantic question remains of how the English word "believe" relates to the model. We will put off adressing that question until Section IV.

As we said in the preceding section, belief will be explained in our model in terms of a system's being in a certain computational relation to expressions in an internal language. We will call the set of expressions to which a system is so related the *belief set* of the system. The exact relationship between the expressions in this set and what we would intuitively call the beliefs of the system will be left unspecified until we discuss the semantics of belief sentences in Section IV. We will also be somewhat vague as to just what computational relation defines the belief set, but we can name some of the constraints it must satisfy. First of all, we will stipulate that, to be in the belief set of a system, an expression must be explicitly stored in the system's memory. It may turn out that we want to say the system has beliefs that would correspond to expressions that are not explicitly stored, but can be derived from stored expressions. In that case, the relationship between the system's beliefs and its belief set will be more complicated, but it will still be important to single out the expressions that are explicitly stored.

The fact that an expression is stored in the memory of the system cannot be sufficient, however, for that expression to be in the system's belief set. If the system is to be even a crude model of an intelligent organism, it will need to have propositional attitudes besides belief, which we would also presumably explain in terms of expressions in its internal language stored in its memory. We can account for this by treating the memory of the system as being logically partitioned into different spaces – one space for the expressions corresponding to beliefs, another for desires, another for fears, etc. These various spaces will be functionally differentiated by the processes that operate on them and connect them to the system's sensors and effectors. For example, perceiving that there is a red block on the table might directly give rise to a belief that there is a red block on the table, but probably not the desire or fear that there is a red block on the table. Similarly, wanting to pick up a red block might be one of the immediate causes of trying to pick up a red block, but imagining picking up a red block would presumably not.

This is a bit oversimplified, but not too much. Although it is true that perceiving a red block on the table could cause a fear that there is a red block on the table, this would need to be explained by, say, a belief that red blocks are explosive. In going from perception to belief, no such additional explanation is necessary. It seems completely compatible with our pretheoretical notions (which our model is supposed to reflect) to assume that we are simply built in such a way that we automatically accept our perceptions as beliefs unless they conflict with existing beliefs. (Anyone who does not think we are built this way should look out his window and try to disbelieve that what he sees is actually there.)

As to the internal language itself, we will again leave the details somewhat sketchy. For the purposes of this discussion, it will be sufficient to assume that the language is that of ordinary predicate logic augmented by intensional operators for propositional attitudes. The expressions in a belief set would be well-formed formulas in this language. The basic inference procedures should certainly be inclusive enough so that there is some way of applying them to generate any valid inference, but they could include procedures for generating plausible inferences as well. The important point is that, to interpret a set of formulas as a belief set, there had better be a well-defined notion of inference for them, since people clearly draw inferences from their beliefs. It is equally important, moreover, that there be a notion of an inference process in the model. The basic inference procedures merely define what inferences are possible, not what inferences will actually be drawn. There must be a global inference process that applies specific inference procedures to the formulas in the belief set and adds the resulting formulas to the belief set.

As simple as this model is, it seems to account fairly well for the obvious facts about belief. For example, it explains how "one-shot" learning can occur when one is told something. The explanation is that the hearer of a natural-language utterence decodes it into a formula in his internal language and adds the formula to his belief set. This idea, which seems to be almost universally accepted in generative linguistics and cognitive psychology, would hardly be worth mentioning if it were not for the fact that it differs so radically from the view presented in behaviorist psychology. According to standard behaviorist assumptions, we would expect that repeated trials and reinforcements would be necessary for learning to occur. This has some plausibility in the case of complex skills or large bodies of information, but a moment's reflection will show that very little learning fits this picture. Most "learning" consists of acquiring commonplace information such as where the laundry was put and what time dinner will be ready. Our model seems to explain this type of learning much better than does reinforcement of responses to a given stimulus.

A slightly less trivial, but still fairly obvious comment is that this model has no difficulty explaining how the system could accept one belief, yet reject another that is its logical equivalent. Suppose that beliefs are individuated more or less as are formulas in the internal language. Suppose further that the system has a particular formula *P* in its belief set that is logically equivalent to another formula *Q*, in the sense there is some way of applying the basic inference procedures of the system to infer *Q* from *P* and vice versa. The system may not put *Q* in its belief set, however, because it never tries to derive *Q*, or because its heuristics for applying its inference procedures are not sufficient to find the derivation of *Q*, or because the derivation of *Q* is so long that it exhausts the system's resources of memory and time. We raise this point because the possibility that "*A* believes *P*" is true and "*A* believes *Q*" is false, even though *P* and *Q* are logically equivalent, is currently considered to be a major problem in the semantics of belief sentences, especially for theories based on possible-world semantics. In view of the voluminous literature this problem has generated (Montague, 1970; Partee, 1973, 1978; Stalnaker, 1976; Cresswell, this volume), it is striking to note that, if reality is even vaguely like our computational model, this is no problem at all for the psychology of belief. This suggests to us that the problem is artificial, a point we will return to in Section V.

A more serious problem that can be handled rather nicely in this model is the question of what beliefs are expressed by sentences containing indexicals such as "I," "now," and "here." This is particularly troublesome for theories that take the language of thought to be identical to the external natural language. To take an example suggested by the work of Perry (1977, 1979), suppose that Jones has a belief he would express by saying "I am sitting down." We would take Jones's use of the word "I" to be a reference to Jones himself and take Jones's belief to be about himself. What is it that makes Jones's belief a belief about himself? It can't be simply that he has used the word "I" to express it, because he might not be using "I" as it is normally used in English; he must also believe or intend that in using "I" he refers to himself. But if this belief or intention consists in having certain English sentences stored in the appropriate space in his memory, it is hard to see how the explanation can avoid being circular. It is certainly not sufficient for Jones to believe "When I use 'I,' it refers to me," because this doesn't express the right belief or intention unless it has already been established that Jones uses "me" and "I" to refer to himself.

One way to try to get out of this problem is to say that Jones has some nonindexical description of himself and this his use of "I" is shorthand for this description. But, as Perry points out, having such a description is neither necessary nor sufficient to account for his use of "I." To see that it is not necessary, suppose Jones is the official biographer of Jimmy Carter, but he becomes insane and begins to believe that he actually is Jimmy Carter. Thus his beliefs include things he would express by "My name is 'Jimmy Carter,'" "I am a former President of the United States," "My daughter is Amy Carter," and so forth, in great detail. It does not seem to be logically impossible that *all* the nonindexical descriptions he attributes to himself are in fact true of Jimmy Carter and not true of him. On the description theory of indexicals, this should mean that Jones uses "I" to refer to Jimmy Carter and that his beliefs are all true. But it is intuitively clear that he still uses "I" to refer to himself, and that his beliefs are all delusional and false. On the other hand, suppose he is not insane, but uses "I" as a shorhand for some true description of himself such as "Jimmy Carter's biographer." Hence, when he says "I am sitting down" he expresses the belief "Jimmy Carter's biographer is sitting down." This does not explain his belief that he is sitting down, however, unless he also believes that *he* is Jimmy Carter's biographer.

In view of Kripke's (1972) critique of the description theory of proper names, it is not surprising that the description theory of indexicals doesn't work either. Nevertheless, it is interesting that Kripke's alternative, which does seem to work for proper names, still does not work for indexicals. Kripke's theory is essentially that when someone uses a proper name, it derives its reference from the occasion on which he acquired the use of the name, and that this creates a causal chain extending back to the original "dubbing" of the individual with that name. Thus, our use of "Kripke" refers to Kripke because we have acquired the name from occasions on which it was used to refer to Kripke. But this can't explain the use of the word "I," because no one *ever* acquires the use of "I" from an occasion on which it was used to refer to him.

In our computational model we can explain the use of "I" by assuming that the system has an individual constant in its internal language – call it SYS – that intrinsically refers to the system itself, and that the system uses "I" to express in English formulas of its internal language that involve this individual constant. This may seem to be no progress, since we are left with the task of explaining how SYS refers to the system. This is an easier task, however. A substantial part of the problem posed by "I" is that it is part of a natural language, and natural languages are acquired. The problem about beliefs being English sentences in the mind is that the person might have acquired a nonstandard understanding of them. Similarly, Kripke's causal-chain theory fails to explain the reference of "I" because "I" doesn't fit the assumptions the theory makes about how terms are acquired. As Fodor (1975) points out, however, if the internal language of thought is in fact not an external natural language, then we can assume that it is innate, and we are relieved of the problem of explaining how the expressions in it are acquired.

We can explain how SYS refers intrinsically to the system in terms of the functional role it plays. The system can be so constructed that, when it seems to see a red block, a formula roughly equivalent to "SYS seems to see a red block" is automatically added to the belief set, or at least becomes derivable in the belief space. Similarly, wanting to pick up a red block is intrinsically connected to "SYS wants to pick up a red block," and so forth. If the meaning of SYS is "hard-wired" in this way, then learning the appropriate use of "I" requires only learning something like "Use 'I' to refer to SYS." This type of explanation cannot be given in terms of the word "I" alone, because people are not hard-wired to use "I" in any way at all.

IV. THE SEMANTICS OF BELIEF SENTENCES

We hope the picture that we have presented so far is plausible as a model of the psychology of belief. If it is, then we have solved a number of interesting conceptual problems. That is, we have given at least a partial answer to the original question of how any physical system could have the properties that cognitive systems appear to have. Of course, solving conceptual problems is different from solving empirical problems; we have very little evidence that human cognitive systems actually work this way. On the other hand, we tend to agree with Fodor (1975, p. 27) that the only current theories in psychology that are even remotely plausible are computational theories, and that having remotely plausible theories is better than having no theories at all.

In light of the foregoing, there is a truly remarkable fact: although the psychology of belief is relatively clear conceptually, the semantics of belief sentences is widely held to suffer from serious conceptual problem. This might be less remarkable if the authors who find difficulties with the semantics of belief sentences rejected our conceptual picture, but that is not necessarily the case. For instance Cresswell (this volume, p. 73) acknowledges that "it is probably true that what makes someone believe something is indeed standing in a certain relation to an internal representation of a proposition," and it appears that Partee (1979) would also be favorably inclined towards this kind of approach.

It seems to us that, if we have a clear picture of what the psychology of belief is like, it ought to go a long way towards telling us under what condition attributions of belief are true. That is, it ought to give us a basis for stating the truth-conditional semantics of belief sentences. Our general view should be clear by now: if our computational model of belief is roughly the way people work, then "*A* believes that *S*" is true if and only if the individual denoted by "*A*" has the formula of his internal language that corresponds appropriately to "*S*" in his belief set, or perhaps "*S*" can be derived in his belief set with limited effort. This latter qualification can be included or excluded, according to whether one wants to say that a person believes things he may never have thought about but that are trivial inferences from his explicit beliefs, such as the fact that 98742 is an even number, or that Anwar Sadat is a creature with a brain.

To complete this view we have to specify the relation between an attributed belief and the corresponding formula in the belief set. As a first approximation, we could say that "*A* believes that *S*" is true if and only if the individual denoted by "*A*" has in his belief set a formula he would express by uttering "*S*." For example, "John believes that Venus is the morning star" would be true if and only if the person denoted by "John" has a formula in his belief set that he would express as "Venus is the morning star." We believe this formulation is on the right track, but it has a number of difficulties that need to be repaired. For one thing, it is obviously not right for *de re* belief reports, such as "John believes Bill's mistress is Bill's wife." On its most likely reading, "Bill's mistress" is a description used by the speaker of the sentence, not John. We would not expect John to express his belief as "Bill's mistress is Bill's wife." We will return to the issue of *de re* belief reports later, but for now we will confine ourselves to *de dicto* readings.

Another apparent problem is the notion of a sentence in an external language expressing a formula of an internal language, but this can be dealt with by the same sort of functional explanation that we used initially to justify the notion of a belief set. A sentence expresses the internal formula that has the right causal connection with an utterence of the sentence. That causal connection may be complicated, but it is basically like the one between the contents of a computer's memory and a print-out of those contents. We will therefore assume that, given a causal account of how the production of utterances depends on the cognitive state of the speaker, there is a best interpretation of which formula in the internal language is expressed by a sentence in the external language.

A genuine problem in our current formulation is the fact that a person cannot be counted on to express his belief that Venus is the morning star as "Venus is the morning star," unless he is a competent speaker of English. A possible way around this would be to say that *A* believes that *P* if *A* has in his belief set a formula of his internal language that a competent speaker of English would express by uttering "*S*." This would be plausible, however, only if we assume that every person has the same internal language, and that expressions in the language can be identified across individuals. It might well be true that the internal language has the same syntax for all persons, since this would presumably be genetically determined, but that is not enough. We would have to further assume that a formula in the internal language means the same thing for every person.

This is clearly not the case, however, as many examples by Putnam (1973, 1975), Kaplan (1977), and Perry (1977, 1979) demonstrate. What these examples show is that two persons can be in exactly the same mental state (which, on our view, would require having the same belief sets), yet have different beliefs, because their beliefs are about different things. This should not be surprising, since there is nothing in our computational model to suggest that the reference or semantic interpretation of every expression in the language of thought is innate. Some expressions can be considered to have an innate interpretation because of the functional role they play in the model. Logical connectives and quantifiers in the internal language might have an *a priori* interpretation because of the way they are treated by innate inference procedures, and we have already discussed the idea that a cognitive system could have a constant symbol that intrinsically refers the system. Predicates and relations for perceptual qualities, such as shapes and colors, would also seem to have a fixed interpretation based on the functional role they play in perception.

For most other expressions, including most individual constants and nonperceptual functions, predicates, and relations, there seems no reason to suppose that the interpretations are innately given. In fact, "concept learning" seems to be best accounted for by assuming that the internal language has an abitrarily large number of "unused" symbols on which information can be pegged. Acquiring a natural-kind concept might begin by noticing regularities in the perceptual properties of certain objects and deciding to "assign" one of the unused predicate symbols to that type of object. Then one could proceed to investigate the properties of these objects, adding more and more formulas involving this predicate to his belief set. Note that there is no reason to assume that the formulas added to the belief set constitute a biconditional definition of the concept; hence this picture is completely compatible with Wittgenstein's (1953) observation that we typically do not know necessary and sufficient conditions for application of the concepts we possess. Furthermore, since it is the acquisition process that gives the predicate symbol its interpretation, we can accomodate Putnam's (1973, 1975) point that a concept's extension can be partly determined by unobserved properties of the exemplars involved in the its acquisition. This also demonstrates, contrary to Fodor (1975), that concept learning can be explained in terms of an internal language, without assuming that the language already contains an expression for the concept.

It appears that concept acquisition processes like the one suggested above could provide the symbols of the internal language with a semantic interpretation via the sort of causal chain that Kripke and Putnam discuss in connection with the semantics of proper names and natural kind terms. Assuming the details can be worked out, we can use this semantic interpretation to try to define sameness of meaning across persons for expressions in the internal language. We can do this along lines suggested by Lewis's (1972) definition of meaning for natural languages: an expression P has the same meaning for A as Q has for B if P and Q have the same syntactic structure and each primitive symbol in Q has the same intension for A as the corresponding symbol in Q has for B. We take an intension to be a function from possible worlds to extensions, and we assume that the intension of a primitive symbol is either innate, because of the functional role of the symbol, or is acquired in accordance with the causal-chain theory.

The problem with this definition is that two primitive symbols can have the same intension, but differ in what we would intuitively call meaning. Suppose John believes that Tully and Cicero are two different people. He might have in his belief set expressions corresponding to:

NAME(PERSON3453) = "TULLY"
NAME(PERSON9876) = "CICERO"
NOT(PERSON3453 = PERSON9876)

The best that the causal-chain theory can do for us is to provide the same intension for both PERSON3453 and PERSON9876, a function that picks out Cicero in all possible worlds. But clearly, these two symbols do not have the same meaning for John. In general, we probably would want to say that two symbols differ in meaning for an individual unless they have the same intension *and* are treated as such in the person's belief set (e.g., by having a formula asserting that they are necessarily equivalent).

To accomodate this observation, we will say that if the primitive symbol *P* has the same intension for *A* that the primitive symbol *Q* has for *B*, then *P* has the same meaning for *A* that *Q* has for *B*, providing either that these are the only symbols having that intension for *A* and *B*, or that the same expression in a common external language expresses *P* for *A* and *Q* for *B*. This latter condition may seem arbitrary, but it will allow us to say that if Bill and John both believe that Cicero denounced Catiline and Tully did not, then both believe the same things. To use Quine's (1971, p. 153) phrase, this amounts to "acquiescing in our [or in this case, Bill and John's] mother tongue."

These criteria obviously do not guarantee that, if two persons possess symbols with the same intension, there is some way to determine which ones have the same meaning. There may be other conditions that would allow us to do this that we have not thought of, but there will undoubtedly be residual cases. Suppose a language has two terms, *P* and *Q*, that, unknown to the speakers of the language, are rigid designators for the same natural kind, and so have the same intension. In a language that has only one term for this natural kind, it might well be impossible to express the belief that these speakers express when they say, "Some *P*'s are not *Q*'s." Imagine a culture in which the idea of the relativity of motion was so deeply embedded that they had no concept of *X* going around *Y* rather than *Y* going around *X*, but only *X* and *Y* being in relative circular motion. How would we go about explaining to them what it was that got Galileo into trouble?

We are finally in a position to state the truth conditions for *de dicto* belief reports that seem to follow from our computational model. First, we will say that an English expression "*S*" expresses the meaning of an internal expression *P* for an individual *A* just in case, for any competent English speaker *B*, there is an internal expression *Q* that has the same meaning for *B* as *P* has for

A, and "*S*" expresses *Q* for *B*. Then a *de dicto* belief report of the form "*A* believes that *S*" is true if and only if the individual denoted by "*A*" has in his belief set a formula *P* such that "*S*" expresses the meaning of *P* for him.

To modify has theory to account for *de re* belief reports we will essentially reconstruct Kaplan's (1969) approach to apply to the internal language. According to our computational model, having a belief comes down to having the right formula in in one's belief set, and a belief report tells us something about that formula. A *de dicto* belief report, such as "John believes Venus is the morning star," provides us with a sentence that expresses the meaning of the formula in the belief set. In a *de re* belief report, such as "John believes Bill's mistress is Bill's wife," part of the sentence, in this case "Bill's wife," need not express the meaning or intension of any part of the corresponding formula. Instead, it expresses the reference of part of the formula. Suppose that the relevant formulas in John's belief set are something like:

NAME(PERSON55443) = "BILL"
WIFE(PERSON55443) = PERSON12345

If these formulas are the basis for the assertion that John believes Bill's mistress is Bill's wife, then it must at least be the case that the occurences of PERSON12345 in John's belief set refer to Bill's mistress. Otherwise, if John's belief is about anybody at all, then it is that person rather than Bill's mistress whom John believes to be Bill's wife. Something more than this is required, though. *De re* belief reports are generally held to support existential generalization. That is, from the fact that John believes Bill's mistress is Bill's wife we can infer that there is someone whom John believes to be Bill's wife. Phrasing it this way, however, we seem to be saying that John not only believes Bill is married, but he can pick out the person he thinks Bill is married to. If John has merely been told that Bill has been seen around lately with a beautiful woman and he has inferred that she must be his wife, then we could not really say that there is some specific person that he believes to be Bill's wife. There seems to be a certain amount of identifying information that John must have about PERSON12345 for his belief set to justify a *de re* belief report, although it is not always clear exactly what this information would be.

Now we can fully state our theory of the semantics of belief sentences. A sentence of the form "*A* believes *S*" is true if and only if the individual denoted by "*A*" has in his belief set a formula *P* that meets the following two conditions: first, the subexpressions of "*S*" that are interpreted *de dicto* must express the meaning for him of the corresponding subexpressions of *P*;

second, the subexpressions of "*S*" that are interpreted *de re* must have the reference for him of the corresponding subexpressions of *P*, and he must be able to pick out the reference of those subexpressions of *P*.

V. CONCLUSION

The truth-conditional semantics for belief sentences presented above is a fairly complicated theory, but that really should not count against it. Most of its complexity was introduced to explain how a belief report in English could be true of someone who is not a competent speaker of that language. Most alternative theories of belief ignore this question entirely. All the formulations of possible-world semantics for belief that we know of, for instance, assume an unanalyzed accessibility relation between a person and the possible worlds compatible with his beliefs. That relation must surely be mediated somehow by his psychological state or his language, but no explanation of this is given. Furthermore, the most serious problem that plagues possible-world theories, the problem of distinguishing among logically equivalent beliefs of the same person, is no problem at all in our theory.

The really interesting question for us, though, is not whether one particular semantic theory is superior to another, but why so little effort has been made thus far to develop an account of the truth conditions of belief sentences in terms of psychological states and processes. Since belief is a psychological state, it seems that this would be the most natural approach to follow. Almost all the recent work on the semantics of belief sentences, however, appears to strive for independence from psychology. Most of this work tries to define belief in terms of a relation between persons and some sort of nonpsychological entities, with the relation either left unanalyzed or analyzed in nonpsychological terms (e.g., Hintikka, 1962, 1969; Montague, 1974; Partee, 1973, 1979; Stalnaker, 1976; Cresswell, this volume; Quine, 1956, 1960). We can only speculate as to why this is the case, but we can think of at least two probable motivations.

One motivation is what Cresswell calls "the autonomy of semantics" – the idea that the goal of semantics is to characterize the conditions under which a sentence of a language is true, and that this can be done independently of any considerations as to how someone could know what the sentence means or believe that what the sentence says is true. Thus we can say that "The cat is on the mat," is true if and only if the object referred to by "the cat" bears the relation named by "is on" to the object referred to by "the mat", without raising or answering any psychological questions. The point that the truth conditions of sentences do not in general involve psychological notions seems well taken, but it surely does not follow that they *never* do. No one seems to object to giving the truth conditions of sentences about physical states in terms of physical relations and physical objects, as in the example above. Why then, should there be any objection to giving the truth conditions for sentences about psychological states in terms of psychological relations and psychological objects?

To look at the matter a little more closely, the possible-world theories attempt to give the semantics of belief sentences in terms of *semantic* rather than psychological objects. That is, these theories claim that the objects of belief are built out of the constructs of the semantic theory itself. This would be a very interesting claim if it were true, but the failure up to now to make such a theory work suggests that it is probably not. If this assessment is correct, it seems natural to assume that the truth conditions of sentences about belief and other psychological states will involve the objects described by true psychological theories. If a true theory of the psychology of belief turns out to require the notion of an internal language, then it is probable that the truth conditions for belief sentences will involve expressions of that language.

The other motivation for seeking a nonpsychological semantics for belief sentences is the desire to unify the kind of truth-conditional semantics that we have been discussing with what is sometimes called "linguistic semantics," the task of characterizing what competent speakers know about the "meaning" of the sentences of their language. The most straightforward way to make this unification is to assume that the semantic knowledge that competent speakers of a language have is knowledge of the truth conditions of the language's sentences – a view that is, in fact, widely endorsed (Davidson, 1967; Moravcsik, 1973; Partee, 1979; Woods, 1981). It is quite implausible, however, that the kind of theory we have been sketching is what people know about belief or belief sentences. The root of the problem is our claim that the truth conditions for belief sentences can ultimately be stated only in terms of a true theory of the psychology of belief. But it is no more plausible that all speakers know such a theory than that all speakers know true theories of physics, chemistry, or any other science.

Our answer to this objection is that the idea that the semantic knowledge of speakers amounts to knowledge of truth conditions is simply mistaken. This is a general point that applies not only to sentences about psychological states, but to many other kinds of sentences as well. As we mentioned in Section IV, Putnam has convincingly argued that the extension of natural-kind terms generally depends not simply on what speakers of a language know or believe about the extension of the term, but also on what properties the objects that the term is intended to describe actually possess. But this means that speakers do not, in fact, know the truth-conditions of sentences that involve natural kind terms. The properties that speakers believe characterize the extension of a natural kind term may turn out to be incomplete or even wrong. When it was discovered that whales are mammals, what was discovered was just that. It was not discovered that whales did not exist, even if being a fish was previously central to what speakers of English believed about the truth conditions of "X is a whale." In general, the truth conditions for a natural-kind term depend not so much on the knowledge of competent speakers as on true scientific theories about the natural kind in question. Viewed from this perspective, the truth conditions of belief sentences depend on what turns out to be true in psychology because belief states form natural kinds in the domain of psychology.

According to our computational model, what a competent speaker of a language needs to know about the meaning of a sentence is not its truth conditions, but what formula in his internal language the sentence expresses in a given context. Of course, as we discussed in Section IV, this formula has truth conditions, and it seems plausible to say that the truth conditions of a sentence in a context are the same as those of the formula it expresses in that context. Now, knowing a formula in the internal language that has the same truth conditions as the sentence is something like knowing the truth conditions of that sentences, but not very much like it. In particular, it is nothing like knowing the statement of those truth conditions in any of the semantic theories we have discussed.

In the case of a belief sentence, the corresponding formula in the internal language might be thought of as an expression in a first-order language with a belief operator. If the hearer of "John believes that snow is white," takes "John" to refer to the same person as his internal symbol PERSON98765, and takes "snow is white" to express WHITE(SNOW), then the whole sentence might express for him the formula BELIEVE(PERSON98765, WHITE (SNOW)). The functional roles and causal connections of the symbols in this formula determine its truth conditions, and those must be right for this formula to actually have the meaning for the hearer that John believes snow is white. Otherwise the hearer has not understood the sentence. To get those truth conditions right the hearer might have to have a lot of knowledge about belief, such as that people generally believe what they say, that they often draw inferences from their beliefs, and that they usually know what they believe. Knowing these properties of belief would help pin down the fact that belief is the psychological state denoted by BELIEVE, yet these properties do not by any means constitute necessary and sufficient truth conditions for formulas involving BELIEVE. But it is only required that these formulas have such truth conditions, not that the hearer *know* them.

The mistaken attempt to identify truth conditions with what speakers know about the meaning of sentences in their language had led to many pseudoproblems. For instance, Partee (1979) raises the question of whether for possible-world semantics to be correct, an infinite number of possible-world models would have to exist in our heads. She concludes that they would not because "performance limitations" could let us get by with a finite number of finite models. This whole issue seems to be pretty much beside the point, however. Even for notions for which possible-world semantics appears to be adequate, such as the concept of necessity, nothing approximating possible worlds needs to be in our heads, although something like modal logic might.

Another example of the confusion that results from trying to unify these two notions of semantics is Woods's (1981) attempt to base a theory of meaning on "procedural semantics." Woods tries to identify the meaning of a sentence with some sort of ideal procedure for verifying its truth, saying that this procedure is what someone knows when he knows the meaning of the sentence. This has an advantage over possible-world semantics in that it can provide distinct meanings for logically equivalent sentences, since two different procedures could compute the same truth value in all possible worlds. The "procedures" that Woods is forced to invent, however, are not computable in the usual sense, even in principle. For example, to account for quantification over infinite sets he proposes infinite computations, while for propositional attitudes he suggests something like running our procedures in someone else's head. The sense in which these nonexecutable procedures are procedures at all is left obscure.

Partee starts from a particular notion of truth conditions, that of Montague semantics, and asks how such conditions could be represented in the head of a speaker. Woods starts from something that could be in the head of a speaker, procedures, and tries to make them yield truth conditions. In both cases, unlikely theories result from trying to say that it is truth conditions that are in the head, when all that is required is that what is in the head *have* truth conditions.

In this paper we have examined a wide range of issues from the perspective of computational models of psychological processes and states. These issues include the legitimacy of psychological models based on internal languages, the problem of distinguishing logically equivalent beliefs, the psychology of having beliefs about oneself, belief reports about a nonspeaker of the language of the report, and the relation between truth-conditional and linguistic semantics. We do not claim to know whether the computational models we have proposed provide a correct account of all the phenomena we have discussed. What we do claim, however, is that many abstract arguments as to how things must be can be shown to be incorrect, and that many confusing conceptual problem can be clarified when approached from the standpoint of the concrete examples that computational models can provide.

SRI International

REFERENCES

Chomsky, N.: (1975) *Reflections on Language*, Pantheon Books, New York.

Cresswell, M. J.: (1982) 'The autonomy of semantics,' this volume, pp. 69–86.

Davidson, D.: (1967) 'Truth and meaning,' *Synthese* 17, pp. 304–323.

Fodor, J. A.: (1975) *The Language of Thought*, Thomas Y. Crowell Company, New York.

Hintikka, J.: (1962) *Knowledge and Belief: An Introduction to the Logic of the Two Notions*, Cornell University Press, Ithaca, New York.

Hintikka, J.: (1969) 'Semantics for propositional attitudes,' in L. Linsky (ed.), *Reference and Modality*, pp. 112–144, Oxford University Press, London, England, 1971.

Kaplan, D.: (1969) 'Quantifying in,' in L. Linsky (ed.), *Reference and Modality*, pp. 112–144, Oxford University Press, London, England, 1971.

Kaplan, D.: (1977) 'Demonstratives: An essay on the semantics, logic, metaphysics, and epistemology of demonstratives and other indexicals,' unpublished manuscript, March 1977.

Kripke, S. A.: (1972) 'Naming and necessity,' in D. Davidson and G. Harman (eds.), *Semantics of Natural Language*, pp. 253–355, D. Reidel Publishing Co., Dordrecht, Holland, 1972.

Lewis, D.: (1972) 'General semantics,' in D. Davidson and G. Harman (eds.), *Semantics of Natural Language*, pp. 169–218, D. Reidel Publishing Co., Dordrecht, Holland, 1972.

Lucas, J. R.: (1961) 'Minds, machines and Goedel,' in A. R. Anderson (ed.), *Minds and Machines*, pp. 43–59, Prentice-Hall, Inc., Englewood Cliffs, New Jersey, 1964.

Montague, R.: (1970) 'Pragmatics and intensional logic,' *Synthese* 22, pp. 68–94.

Montague, R.: (1974) *Formal Philosophy: Selected Papers of Richard Montague*, R. H. Thomason (ed.), Yale University Press, New Haven, Connecticut.

Moravcsik, J.: (1973) 'Comments on Partee's paper,' in K. J. J. Hintikka et al. (eds.), *Approaches to Natural Language*, pp. 349–369, D. Reidel Publishing Co., Dordrecht, Holland, 1973.

Partee, B. H.: (1973) 'The semantics of belief-sentences,' in K. J. J. Hintikka et al. (eds.), *Approaches to Natural Language*, pp. 309–336, D. Reidel Publishing Co., Dordrecht, Holland, 1973.

Partee, B. H.: (1979) 'Semantics-mathematics or psychology?', R. Bauerle, U. Egli and E. von Stechow (eds.), *Semantics from Different Points of View*, Springer-Verlag, Berlin, pp. 1–14.

Perry, J.: (1977) 'Frege on demonstratives,' *The Philosophical Review* 86.

Perry, J.: (1979) 'The problem of the essential indexical,' *Nous* 13.

Putnam, H.: (1973) 'Meaning and reference,' in S. P. Schwartz (ed.), *Naming, Necessity, and Natural Kinds*, pp. 118–132, Cornell University Press, Ithaca, New York, 1977.

Putnam, H.: (1975) 'The meaning of "meaning",' in K. Gunderson (ed.), *Minnesota Studies in the Philosophy of Science, Vol. VII, Language, Mind, and Knowledge*, pp. 131–193, University of Minnesota Press, Minneapolis, Minnesota, 1975.

Quine, W. V. O.: (1956) 'Quantifiers and propositional attitudes,' in L. Linsky, (ed.), *Reference and Modality*, pp. 112–144, Oxford University Press, London, England, 1971.

Quine, W. V. O.: (1960) *Word and Object*, The M.I.T. Press, Cambridge, Massachusetts.

Quine, W. V. O.: (1971) 'The inscrutability of reference,' in D. D. Steinberg and L. A. Jakobovits (eds.), *Semantics*, Cambridge University Press, London, England, 1971.

Quine, W. V. O.: (1972) 'Methodological reflections on current linguistic theory,' in D. Davidson and G. Harman (eds.), *Semantics of Natural Language*, pp. 442–454, D. Reidel Publishing Co., Dordrecht, Holland, 1972.

Ryle, G.: (1949) *The Concept of Mind*, Barnes and Noble, Inc., New York.

Stalnaker, R. C.: (1976) 'Propositions,' in A. F. Mackay and D. D. Merrill (eds.), *Issues in the Philosophy of Language*, pp. 79–91, Yale University Press, New Haven, Connecticut, 1976.

Wittgenstein, L.: (1953) *Philosophical Investigations*, Blackwell, Oxford, England.

Woods, W. A.: (1981) 'Procedural semantics as a theory of meaning,' in A. Joshi, *et al.* (eds.), *Elements of Discourse Understanding*, pp. 300–332, Cambridge University Press, Cambridge, England, 1981.

JANET DEAN FODOR

THE MENTAL REPRESENTATION OF QUANTIFIERS

1. DESIDERATA

The system of semantic representation for quantified sentences that I shall propose in this paper is an unconventional one and looks very naive in comparison with the elegant formalism of standard quantificational logics. My excuse for presuming to tamper with the standard formalism is that, though it may meet the needs of logicians,[1] it by no means obviously meets the needs of psychologists. I include linguists among psychologists, and assume that their common goal is to develop an integrated model of what native speaker/hearers know about their language and how they put this knowledge to work in speaking and understanding.

I take it for granted that the findings of linguistics and experimental psychology will, as they are sharpened over time, eventually prove to be compatible; this is simply a declaration of faith in the coherence of the joint project. A much more ambitious assumption is that we can find a single system of semantic representation which meshes with formal rules of grammar and inference to mimic the competence of the ideal speaker/hearer, and also meshes with the computational processes involved in sentence production and comprehension and reasoning to mimic the typical behaviour of a real speaker/hearer. There is no guarantee at all that the search for such a system will be successful, since the relation between the grammars that linguists construct and the mental processes that psycholinguists uncover could turn out to be very indirect. Early work in psycholinguistics suggested that this was indeed the case. But as Bresnan (1978) has emphasized, the apparent mismatch between grammars and performance models depends as much on the grammars we assume as on psychological discoveries about performance. We may be able to develop grammars – and we may even be able to find independent evidence for them – which can play a much more central role than at present in models of linguistic performance. Also, as Fodor, Bever and Garrett (1974) have noted, there might well be a close correspondence between the grammatical and the mental *representations* of sentences, especially at significant levels of the grammar, even if there is little relation between grammatical rules and mental processes. So

S. Peters and E. Saarinen (eds.), Processes, Beliefs, and Questions, 129–164.

the search I am embarked on, though it may fail, is not an obviously foolhardy one.

My goal is to find a system of semantic representations which satisfies all of the following conditions.

(i) It is rich enough to capture all interpretations of all sentences in the language.

(ii) It is restricted enough to exclude impossible interpretations of sentences.

(iii) It permits the formulation of inference rules which specify the entailment relations between sentences.

(iv) It permits the formulation of grammatical rules which correlate semantic representations with the surface forms of sentences.

(v) It can serve as a basis for predicting which entailment relations between sentences are easy for speaker/hearers to recognize.

(vi) It can serve as a basis for predicting which interpretations of which sentences are easy for hearers to compute, and which sentences with which interpretations are easy for speakers to construct.

(vii) It permits a plausible account of how speaker/hearers translate between semantic representations and perceptions of the world.

The development of modern quantificational logic has been responsive to conditions (i), (ii) and (iii), though the full semantic richness of natural languages has not yet been formally characterized. Linguists have added condition (iv). Both within the framework of generative semantics (Lakoff, 1965) and within the extended standard theory (May, 1977), logical formulae have been adopted as semantic representations, though modified in various details to make them more consonant with the syntactic representations with which they are correlated by the rules of the grammar.

Conditions (v) and (vi) are the performance analogues of conditions (iii) and (iv). Condition (vi) is the one that I shall rely on most heavily in what follows; in particular, my concern will be with what goes on inside people's heads as they listen to and understand quantified sentences. Condition (v) has been taken seriously by some cognitive psychologists, including Johnson-Laird (1975) whose conclusions about the mental representations of quantified sentences in reasoning tasks are encouragingly similar to my own conclusions based on data about sentence comprehension.

Condition (vii) may be the most interesting one of all but at present it is the least constraining, simply because we are so far from understanding the psychological mechanisms which mediate between sentences and the nonlinguistic information that they are used to convey. We know that people can form mental representations of actual and possible states of affairs. And we have reason to believe that these representations are both richer and different in kind from the relatively orderly propositional representations that can be put into correspondence with syntactically structured strings of lexical items in the language. About what happens in between these two we can only make vague conjectures. It seems that a child acquiring language must learn to subject his perceptions, in all their wealth of detail, to a set of linguistically prescribed 'sieves', which isolate just those features which can or must be encoded in sentences. To use the language to receive and transmit information, one must be able to recognize a complex event as, for example, an instance of giving, and one must identify the participants in this event and distinguish their roles as agent, recipient, theme (that which is given), and so forth. (These analytic skills no doubt develop, at least to some degree, even without the stimulus of language learning, though it also seems to be true that different languages demand slightly different sieves. See Goldin-Meadow, forthcoming, on the encoding of thematic relations by deaf children who have invented their own sign language.)

Though much of syntax is concerned with the coding of who did what to whom, the role of quantifiers is to specify how many acts or participants were involved in the situation described. Seen from this point of view, quantifier scope contrasts are not a wayward creation of the human mind but are a perfectly natural consequence of the fact that how a situation is parsed into its component parts inevitably affects how those components are to be counted. In a situation in which Susan, Mary and Jane each give candy to Bill, there are (at least) three acts of giving, for each one of which there must be a recipient. Yet the number of recipients in this situation is not three, but one. These different ways of counting correspond to the two interpretations of the sentence *Each of three girls gave candy to a boy*. The point to be emphasized is that this ambiguity is exactly what would be expected if the transition between a perceptual representation and a sentential structure is effected by identifying and counting selected components (acts and participants) of the situation represented and then inserting both the numerical and the descriptive specifications into appropriate role-designated slots in a syntactic structure. A variety of more complex syntactic devices have evolved in natural languages to permit the disambiguation of quantifier scopes, but in the simplest case it seems that scope ambiguity is a rather direct reflection of the degrees of freedom inherent in the process of 'sieving' a complex percept so that it can be encoded in language.

Many of the achievements of generative linguistics have stemmed from its emphasis on the peculiarities of natural languages, characteristics which must be explained in terms of the structure of the human mind rather than in terms of general requirements on any effective system of communication. But I wonder whether, in the area of semantics, the deviousness of natural languages hasn't been exaggerated. It often looks as if sentence structures and the mental representations of the world that they are used to transmit are two entirely different kinds of beast, but this may be in part because we have interposed between them a system of semantic representations which is not congruent with either and which thus masks the natural relation between them. This, at least, is the hunch that I shall pursue: that our picture of how linguistic and nonlinguistic representations engage with each other has been led astray in the middle by the assumption that semantic representations resemble the formulae of standard logic.

What I shall do is review a number of rather different systems for representing quantifier scope, and confront each one with some general observations about how readily certain interpretations are assigned to quantified sentences by hearers. The data that I shall appeal to are derived from intuition and have not yet been experimentally confirmed, but some of them at least seem to be quite secure.

2. PREFIXED QUANTIFIER REPRESENTATIONS

The essence of what I have been calling 'standard quantificational logic' is that a quantified noun phrase has a dual representation: the quantifier (or, in some versions, the whole of the quantified noun phrase) appears at the front of the clause or sentence, where its position indicates its scope relative to other quantifiers, negation, and so on; a related variable appears within the main body of the sentence representation and indicates the role of the noun phrase in the predicate-argument structure for the sentence. Linguists have generally assumed that the prefixed quantifiers are not only sequentially ordered but are also hierarchically structured, but I think it is true that, as far as scope relations are concerned, the domination relations in the tree structure are redundant with the left-to-right order relations and do not contribute anything crucial to the expressive power of the system.

Though doubts have been raised recently concerning partially ordered quantifiers (see Hintikka, 1974), this kind of system generally does provide representations for all of the discernible readings of quantified sentences. Since there are $n!$ way of ordering n quantifiers, a sentence with one quantifier is assigned one reading, a sentence with two quantifiers is assigned two readings, a sentence with three quantifiers is assigned six readings, and so on. The fact that not all of these logically possible readings are actually available for some sentence forms is handled by imposing constraints on the syntax-to-semantics mapping rules, to block the derivation of certain quantifier sequences.

As has often been noted, however, there are many conceivable notational variants of this system which have the same expressive power but which do not make use of prefixed quantifiers. We might, for example, leave the quantifiers in their surface positions and simply assign numerical subscripts to indicate their relative ordering. For psychological purposes the differences between notationally variant systems of representation can be quite significant. What is needed, therefore, is not just an argument that quantifier scope is to be captured by ordering the quantifiers, but some positive motivation for representing these ordering relations by lining up the quantifiers at the front of the clause. This does, after all, have implications for what mental computations a hearer must perform in recovering the semantic representation for the sentence.

Explicit arguments for prefixing quantifiers in semantic representations are surprisingly hard to find in the literature. The only serious candidate, I believe, is the argument that the grammatical rules that relate surface structures to semantic representations by prefixing the quantifiers exhibit formal similarities to syntactic transformations, similarities which are too close to be regarded as coincidental. (In generative semantics grammars the rules lower quantifiers in the semantic representation into their surface positions, but I will focus here on more recent treatments within the extended standard theory.)

May (1977) has argued, for example, that the quantifier prefixing rule is governed by Subjacency, as syntactic transformations are. This conclusion depends, however, on a particular way of parcelling out the facts to be accounted for: May's system is designed to predict the unmarked interpretations of quantified sentences, and other principles have to be invoked to account for marked interpretations. Also, May regards as unmarked both interpretations of a sentence with two quantifiers in the same clause, as in (1), though when the second quantifier is in a subordinate clause, as in (2), he regards the reading in which this quantifier has wide scope as marked.

(1) Every child saw a squirrel.
(2) Every child knew a squirrel was in the tree.

But there seem to be no grounds for drawing this sharp distinction.

Sentence (2) is more complicated than (1) because it has three possible readings: one in which *a squirrel* is interpreted as non-specific, i.e., as having scope only over the embedded clause; one in which *a squirrel* is interpreted as specific but within the scope of *every child*; and one in which *a squirrel* is interpreted as specific and with wide scope over *every child*. May's Subjacency approach excludes the second and third of these readings entirely, except insofar as they can be generated by special principles outside of core grammar. The justification given for this is that the specific readings are more marked than the non-specific one. However, the claim that the readings differ in markedness appears to be based only on the fact that the non-specific reading is more natural, more likely to be computed by hearers, than the others are.[2] An exactly comparable asymmetry is observable in sentence (1), however. The reading in which the later quantifier has wide scope is generally less preferred than the reading in which it has narrow scope. To be consistent, therefore, it would seem that the Subjacency account of quantifier scope should either undertake to derive all possible readings of all sentences, and thus permit the specific readings of (2), or else should continue to derive only unmarked readings, and thus block the reversed reading of (1).

The reversed reading of (1), in which the quantifiers are in the same surface clause, could be blocked by appeal to some kind of precedence constraint (as in Lasnik and Kupin, 1977), to ensure that the quantifier fronting rule is applied first to the leftmost quantifier in the surface structure, then to the quantifier that follows it, and so on. By itself this would not guarantee any relation between the sequence of quantifiers in surface structure and their sequence in the preferred semantic representation, for whatever the order in which they were moved, the sequence of quantifiers could still be rearranged as they move.

But the surface sequence could be preserved if there were also some kind of constraint on where each quantifier can end up, a constraint requiring a quantifier to be adjoined below (and to the right of) all other quantifiers that have previously been moved. The Subjacency principle looks to be just the right sort of constraint for this purpose, but as May formulates it it will not do the job. Subjacency is said to be a condition not on rule applications but on the relations between quantifiers and their associated variables in logical form (the semantic representation): a quantifier is not permitted to bind a variable across more than one S node. In this form, Subjacency would block *all* interpretations of sentences with two or more quantifiers, since quantifiers are Chomsky-adjoined to S, and there would therefore be two S nodes between the wide scope quantifier and its variable (the original S node over the clause, and another S node introduced by adjunction of the narrow scope quantifier). For this reason May permits, as non-violations of Subjacency, just those structures in which the S nodes intervening between a quantifier and its variable stand in an immediate domination relationship, i.e., just those structures in which the intervening S nodes are due to prior quantifier adjunction. This weakening of Subjacency means, however, that it will not, after all, force later moved quantifiers to have narrower scope than earlier moved quantifiers; *both* interpretations of sentence (1) would now be permitted.

This problem could be solved by construing Subjacency, after all, as a condition on rule applications. Sentence (1) would be assigned representation (3), by first fronting *every child*, in accord with the precedence condition, and then fronting *a squirrel* to a position beneath it, in accord with Subjacency.

(3) $_S$[every child$_x$ $_S$[a squirrel$_y$ $_S$[x saw y]]]

The derivation of representation (4) would involve first fronting *every child*, in accord with the precedence condition, and then moving *a squirrel* over it, in violation of Subjacency.

(4) $_S$[a squirrel$_y$ $_S$[every child$_x$ $_S$[x saw y]]]

If Subjacency were also construed as a markedness principle rather than as an absolute constraint, then the origin of the less preferred scope readings could also naturally be accounted for. Both (3) and (4) would be permitted as readings for sentence (1), but (4) would be less preferred because it violates Subjacency. And exactly the same considerations would apply to sentence (2), in which the quantifiers are in different clauses. Readings (5), (6) and (7) would all be available for sentence (2), but (6) and (7) would be less preferred because their derivations violate Subjacency.

(5) $_S$[every child$_x$ $_S$[x knew $_S$[a squirrel$_y$ $_S$[y was in the tree]]]]
(6) $_S$[every child$_x$ $_S$[a squirrel$_y$ $_S$[x knew $_S$[y was in the tree]]]]
(7) $_S$[a squirrel$_y$ $_S$[every child$_x$ $_S$[x knew $_S$[y was in the tree]]]]

These modifications to May's Subjacency condition on quantifier movement thus lead to greater descriptive adequacy, but the formal similarity between the quantifier movement rule and syntactic rules such as WH-Movement is now very slight. For syntactic rules, Subjacency is an absolute condition, the relevant bounding nodes include NP as well as $\bar{S}$ and/or S, and it is arguably a condition on representations at the level of logical form – if, indeed, it exists as an independent condition at all (see Koster, 1978). For the quantifier prefixing rule, Subjacency is not an absolute constraint, the only relevant bounding node is S, and it must be a condition on the syntax-to-logical form mapping rules rather than on logical forms themselves.

It may also be noted that the effect of Subjacency on quantifier scope interpretation in this system is to ensure that in the unmarked case, overlapping applications of the quantifier movement rule are intersecting rather than nested. But there seems to be a general tendency among natural languages, wherever the domains of movement rules are not prevented from overlapping by other constraints, for nested applications to be permitted and intersecting ones to be excluded. In Fodor (1978) I discussed a range of examples in English, including sentences like (8), which are acceptable for at least some speakers of English, and sentences like (9), which are not acceptable in any dialect.

(8) Who$_i$ was John wondering what sort of present$_j$ to send t_j to t_i?

(9) *What$_i$ was John wondering which person$_j$ to send t_i to t_j?

Bordelois (1974) describes a similar phenomenon in Spanish, Napoli (1974) provides examples from Italian, and Engdahl (1979) gives examples from Swedish and Norwegian. The details differ somewhat from language to language, but it seems hard to resist the conclusion that for genuine syntactic movement and deletion rules (or their counterparts in an interpretive treatment of the phenomena), a mirror image relation between binding phrases and bound variables is what natural languages overwhelmingly prefer. This casts serious doubt on the assumption that quantifier scope relations are to be captured by prefixed quantifiers whose ordering is determined by a movement rule.

The linguistic evidence for a quantifier prefixing rule thus seems shaky at best. But perhaps a psycholinguistic defence for a prefixed quantifier system can be constructed. The precedence condition on quantifier movements could be seen as a natural reflection of the on-line, 'left-to-right' character of sentence comprehension processes; each quantifier would be assigned to its proper position in the semantic representation as it was encountered in the word string. Furthermore, the net effect of the Subjacency condition, when permitted but less preferred readings are taken into account, seems to be exactly what would follow from a principle stating that sentence readings are marked to the extent that quantifiers have been moved further than necessary from their surface positions. And this principle would have a very plausible basis in the sentence comprehension routines if we could assume that leftward movement of constituents is a costly operation for hearers to perform.

In the syntactic component, leftward movement rules are clearly favored over rightward movement rules – leftward movements are more common, and unlike rightward movements they can be unbounded (can be successive cyclic). But it is important here to bear in mind the difference between syntactic transformations, which have to be unpicked by the sentence comprehension device, and the putative quantifier prefixing rule, which has to be applied during sentence comprehension. On the assumption that syntactic parsing involves the replacement of moved constituents into their associated 'gaps' (see Fodor, 1978, 1979), the preference for leftward movement rules in the grammar amounts to a preference for rightward movement operations by the hearer.[3] Thus we might well expect the leftward movement of quantifiers by the hearer to be a relatively unfavored operation. This reasoning may make it difficult to see why the language should rely on leftward movement to disambiguate quantifier scope, but it does have the virtue of predicting that the preferred scope readings will be those in which quantifiers move as short a distance as possible.

The prefixed quantifier system thus seems to be compatible with performance considerations even if there is little direct linguistic evidence for it. However, there is a collection of other facts about performance which receive no satisfactory explanation on this theory. There may not *be* any explanation for them, of course, at least in terms of the properties of semantic representations; but I hope to show that some of them do fall naturally into place on the basis of other conceptions of what semantic representations are like.

One fact is that the comprehension difficulty of quantified sentences accelerates sharply with the number of quantifiers that are present. If there is just one quantifier, the sentence is not noticeably more difficult to understand than a comparable sentence with a proper name, for example, in the same position; *I saw a squirrel* seems not to be any harder than *I saw John*. Sentences with two quantifiers generally do seem to be harder to understand than sentences with only one, and sentences with three or more quantifiers are notoriously difficult to interpret. In a standard prefixed quantifier system, every quantifier has to be fronted, whether or not there are other quantifiers in the same sentence with which it could interact, and whether or not it already precedes and c-commands other quantifiers that it has scope over. Thus each quantifier in a sentence should add a constant increment to the amount of processing involved in computing the semantic representation from the surface word string, and processing difficulty should (other things being equal) be a linear function of the number of quantifiers. The only possible explanation of the observed rapid increase in difficulty would be that the comprehension device is confused, while computing any one reading of a multiply quantified sentence, by the number of alternative readings that it could in principle be assigned. However, many speakers of English are inclined to judge that the difficulty of the individual readings themselves increases sharply with the number of quantifiers. This intuition may be a slim basis for objecting to the prefixed quantifier system, but it connects with another point that this system also does not handle quite convincingly. This is that a sentence with two existential quantifiers (e.g. *A child saw a squirrel*) or with two universal quantifiers (e.g. *Every child saw every squirrel*) is not ambiguous. Nothing in the semantic representation system or in the syntax-to-semantics mapping rules distinguishes these sentences from sentences with quantifiers that differ in kind; since there are two quantifiers, they can be ordered in two different ways at the semantic level, and it is left to the inference rules to specify that these two orderings are logically equivalent. But this is at odds with the intuitive judgement that sentences with quantifiers of the same kind (especially sentences where all the quantifiers are existential) are not as difficult to comprehend as sentences with the same number of quantifiers of different kinds.

Finally, there are prosodic effects to be accounted for. It has often been observed (see, for example, Jackendoff, 1972; Lasnik, 1975) that a scope ambiguity can be resolved by the prosodic contour of the sentence. In particular it appears that for the reversed reading of a sentence with a universal quantifier followed by an existential quantifier, there is often a characteristic prosodic break before the existentially quantified phrase. Since the prefixed quantifier system can, as I have argued, be made to predict that a reversed quantifier reading is a non-preferred reading, it does offer some explanation for why this reading should be the one that is associated with a marked prosodic contour. But there is no obvious explanation for why a violation of the 'minimal movement' principle for quantifiers should lead to a marked contour of just this kind (or for why a *different* marked contour is associated with the reversed reading of a sentence in which a universal quantifier follows an existential quantifier; see section 5 below).

3. HIERARCHICAL SYSTEMS

The prosodic data suggest a rather different approach to the semantic representation of quantifiers, an approach in which domination relationships alone serve to specify quantifier scope. Since the normal prosodic unit is a surface phrase, the prosodic break before the second quantifier on the marked interpretation of a sentence can be taken as a sign that the normal phrasal structure of the sentence is being overruled. In the normal case, the sentence *Every child saw a squirrel* will be parsed as in (10), but the marked prosodic contour signals that it is to be parsed as in (11).

(10)

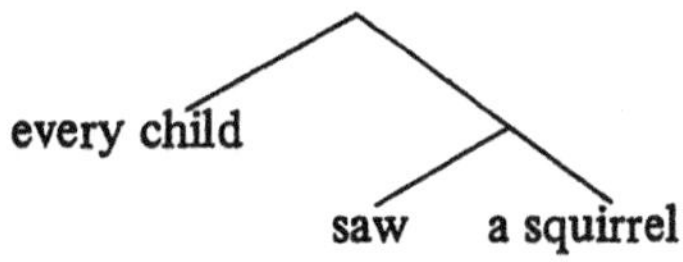

(11)

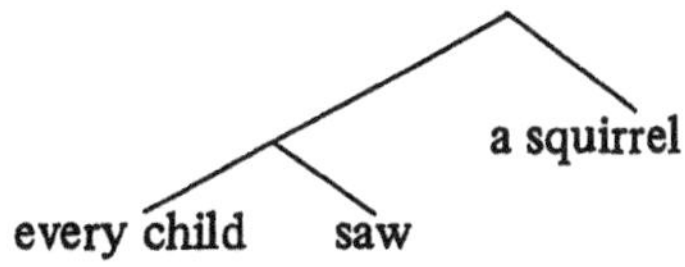

We may consider the possibility, then, that there is no leftward movement of quantifiers in the derivation of semantic representations from surface forms, but only the rearrangement of the c-command relations between constituents. A quantifier will have scope over another quantifier that precedes or follows it, just as long as it c-commands that quantifier in the semantic representation. In the unmarked case, the structure of the semantic representation will be exactly congruent with the surface structure of the sentence; in the marked case, the semantic structure (left branching) is a distortion of the syntactic structure (right branching).[4]

This system is appealing because it comes to grips with one basic mismatch between syntactic and semantic structures in natural languages. Though the evidence could be stronger, it does appear that syntactic structures favor binary branching. But the semantic structure of a clause can generally be captured by a multiply branching representation in which the predicate and its various arguments are sisters. This was Fillmore's claim, and though Davidson (1967) has emphasized the problems (e.g. a variable number of arguments for the same predicate), it is extremely difficult to find any evidence that in the *semantic* representation of a sentence like *Jones buttered the toast at midnight* the phrases *Jones* and *the toast* must be represented at different levels. (The position of *at midnight* is another matter, on which there might well be disagreement.)

The relational system of representation under consideration offers a compromise between the demands of syntax and semantics. For a simple sentence without quantifiers, the configuration of constituents in the semantic representation will have no import: [*Jones* [*buttered the toast*]], [[*Jones buttered*] *the toast*], and [*Jones buttered the toast*] will all serve equally well as semantic representations. Which of them is actually generated by a hearer could depend on how much work is required to derive them from the syntactic structure; for a syntactically right branching language like English the right branching semantic representation might be the easiest for a hearer to compute, while for a left branching language such as Japanese a left branching semantic representation would be more natural. Only for quantified sentences would these natural computational tendencies have to be overcome, and then only for the marked readings of sentences with two or more quantifiers of different kinds.

A system of this kind may also be appropriate for the representation of opaque constructions. Quine (1956), and other since, have referred to the specific interpretation of a sentence like *John wants to catch a fish* as the *relational* interpretation. In other words, *wants to catch* is construed as designating a complex relation which is being asserted to hold between John and a fish. This (marked) interpretation would be very naturally captured by bracketing the sentence as [*John* [*wants to catch*] *a fish*] where *a fish* has been lifted out of the lower verb phrase and placed on a level with the argument *John*.

This kind of hierarchical-restructuring-without-reordering system thus looks very promising, but I have been unable to extend it to account for the full range of interpretation preferences. The basic idea is that each language exhibits a preferred syntactic branching pattern, and that mismatches between this and the semantic branching pattern for a sentence put the performance mechanisms under strain. It might have been expected that discontinuous constituents in the semantic representation would be a source of even greater strain, but this is not borne out by a comparison between sentences such as (12) and (13).

(12) Every child saw a squirrel.
(13) Every child pointed out a squirrel to the teacher.

Both sentences have a non-preferred interpretation on which *a squirrel* has scope over *every child*, and the difficulty of this interpretation seems to be much the same for both sentences – even though in (13), though not in (12), the raising of *a squirrel* so that it c-commands *every child* would lead to crossed branches in the semantic representation. There are some possible moves here which might be worth exploring (e.g., that the whole of the verb phrase is raised in the marked semantic representation for (13), rather than just the direct object), but the prospects for finding a general metric for perceptual complexity based on complexity of the tree structure do not look to be good. There is also the problem of characterizing the class of possible complex predicates. *Wants to catch* can be interpreted as designating a relation holding between John and a fish, and it also permits a reversed reading of quantifiers in its two argument positions (as in *A child wants to catch every fish*), but *wants to meet the man who caught* can be construed in this way only with great difficulty, if at all. Some constraints on the constituent raising rule with derives semantic representations from surface structures thus seem to be called for, but there is no more precedent for the exact form of the necessary constraints in this system than in the prefixed quantifier system.

One final worry is that this hierarchical rearrangement approach to the representation of quantifier scope predicts that in languages whose syntactic phrase markers are predominantly left branching, the preferred interpretation of a sentence with several quantifiers should be the one in which later quantifiers have wide scope over earlier quantifiers. This is such a counterintuitive prediction that it would be very impressive if it were confirmed, but I suspect that it would have been reported long before now if it were true.

4. FEATURE REPRESENTATIONS

In the system described in the previous section, certain interpretations of quantified sentences demand no special mental computations at all. Those which do require modifications of the surface structure are just those which are marked, or judged to be difficult to compute. Certain kinds of feature representation systems share this property, while not being open to the same objections.

The features used to capture quantifier scope cannot be binary features. To use features such as [± specific] or [± wide scope] would be to predict that a sentence containing n quantifiers has 2^n logically possible distinct interpretations (though some of these might be excluded for a given sentence by constraints on the syntax-to-semantics mapping rules). This is just false: a sentence with one quantifier has only one interpretation, not two; and for a sentence with three quantifiers, for example, a maximum of six distinct interpretations can be distinguished. To make the number of predicted interpretations increase in the proper way with the number of quantifiers in the sentence, the features must be generated for each individual sentence, and must express relations between pairs of quantifiers. For example, each universal quantifier in a sentence might be assumed to give rise to a feature [$\pm \forall_i$], one value of which is then assigned to each existential quantifier in the sentence. An existential quantifier bearing the feature [+ $\forall_i$] would be interpreted as within the scope of the *i*th universal quantifier in the sentence. To avoid redundancy, we could further assume that the feature [– $\forall_i$] need not be explicitly represented; it would be entailed by the absence of the feature [+ $\forall_i$]. For the sentence (14), the forwards reading in which the universal quantifier has narrow scope would be represented with no marked features at all, as in (15), and the reversed reading in which the universal quantifier has wide scope would be represented with one marked feature, as in (16). (Note: for convenience I shall use the notations $\exists\forall$ and $\forall\exists$ to designate these two readings in what follows, but without intending any commitment to the prefixed quantifier system.)

(14) A child saw every squirrel.
(15) A child saw every squirrel. $\exists\forall$
(16) A child $_{[+\ \forall]}$ saw every squirrel. $\forall\exists$

Clearly there are other conceivable feature systems of this general kind – systems in which features are generated from the existential quantifiers in the sentence, or systems in which the negative value of the feature is taken as the marked value. But the variant that I have outlined here has special claim to attention since it exhibits (I believe) the essentials of representations using Skolem functions. (On Skolem functions see, for example, Enderton, 1972). These representations capture the fact that scope relations between quantifiers are dependence relations. The interpretation of a quantifier *A* that is within the scope of a quantifier *B* is dependent on the presence of *B*. In the reading (16) of sentence (14), for example, the phrase *a child*, which is within the scope of *every squirrel*, does not receive the same interpretation as it does when it is the only quantified phrase in a sentence, or when it has scope over all other quantifiers in its environment. It is to be instantiated not just once, but multiply, with one child for each of the squirrels instantiating the phrase *every squirrel*. By contrast, the interpretation of the wide scope phrase *every squirrel* is not context dependent; this phrase is interpreted exactly as it would be if it were the only quantifier in the sentence.

This is not a novel observation, but it does serve to point up the fact that the sequential ordering of prefixed quantifiers in standard logical formulae is simply a conventional device for indicating the dependence of one quantifier on another in the assignment of truth and reference conditions to the sentence. The Skolem-type feature system I have described represents these dependencies more directly; its representations are closer (in a sense which is difficult to define precisely but is, I think, intuitively clear) to the nonverbal representations of states of affairs that quantified sentences describe. A quantifier in a semantic representation will be marked with a feature only when its interpretation differs from its normal interpretation in isolation, i.e. only when it does not represent a straightforward count of the number of individuals filling a certain role in the event described by the sentence. This characteristic of the system stems from the two choices that were made in the selection of the marked feature values. The use of the positive rather than the negative values of the quantifier features means that it is dependence rather than independence of interpretation that is explicitly marked. The use of universal rather than existential quantifiers as the source of the features means that $\forall\exists$ readings of sentences will always be marked, while $\exists\forall$ readings will always be unmarked. As we have noted, the interpretation of the $\exists$ quantifier of a $\forall\exists$ reading is context dependent, though the interpretation of the $\forall$ quantifier is context free. But in a $\exists\forall$ reading, *both* quantifiers are interpreted as they would be if they had occurred alone. For example, on reading (15) of sentence (14) above, the phrase *every squirrel* is to be instantiated, just as usual, by all (contextually relevant) squirrels, and the phrase *a child* is to be instantiated, just as usual, by just one child (not by one child for each of the squirrels). To put it more generally: a wide scope existential quantifier does not affect the interpretation of other quantifiers within its scope. The traditional prefixed quantifier representations obscure this difference between wide scope universal quantifier readings and wide scope existential quantifier readings; in both cases the quantifiers are explicitly ordered in the semantic representation, though only in the first case does the ordering capture a genuine dependence between the quantifiers.[5] (Note that the feature system automatically predicts the equivalence of $\exists x \exists y$ and $\exists y \exists x$, and of $\forall x \forall y$ and $\forall y \forall x$. It also permits the representation of partially ordered quantifiers.)

A Skolem-type feature system is thus more sensitive to the semantic facts than more traditional representation systems are. Unfortunately, it is not simultaneously sensitive to the left-to-right asymmetries which determine the preferred readings for scope ambiguous sentences. Our working assumption is that these preferences are due to sentence comprehension processes, with the preferred reading being the one that hearers find easiest to compute on-line. For a feature system, it is natural to assume that it is psychologically more costly to assign a feature than not to assign a feature, and also that it is more costly to have to go back and assign a feature derived from the quantifier currently being processed to a quantifier that was previously processed, than to assign a feature derived from an earlier quantifier to the quantifier that is currently being processed. These assumptions lead to the correct prediction for sentence (14), that reading (15) is preferred to reading (16). But for sentence (17), they lead to the incorrect prediction that reading (18) is preferred to reading (19), i.e. that the reversed reading is preferred to the forwards reading.

(17)	Every child saw a squirrel.	
(18)	Every child saw a squirrel.	$\exists\forall$
(19)	Every child saw a $\text{squirrel}_{[+\ \forall]}$.	$\forall\exists$

This incorrect prediction is simply one instance of the generalization noted above, that a $\forall\exists$ reading is always predicted to be more complex than a $\exists\forall$ reading, regardless of the sequence of the quantifiers in the surface sentence. In fact, as we know, the observed preference is a function not of the form of the semantic representation alone, but of the *relation* between the semantic representation and the surface structure from which it is derived: the earlier the quantifier occurs in the surface sentence, the wider its semantic scope tends to be.

There are ways of patching up the feature representation system to make it responsive to the surface form of the sentence. We could, for example, use features derived from both universal and existential quantifiers, and assign positive values from later quantifiers in the sentence to earlier quantifiers which would then be construed as within their scope. The representations for our example sentences would then be as in (20)–(23), with the unmarked reading for each sentence being its forwards reading.

(20)	A child saw every squirrel.	$\exists\forall$
(21)	A $\text{child}_{[+\ \forall]}$ saw every squirrel.	$\forall\exists$
(22)	Every child saw a squirrel.	$\forall\exists$
(23)	Every $\text{child}_{[+\ \exists]}$ saw a squirrel.	$\exists\forall$

This system is of course explicitly designed to capture left-to-right asymmetries, but in doing so it loses the fundamental semantic insight of the Skolem systems, viz., that only universal quantifiers (or other 'multiple' quantifiers such as *many, several, most, seventeen,* etc.) impose a special interpretation on other quantifiers within their scope.

A more promising alternative would be to use only features derived from universal quantifiers but to use both positive and negative values, assigning the positive value to an *earlier* quantifier in the sentence which *is* within the scope of the universal quantifier, and the negative value to a *later* quantifier in the sentence which is *not* within the scope of the universal quantifier. The representations would then be as in (24)–(27), with the forwards reading again being the unmarked one for both example.

(24)	A child saw every squirrel.	$\exists\forall$
(25)	A child$_{[+\ \forall]}$ saw every squirrel.	$\forall\exists$
(26)	Every child saw a squirrel.	$\forall\exists$
(27)	Every child saw a squirrel$_{[-\ \forall]}$.	$\exists\forall$

In terms of sentence processing, this system implies that a hearer who has encountered a universal quantifier in a sentence will find it easiest to extend the scope of this quantifier indefinitely far forwards over later constituents, but not backwards over any earlier constituents; deviations from this pattern are what demand special mental computations.

That it is costly to extend the scope of a quantifier backwards in the sentence is easy enough to understand; as we have noted, for an on-line comprehension routine this would entail revising a part of the semantic representation that has already been constructed. But it is much less clear why it should be costly to the comprehension routines to terminate the forwards scope of a universal quantifier. This may seem a minor objection to the system. However, it is worth pressing for an explanation, because the use of the $[-\ \forall]$ feature is the one point of divergence from the general assumption that it is the dependence of one quantifier on another, rather than their independence, that should be explicitly marked in semantic representations. I turn now to a system which preserves the desirable properties of this one, but also offers a possible explanation for the psychological cost of terminating forwards scope.

5. MODEL-OF-THE-WORLD REPRESENTATIONS

The general outlines of the representation system I shall propose here will be familiar to anyone who has taught introductory logic. In an attempt to get across to beginning students the difference between $\forall\exists$ and $\exists\forall$ readings, we often resort to schematic pictures of the individuals described and the relations asserted to hold between them. To distinguish the readings of *Every child saw a squirrel*, for example, we might use diagrams such as (28) and (29).

(28)

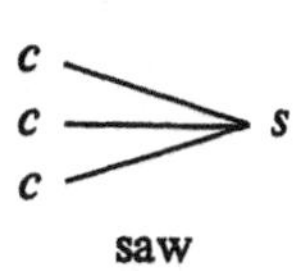

$\exists\forall$

(29)

We explain that the *c*'s stand for children, and that although there are only three of them in the picture this is not meant to restrict the sentence to situations involving only three children – the three are merely illustrative of as many children as the universal quantifier is taken to range over. We also point out that the *s*'s stand for squirrels, and that the single *s* in (28) *is* significant since it *is* intended to restrict the sentence to situations in which one and the same squirrel was seen by every child, though the three distinct *s*'s in (29) are not intended to restrict the sentence to situations in which a different squirrel was seen by each child – the three distinct *s*'s might or might not correspond to three distinct squirrels.

Although these diagrams must be governed by interpretive conventions of this kind, they obviously represent the truth and reference conditions on sentences much more directly than any of the representation systems we have considered so far. It is not just that they are two-dimensional, like a real picture or photograph. The crucial point, I think, is that phrases that are to be multiply instantiated are represented alike, and unlike phrases that are to have a singular instantiation. This is so whether the multiple instantiation is due to a multiple quantifier within the phrase itself (e.g., *every child, several squirrels, three hotdogs*), or whether it is due to the phrase being within the scope of another multiply quantified phrase (e.g., *a squirrel* in the forwards reading of *Every child saw a squirrel*, or *himself* in *Each man admires himself*).[6]

In the traditional prefixed quantifier representations, multiple (universal) and nonmultiple (existential) quantifiers are not structurally distinguished; the difference between them emerges only in the assignment of truth conditions, where the symbol ∀ is – as a matter of convention – construed as *for all*, and the symbol ∃ as *for some*. There is also no formal distinction between the variables bound by these different quantifiers. The *he* in sentence (30) and the *he* in sentence (31) are represented in exactly the same way (except for the difference in the quantifier at the front of the formula), even though the first stands for just one individual and the second for many.

(30) A boy was given a card and he was asked to draw a frog on it.
(31) Each boy was given a card and he was asked to draw a frog on it.

In the Skolem-type feature representations, as we have noted, multiple and nonmultiple quantifiers have different formal roles, and some of the context dependence of the standard logical formulae is unpacked. But a multiply quantified phrase is still formally distinguished from a phrase within the scope of another multiply quantified phrase, so the relation between phrases and the individuals or sets of individuals that instantiate them is still not fully transparent. It is to emphasize the difference between such representations and diagrams like (28) and (29) that I have termed the latter 'models of the world'.[7] Though schematic and conventionalized, the diagrams indicate quite transparently how each phrase is to be instantiated, and scope ambiguities are clearly revealed as ambiguities in the counting of the participants in an event. These diagrams could indeed be the output of a mental 'sieve' which filters full-blooded perceptions of the world for the purposes of linguistic encoding.

These diagrams are typically employed only as pedagogic aids in the presentation of the accepted logical representations with prefixed quantifiers and variables. They are assumed to have no place in a formal linguistic description of a language. If they are held to be psychologically real at all, it would probably be assumed at most that they correspond to visual images which some speaker/hearers may sometimes construct in addition to the 'real' semantic representations for sentences. What I wish to argue is that these schematic representations of events in the world (real or imaginary) themselves constitute the semantic representations for quantified sentences in natural languages. They may or may not be realized as visual images; whether or not they are is irrelevant to their status as the formulae of a well-defined formal language which captures quantifier scope distinctions in a different way, but just as effectively, as the more standard prefixed quantifier language.

In evaluating other systems of representation I have drawn attention to a number of facts which, ideally, we would like to be able to explain. Somewhat to my own surprise, I find that explanations for all of these facts, and others too, fall out naturally from this model-of-the-world representation system.

As in the feature systems of the previous section, quantifiers are interpreted *in situ*; they do not move, and hence there is no problem of determining where they may move to or whether their sequence may be jumbled up as they move. The scope of a quantifier may extend forwards or backwards over other constituents in the sentence. As in the Skolem-type feature system, it is just universal (or other multiple) quantifiers that can have scope over others; for a multiple quantifier to have scope over a portion of the sentence is for it to induce a multiple representation of that portion of the sentence.

For example, in representation (29) above, the quantifier *every* has induced a multiple representation not only of the noun *child* that it governs, but also of the verb and the object noun phrase; in (28) it has induced a multiple representation of just its own noun and the verb.

The explanation of the relative difficulty of readings in which the scope of a multiple quantifier extends backwards over earlier parts of the sentence is just as before. The $\forall\exists$ reading for sentence (32) will be computed on-line *via* an intermediate step in which *a child* is assigned a singular representation, which must then be revised as in (33) when the universal quantifier is encountered. It would be less costly for the hearer to compute the representation (34), corresponding to the $\exists\forall$ reading, since this demands no backtracking by the comprehension routines.[8]

(32) A child saw every squirrel.

(33)

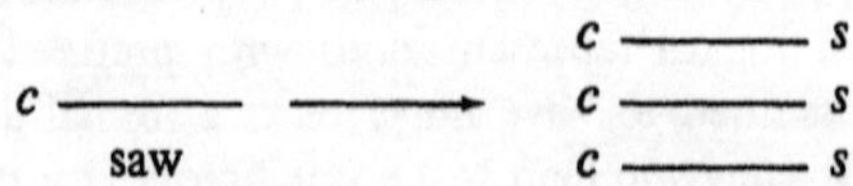

(34)

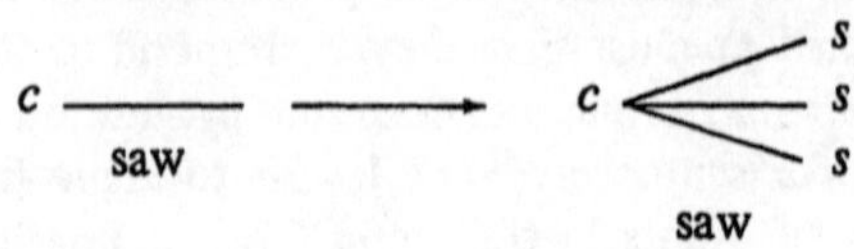

Forwards scope of a multiple quantifier should be relatively easy for a hearer to compute. For a sentence like (35), it requires only that the multiple paths in the representation established for *every child* should be extended to later words of the sentence as they are encountered.

(35) Every child saw a squirrel.

(36)

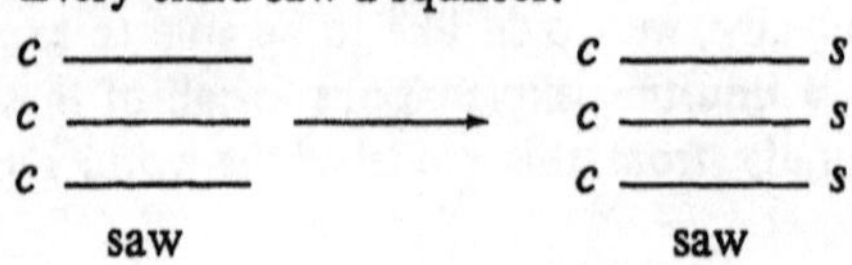

Indeed, we might even assume that to save time and effort on-line, the hearer forms an even more skeletal representation of the form (37), leaving the additional paths in the representation to be filled out as time becomes available and if the details are needed (e.g. for inference tasks); for the moment, he would construct a detailed representation of the activities of just one of the illustrative participants, with the mental footnote that what was true of one was true of each.

(37) *c* ——— *s*
c . . . (ditto)
c . . .
saw

This would explain why the scope of a multiple quantifier tends to extend forwards throughout the sentence. To terminate its scope, the hearer would have to form a representation like (38), in which the multiple paths for the early part of the sentence converge at some point.

(38)
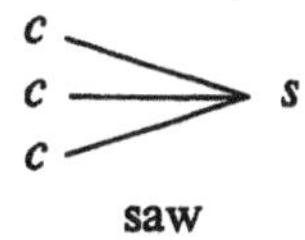

For this, the "ditto" time-saving convention won't do; the multiple paths must be explicitly represented in order for their convergence to be explicitly represented. So a hearer who has lazily made use of the "ditto" abbreviation at an earlier point in processing the sentence will not be able, without further effort, to compute the converging reading.[9]

The marked prosodic contours associated with reversed readings also make sense in this system. When the surface structure contains a multiple quantifier followed by a singular quantifier, the reversed reading will correspond to a converging representation, i.e. a representation in which the singular quantifier is to be dissociated from the multiplicity of paths constructed for the earlier part of the sentence. A prosodic break would be a natural way to signal this dissociation. When the surface structure contains a singular quantifier followed by a multiple quantifier, the reversed reading corresponds to a representation formed by multiplying the representation for an earlier constituent that had previously been assigned a singular representation. The only prosodic contour that could be expected to assist the hearer in this case would be one that encourages him to delay processing the earlier parts of the sentence until the multiple quantifier has been encountered. There is some evidence (Cutler and Fodor, 1979) that focussed phrases are given priority in interpretation, which suggests that the ideal contour would be one in which earlier constituents have less prominence than usual, and the multiple quantifier is stressed.[10] To the extent that there is any generally accepted prosodic convention for these readings, this is just what is observed.

Another bonus of this system is that the collective/distributive distinction falls out automatically, as a scope relation between quantifiers and verbs. In traditional representation systems, quantifiers (and negation operators, etc.) are moved to the front of a clause of the logical formula but the verb remains within the clausal representation; hence every quantifier has scope over the verb of its own clause (and possibly those of other clauses too). The reading of a sentence such as (39) on which the children collectively lifted the rock thus cannot be represented without the addition of some further notational devices; merely prefixing the quantifiers (in whichever order) would imply that there were as many distinct acts of lifting as there were children.

(39) All the children lifted a rock.

The model-of-the-world system, by contrast, provides three distinct representations for this sentence, which differ only with respect to the extent of the forwards scope of the universal quantifier. Representations (40) and (41) correspond to the readings we have been distinguishing so far, with the verb multiply interpreted in both cases, whether or not the object noun phrase is multiply interpreted. In representation (42) the multiple paths associated with the universal quantifier converge before the verb, and this thus represents collective action.

(40)
```
c ... ______ ... r
c ... ______ ... r
c ... ______ ... r
       lifted
```

(41)
```
c ... ______ .
c ... ______ . : r
c ... ______ .
       lifted
```

(42)
```
c .
c . : ______ ... r
c .
       lifted
```

With this unification of scope over verbs (and prepositions, etc.) with scope over other quantifiers, a major difference between the universal quantifiers *each*, *every* and *all* (see Vendler, 1967; Ioup, 1975; VanLehn, 1978) can now be systematically described. The quantifier *each* must take scope over at least one constituent in the sentence other than the nominal that it is associated with. This is why a sentence such as (43), with a verb which can only be taken to designate collective action, is ill-formed; the multiple paths associated with *each* would have to converge immediately after *soldier*, and before any other constituents in the sentence.

(43) *Each soldier surrounded the fort.

(Alternatively, we could construe (43) as well-formed, but descriptive of a pragmatically impossible situation in which each soldier individually surrounded the fort; on this interpretation the requirement on *each* would be met at the expense of the requirement on *surround*.) For the quantifier *every*, there is a similar requirement though it seems to be somewhat less stringent. For the composite forms *everyone, everybody, everything* the requirement is for some reason less stringent still. And for *all* there is no such requirement at all.

(44) ??Every soldier surrounded the fort.
(45) ?Everyone surrounded the fort.
(46) All the soldiers surrounded the fort.

This difference between the multiple quantifiers is just one reflection of a general scale of 'hunger' for inducing multiple interpretations of other constituents; *each* is the hungriest, *all* the least hungry. These lexically determined preferences are orthogonal to the general preference for extending scope forwards rather backwards within the sentence; for example, *each* tends to extend its scope further in both directions than the other quantifiers, but further still in a forwards direction than in a backwards direction. The interplay between these two factors leads to some very delicate predictions of the degree of preference for the various readings of various quantifier sequences, which correspond surprisingly well with intuitive judgements.

A related observation concerns the ease with which a multiple quantifier within a larger noun phrase can take scope over the head of that noun phrase. As VanLehn (1978) has observed, there is a scale extending from quantifiers within prepositional phrase modifiers (which readily take wide scope over the head), through quantifiers within reduced relative clauses, to quantifiers within full relative clauses (which are rarely assigned wide scope over the head). Examples (47)–(49) illustrate this scale.

(47) I spoke to a man from each East European country. (prefers $\forall\exists$)
(48) I spoke to a man representing each East European country. (? preference)
(49) I spoke to a man who was representing each East European country. (prefers $\exists\forall$)

In the prefixed quantifier system, these differences would have to be explained by appeal to constraints on the rules that move quantifiers to derive semantic representations. For example, May (1977) has distinguished examples like (47) and (49) in terms of the presence of an S node within (49), which prevents the extraction of constituents from the complex noun phrase and also provides a locus within it for the adjunction of the quantified phrase. Restrictions on scope interpretations are thus attributed to island constraints comparable (if not identical) to island constraints on syntactic extraction. However, as VanLehn notes, this does not account for the intermediate status of examples like (48). It also does not account for the contrast between (47) and a sentence like (50), which exhibits the opposite preference.

(50) I took a tour through every East European country. (prefers $\exists\forall$)

There is also the fact that a multiple quantifier *can* 'escape' from a relative clause in examples like (51), which are not especially difficult to construe as concerning a different professor for each applicant, i.e. as $\forall\exists$ sentences.

(51) I spoke to $\left\{\begin{matrix}\text{a}\\\text{the}\end{matrix}\right\}$ professor that each applicant had corresponded with.[11]

The squishiness of these contrasts, their dependence on particular lexical choices, and their dependence on the length and complexity of the modifying phrase, all suggest that they belong together with our previous generalizations about quantifier scope preferences within simple sentences. In (47) the multiple quantifier is *each*, which must induce a multiple interpretation of some other constituent(s). Within the prepositional phrase there are few other constituents for it to assuage its hunger on, and in any case a multiple interpretation of these constituents is pragmatically implausible – one man cannot be *from* many countries. (We can say that he is from Bulgaria, if that is where he was born, or that he is from Poland, if that is where he last resided, but even then we would not say that he is from both Bulgaria and Poland.) Thus the only way in which *each* can satisfy its need to induce multiple interpretations of other constituents is for the whole noun phrase to be multiply interpreted; then there will be multiple men, each one from one East European country. In (50), by contrast, we have the quantifier *every*, which is somewhat less energetic in inducing multiple interpretations of other constituents, and a prepositional construction which in any case does lend itself to multiple interpretation – a single tour *can* be through several different countries. Hence there is less pressure for the scope of the embedded quantifier to extend backwards over the head noun phrase. In relative clauses, which are longer and structurally more complex, there is more opportunity for the quantifier to induce multiple interpretations of other constituents within the modifying material, so in (49) there is again less pressure for it to extend its scope over the head noun phrase – though with sufficient pragmatic support it can do so, as (51) shows. A similar account can be given for interpretation preferences for quantifiers inside complement clauses, as in (52).

(52) Someone was aware (of the fact) that John had stolen {each / all} of the paintings.

For facts such as these, then, it appears that structural island constraints are not necessary, and indeed are descriptively inferior to squishy performance-based limitations on the sphere of influence of a quantifier in a given position in a sentence. There do exist some absolute restrictions on the relation between surface forms and semantic representations, but these can be captured in the model-of-the-world system by one very natural restriction, viz., that multiplicity of interpretation can only be inherited through a direct link with a multiple quantifier.

In a structure such as (53), a multiple quantifier in NP_1 can induce a multiple interpretation of NP_3 only by inducing a multiple interpretation of NP_2 – there can be no 'action at a distance' between NP_1 and NP_3.

(53)

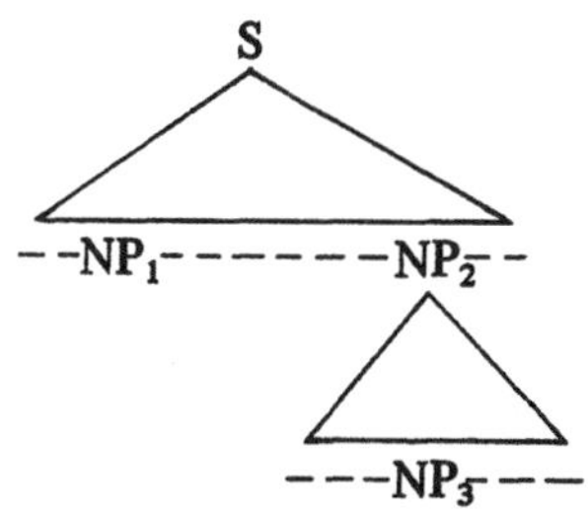

This is illustrated by sentence (54), in which the phrase *an East European country* can receive a multiple interpretation.

(54) Each diplomat spoke to a representative of an East European country.

That this multiple interpretation is attributable to the quantifier *each* in the subject phrase in shown by the fact that there can be no multiple interpretation of *an East European country* in sentence (55).

(55) This diplomat spoke to a representative of an East European country.

But if *an East European country* is multiply interpreted in (54), then *a representative* must also be multiply interpreted (and so must the other linking constituents, *spoke to* and *of*). That is, there can be no interpretation of the kind that would be represented in traditional terms with the quantified phrases prefixed in the sequence *a representative – each diplomat – an East European country*.

Similarly, if NP_3 contains a multiple quantifier, it can induce a multiple interpretation of NP_1 only by inducing a multiple interpretation of the linking NP_2. In (56), *a diplomat* can be multiply interpreted, and (57) shows that this interpretation is due to the multiple quantifier in *each East European country*.

(56) A diplomat spoke to a representative of each East European country.

(57) A diplomat spoke to a representative of that East European country.

But the multiple interpretation of *a diplomat* in (56) is possible only if *a representative* is also multiply interpreted; if the sentence is taken to be about just one representative for all of the East European countries together, then it must be about just one diplomat who spoke to him. The reading that is excluded is the one that would traditionally be represented with the quantified phrases prefixed in the sequence *a representative – each East European country – a diplomat*.

These restrictions on possible interpretations could perhaps be handled in prefixed quantifier systems by various constraints on extraction and the proper binding of variables. But the linkage requirement in the model-of-the-world system is psychologically very natural (multiple paths that have converged in the semantic representation being computed may not diverge again, except in response to a new multiple quantifier in the sentence). It is also extremely general; it applies to all kinds of constructions, some of which would require yet other restrictions in traditional systems. For example, it ensures that a multiply quantified noun phrase will pass on its multiplicity to other noun phrases in its clause only *via* a multiple interpretation of the verb. Sentence (58) can be assigned the semantic representations (59)–(61), but (62) is impossible. (Note that (62) *would* be possible as the representation of the collective interpretation of *All the children lifted all the pianos*, which has a second multiple quantifier.)

(58) All the children lifted a piano.

(59)
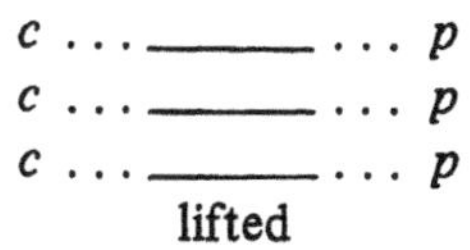

(60)
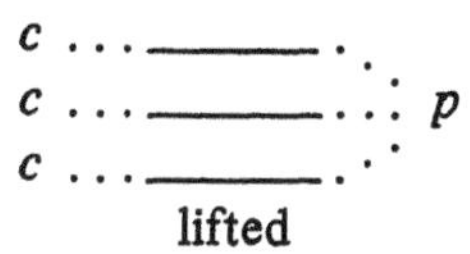

(61)
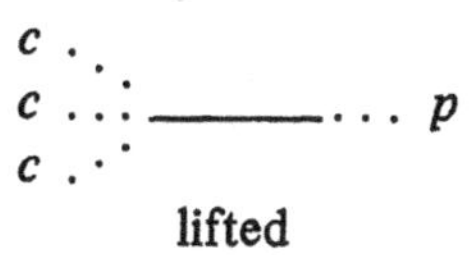

(62)
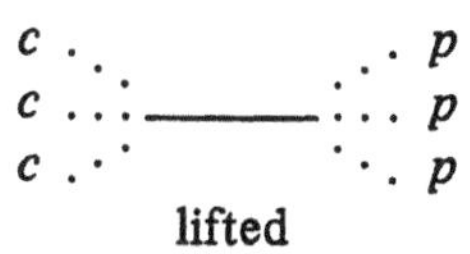

The linkage which permits multiplicity of interpretation to be transmitted from one constituent to another holds between every pair of arguments to a predicate, independently of any other arguments it may have. Thus in (63), *a picture* can be multiply interpreted, even if *a teacher* is not, as long as the verb *showed* which links it to the multiply quantified phrase *every child* is multiply interpreted; if the sentence is construed as about a distinct picture for each child, then there must have been a distinct showing by each child, though there need not have been a distinct teacher for every child.

(63) Every child showed a picture to a teacher.

But it is also true that *a teacher* can be multiply interpreted, even if *a picture* is not, as long as the verb is; the sentence can be construed as about a distinct showing by each child of the same picture to a distinct teacher. Until now, I have considered only predicates with two arguments, and have represented them in the form *aRb*. To extend this by representing three-argument predicates in the form *aRbc* would make the linkage requirement quite untransparent; it would suggest, incorrectly, that *c* cannot inherit a multiple interpretation from *a* unless the intervening *b* as well as *R* is multiply interpreted. The same problem, or a comparable one, arises for all the styles of representation in (64).

(64) *Rabc* *abRc*

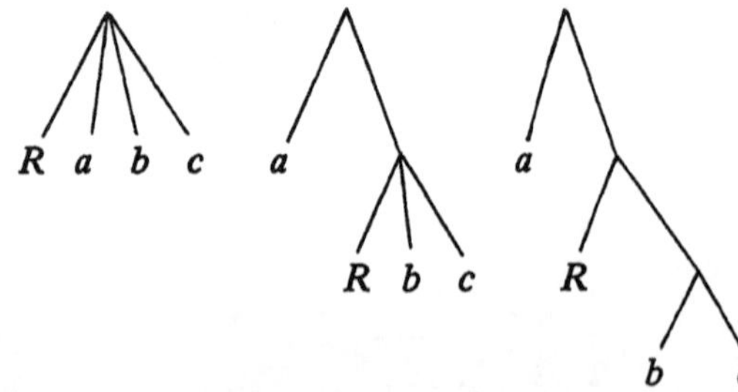

Instead, the structural representation of a predicate and its arguments must (if the linkage requirement is to be simply stated) give each argument equal access to each other argument, but only through the predicate. This suggests that model-of-the-world representations should be of the form (65).[12]

(65)

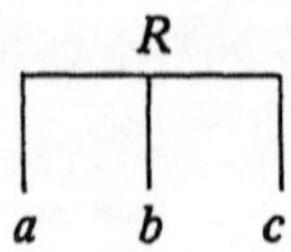

(As a means of distinguishing the thematic roles of the various arguments, we might label the vertical branches with suitable prepositions or semantic case markings.)

I will not attempt here to provide precise well-formedness conditions on the model-of-the-world representations (though preliminary work suggests that they will not be particularly difficult to formulate), but a few points are perhaps worth noting. First, representations like (65), just like more familiar syntactic phrase markers, are hierarchical in structure and thus permit the embedding of relations as arguments to other relations, as in (66).

(66)

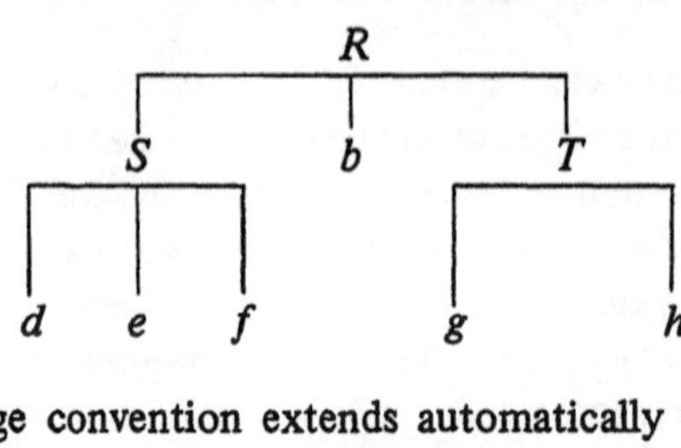

The linkage convention extends automatically to these complex structures (as noted in connection with (53) above), to ensure that a multiple quantifier in phrase *e*, for example, will induce a multiple interpretation of phrase *g*, only if it also induces a multiple interpretation of the predicates *S*, *R* and *T*.

Secondly, representations with multiple paths will now be three-dimensional, as in (67).

(67)

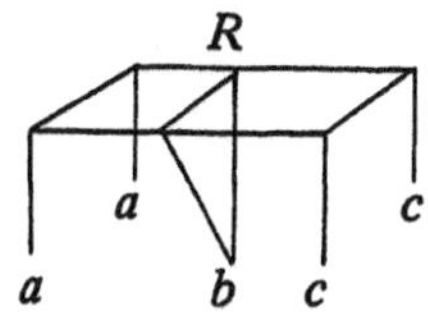

This makes the notation cumbersome to use on paper (and also perhaps difficult for some current computer systems to display), but this of course has no bearing at all on its adequacy as a reconstruction of the mental notation employed by the human sentence comprehension routines.

Another aspect of this system that I have not addressed so far concerns the means by which different quantifiers are to be distinguished representationally. In (67), for simplicity, I included only two paths for multiply interpreted constituents. This is in fact sufficient for distinguishing multiple (two-path) from non-multiple (one-path) quantifiers, and also for indicating the convergence and divergence of multiple paths, which is the basic device for specifying quantifier scope. The use of just one- and two-path representations might also tie in naturally with the singular/plural distinction that is common in human languages. (For languages which distinguish singular, dual and plural, one-, two- and three-path representations would then presumably be appropriate.) Alternatively, we might hypothesize that the number of paths that can be mentally distinguished is 7 ± 2 (see Miller, 1956). Some distinctions within the class of multiple quantifiers could then be captured, but it would still be impossible to distinguish all of *many, most, some, several, seventeen, eighteen, six hundred and forty two*, and so on. There seems to be no alternative to assuming that the basic representations are supplemented by a collection of mental footnotes specifying the number (or proportion) of individuals for which the few individuals that are explicitly represented stand as examplars. Inference which turn on these footnotes (e.g., *At least eighteen people ate asparagus; therefore at least seventeen people ate asparagus*) would have to be governed by meaning postulates rather than by general structural inference principles. It is worth noting that in this respect the model-of-the-world system is no worse off than more conventional systems, which typically distinguish only between *all* and *some*, and can make finer distinctions only by the use of lengthy strings of quantifiers and identity predicates, or by appeal to set theoretic notions, neither of which is at all plausible psychologically (see Martin, 1970).

Despite this limitation, some general inference principles can be defined over the model-of-the-world representations. Setting aside negation (which I plan to discuss in another paper), the main patterns of inference from a single premise involve reduction of the representation, and divergence of paths. The first corresponds to inferences such as *Every child likes John; therefore* (assuming nonemptiness of the set) *some child likes John*, which would be captured by simply deleting part of the representation for the premise, as in (68).[13]

(68)

The second pattern covers inferences from ∃∀ readings to the weaker ∀∃ readings, as in *There is a squirrel that every child saw; therefore every child is such that there is a squirrel that he saw*. This is captured by converting convergent paths into divergent paths, as in (69).

(69)

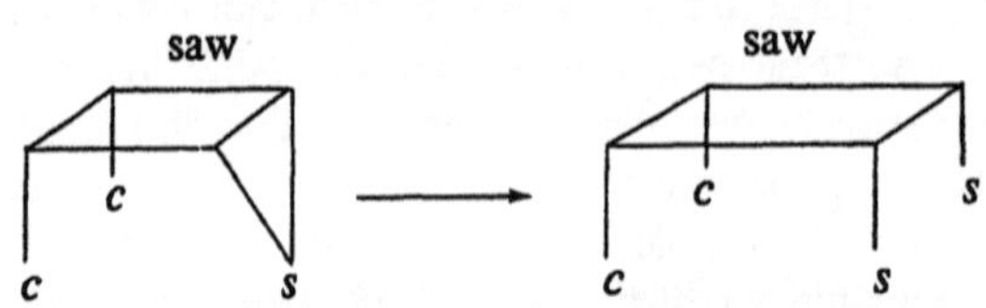

Inferences from two or more premises can be established by combining the representations for the premises, and then simplifying them as above. The model-of-the-world system as I have outlined it so far is intended to provide representations for individual sentences. But I regard it as an asset of the system that these sentential representations can be integrated rather naturally to provide representations of complete discourses, or can be integrated with comparable representations of general background information. (No substantial integration process seems to be possible in the more traditional representation systems; conjunction of separate formulae is the only device available.) Thus the representations for *Every child likes John* and *Sam is a child* can be combined as in (67) (the combination being sensitive to the footnote that the *c*'s are illustrative of all children).[14]

(67)

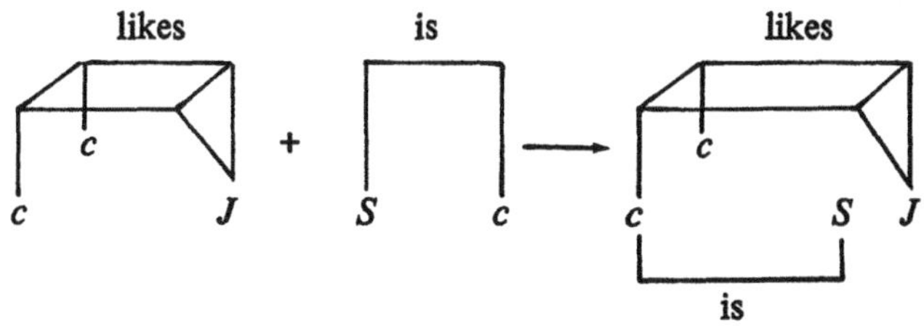

The resulting composite representation can then stand as a unified coding of the information contained in this (very brief) discourse, or it can, if the need arises, be used to generate the conclusions *Sam is a child who likes John* or *Sam likes John*, by simplification of the representation.

A number of psychologists and computer scientists concerned with information storage and retrieval processes have proposed somewhat similar combinatory operations on the representations of individual sentences (see, for example, Anderson and Bower, 1973; Hendrix, 1978). Linguists have not, I think, given a great deal of attention to these proposals about the form in which information is mentally represented – there has seemed to be so little connection between the conceptual representations that have been proposed and the representations that are assigned to sentences by generative grammars. But the model-of-the-world semantic representations that I have been arguing for hold out the hope that linguistics, psycholinguistics and cognitive psychology can, after all, be made to meet in the middle. There are many questions of detail to be worked out, of course, but progress may perhaps be more rapid once we see how linguistic data can contribute to filling in some of these details.

University of Connecticut

NOTES

[1] Some excuse is clearly called for. Even I would hesitate to disagree with Kneale and Kneale (1962, p. 511): "In short, it is no exaggeration to say that use of quantifiers to bind variables was one of the greatest intellectual inventions of the nineteenth century."

[2] This is not quite fair to May, for he offers two other indications of the marked character of the specific readings. One is that their occurrence is highly idiosyncratic and dependent on the 'vividness' of descriptions (see Kaplan, 1969). This point, however, seems to involve a confusion between the possibility of interpreting a noun phrase as specific, and the conditions under which the specific interpretation is true (which was Kaplan's concern). The second observation is that the specific reading is more accessible

when the main verb is one which functions as a 'bridge' for WH-Movement. This is an intriguing point, which does seem to indicate a close association between quantifier scope and syntactic movement rules. However, the correlation is not a very precise one; for example, *Which cheese did John regret that he had eaten?* is well-formed even though *John regretted that he had eaten all the cheese* quite strongly prefers a narrow scope interpretation for *all the cheese*. Since it seems likely that the bridge/non-bridge distinction rests on the semantic properties of predicates, my own suspicion (however heretical) is that the constraints on movement are lexically and syntactically hardened-in reflections of deeper but looser semantic tendencies, which favor semantic associations between some constituents in a sentence but not others.

[3] As noted in Fodor (1979), the syntactic parsing of transformed sentences might involve mental processes analogous to the binding of traces by moved constituents, rather than the replacement of moved constituents into the gaps which represent their deep structure positions. In this case, the formal similarity between the quantifier prefixing rule and leftward syntactic movement rules would be matched by at least a partial similarity of the mental processes engaged in during sentence comprehension, for the binding of variables would be involved in the hearer's mental computations for both types of rule. The assumption that quantifier prefixing is difficult in proportion to the distance that the quantifier is moved might still be motivated by analogies with syntactic parsing, but on the basis of different syntactic facts (e.g., the clause-boundedness of even leftward movement rules in some languages, and the Keenan-Comrie extraction hierarchy).

[4] For unmarked cases, determining quantifier scope by reference to c-command relations in the semantic structure will give the same results as determining scope by reference to c-command relations in the surface syntactic structure, as proposed by Reinhart (1967). Reinhart's c-command conditions are of considerable interest because of their similarity to the conditions on anaphoric phenomena, but it is not clear that they can handle the full range of marked and unmarked readings of quantified sentences. (See May, 1977, and VanLehn, 1978, for discussion of some problematic cases.)

[5] This distinction is clearly drawn in game theoretic semantics (see, for example, Hintikka, 1968). I have not discussed game theoretic semantics in this paper since its emphasis is not on static representations of logical form but on dynamic 'game plans' for such activities as evaluating the truth of sentences. However, flow charts of these game plans exhibit a striking resemblance to the semantic representations that I shall propose in Section 5. (This point emerged from a discussion with Lauri Carlson.)

[6] I think it is correct to regard a phrase within the scope of a multiple quantifier as having been converted, in effect, into a multiply quantified phrase. As will be discussed below, it can pass on its multiplicity of interpretation to other phrases in the sentence, just as it could if it were itself multiply quantified. This would explain, incidentally, why a (specific but) multiple interpretation of *someone* is more natural in the sentence *Each man thought that he had been unfair to someone* than in the sentence *Each man thought that I had been unfair to someone*; the *he* in the first sentence, unlike the *I* in the second, would function like a multiple quantifier and would thus tend to induce a multiple interpretation of the nearby *someone*.

[7] I should make it clear that this designation has nothing to do with model theoretical interpretations for semantic representations. The representation system I shall outline stands in just as much need of such an interpretation as any other system. (I shall not

provide one here, but I have no reason to believe that it cannot be done; indeed, if I am right, it can be done in a psychologically more natural way for this system than for others.)

[8] This is not quite true as it stands because of the lines representing the verb, but I will return to the proper treatment of these below.

[9] A particularly astute participant at the conference observed that this explanation turns on the tacit assumption that "ditto" abbreviates the continuation with distinct paths rather than the continuation with converging paths. I think this assumption is justified. As noted, the convergence of paths carries the specific information that all the paths must be instantiated with the same individual, while separate paths are neutral between identical or different instantiations. Thus the convergence of paths should be regarded as the marked case; without a specific indication to the contrary, separate paths would be constructed when the "ditto" abbreviation is later expanded.

[10] Cutler and Fodor write (p. 56): "Once the focussed segment has been located (usually by tracking the intonation contour to locate the main accent), processing of it begins immediately, even though in some cases processing of preceding segments is not complete."

[11] For a definite noun phrase, a multiple interpretation can be induced by the 'upwards' influence of a multiple quantifier within it more easily than by the forwards or backwards influence of a multiple quantifier in a neighboring phrase. A sentence like *Each child saw the squirrel* is typically interpreted (like *Each child saw John*, but unlike *Each child saw a squirrel*) as requiring a single instantiation of the object noun phrase. Multiple interpretation is natural only for examples like *I petted the squirrel that each child brought me* (or *Each child petted the squirrel he had caught*, which has a multiply interpreted pronoun within the definite phrase).

This difference between definites and indefinites need not be accounted for structurally, for it follows from the uniqueness condition on the referents of definite descriptions. The referent of a complex noun phrase is determined by the referents of its constituents. When a phrase within the definite noun phrase is multiply interpreted, this can lead to multiple interpretation of the whole noun phrase, with the uniqueness condition associated with each individual path in the representation. But a neighboring phrase does not normally influence the referent of the definite description, and so the uniqueness condition must be met independently of multiple interpretations for neighboring phrases.

However, as Keith Stenning has pointed out to me, some discourse contexts are rich enough to permit identification of a unique referent relative to each of a set of individuals that is under discussion. For example, in the discourse *Each child saw a cup. The handle was blue*, the definite description *the handle* can be multiply interpreted *via* the implicit link with *a cup*, which is indefinite and has a multiple interpretation induced in the usual way by *each child*. Similarly, in the discourse *Each child saw a chipmunk and a squirrel. The squirrel was eating a nut*, the definite phrase *the squirrel* can be multiply interpreted *via* coreference with the preceding multiply interpreted indefinite *a squirrel.*

[12] This form of representation incidentally offers at least a partial solution to the problem (see Note 8) of the retroactive multiplication of verb paths by a following quantified phrase (as in *John touched several squirrels*). In the semantic representation, the verb will be adjacent to each of its arguments (even arguments that are some distance from it in the surface structure), and this minimizes the amount of mental backtracking that is necessary in constructing a multiple representation for the verb in response to a multiple

quantifier that occurs later in the sentence. The distances between constituents in representations like (65) are thus consistent with the judgement that the backwards influence of a multiple quantifier on a *verb* gives rise to little or no sensation of mentally reorganizing the interpretation that is being assigned to the sentence on-line, though this sensation typically *is* associated with the backwards influence of a multiple quantifier on an earlier *noun phrase* in the sentence.

However, verb representations raise a host of other questions that I have not yet given sufficient attention to. Why is there apparently no preference at all for a sentence beginning *John touched* ... to continue with a singular object or a multiple object? Could it be that verb representations are not mentally constructed until after all their arguments have been interpreted? If so, how can verbs be the link by which multiplicity of interpretation is passed from one argument to another? Are some verb representations perhaps neutral between a singular and a multiple interpretation? Is this why *John saw several squirrels* is not associated with any clear sense of ambiguity between several acts of seeing one squirrel and one act of seeing several squirrels? But then why is a sentence like *John weighed several squirrels* judged to be ambiguous between several acts of weighing one squirrel and one act of weighing several squirrels? Must verbs be lexically categorized for this ambiguity? Or do the differences between verbs stem from the fact that individual paths in a verb representation correspond to distinct *relations*, rather than to distinct *acts*? (An act of seeing Mary and Bill is not an act of seeing Mary and an act of seeing Bill, but if I stand in the seeing relation to Mary and Bill then I do stand in the seeing relation to Mary and to Bill. However, if I stand in the weighing relation to Mary and Bill (together), it does not follow that I stand in the weighing relation to Mary and to Bill.)

[13] In (68) I have represented the proper name *John* just once, so that the multiple paths for earlier constituents must converge at this point. Since proper names are not associated with any special processing difficulty, even in multiple contexts, this might appear to undercut may explanation (p. 149) of the mental cost of converging representations. However, proper names are unlike quantified nouns in that they refer to specific individuals rather than to illustrative members of a set. It is therefore of no import whether their semantic representations are singular or multiple. A multiple representation might be constructed on-line for *John* in *Every child saw John*, thus continuing the separation of paths for the earlier parts of the sentence; the processing mechanism could subsequently collapse these representations at its leisure on the basis of their referential identity.

A related point concerns sentences like *Every child saw every squirrel*. Left-to-right interpretation would presumably give rise to the representation (i) or (ii), though the equivalent but symmetric representation (iii) would be more useful in arriving at the conclusion that every squirrel was seen by every child.

(i)

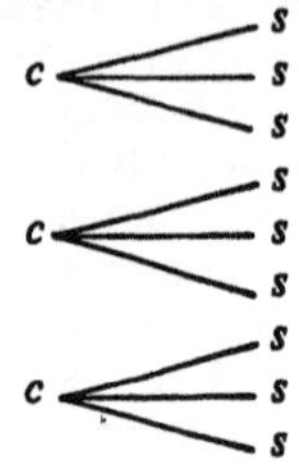

(ii)

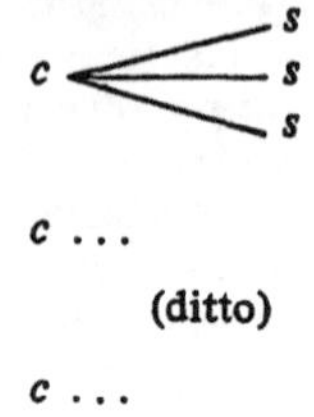

(iii)

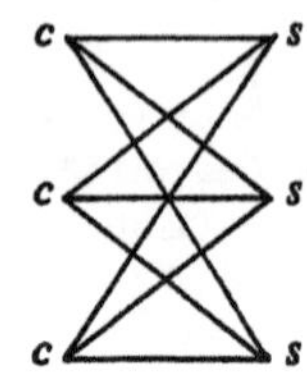

Once again, it is conceivable that the on-line processes do what comes naturally when working from left to right (e.g. construct representation (ii)), and that subsequent rearrangements can be made if and when convenient to make explicit certain inferentially useful connections.

[14] These diagrams will serve to illustrate the general idea that sentential representations are integrated by superimposing parts that are identical, but the treatment of the predicate *is a child* may not be correct. The copula could be construed as expressing an identity relation between the subject and some unspecified member of the set of all children, or as expressing a membership relation between the subject and the set of all children; or the copula could be regarded as semantically empty, and the predicate nominal *a child* could be construed as expressing a singulary property (like *is young*, or *sleeps*). I will not try to adjudicate between these alternatives here, but it should be noted that the choice between them impinges on the details of the representation for quantified phrases like *every child*. The latter may have to be adjusted, if the integration process is to be defined simply, depending on how we decide to represent predicate nominals.

REFERENCES

Anderson, J. R. and G. H. Bower: (1973) *Human Associative Memory*, V. H. Winston and Sons, Washington, D.C.

Bordelois, I.: (1974) *The Grammar of Spanish Causative Complements*, unpublished Ph.D. dissertation, MIT, Cambridge, Massachusetts.

Bresnan, J.: (1978) 'A realistic transformational grammar,' in M. Halle, J. Bresnan and G. A. Miller (eds.) *Linguistic Theory and Psychological Reality*, MIT Press, Cambridge, Massachusetts.

Cutler, A. and J. A. Fodor: (1979) 'Semantic focus and sentence comprehension,' *Cognition* 7, 49–59.

Davidson, D.: (1967) 'The logical form of action sentences,' in N. Rescher (ed.), *The Logic of Decision and Action*, Pittsburgh University Press, Pittsburgh.

Engdahl, E.: (1979) 'The nested dependency constraint as a parsing strategy,' in E. Engdahl and M. J. Stein (eds.) *Papers Presented to Emmon Bach by his Students*, University of Massachusetts, Amherst, Massachusetts.

Enderton, H. B.: (1972) *A Mathematical Introduction to Logic*, Academic Press, New York.

Fodor, J. A., T. Bever and M. Garrett: (1974) *The Psychology of Language: An Introduction to Psycholinguistics and Generative Grammar*, McGraw-Hill, New York.

Fodor, J. D.: (1978) 'Parsing strategies and constraints on transformations,' *Linguistic Inquiry* 9, 427–473.

Fodor, J. D.: (1979) 'Superstrategy,' in W. E. Cooper and E. C. T. Walker (eds.) *Sentence Processing: Studies in Psycholinguistics Presented to Merrill Garrett*, Lawrence Erlbaum Associates, Hillsdale, New Jersey.

Goldin-Meadow, S.: (1979) 'Structure in a manual communication system developed without a conventional language model: language without a helping hand,' in H. A. Whitaker and H. Whitaker (eds.) *Studies in Neurolinguistics*, Vol. 4, Academic Press, New York.

Hendrix, G. G.: (1978) 'Encoding knowledge in partitioned networks,' *SRI International Technical Note 164*, to appear in N. V. Findler (ed.) *Associative Networks – The Representation and Use of Knowledge in Computers*, Academic Press, New York.

Hintikka, J.: (1968) 'Language games for quantifiers,' in N. Rescher (ed.) *Studies in Logical Theory*, Basil Blackwell, Oxford. Reprinted with revisions as Ch. III of J. Hintikka, *Logic, Language-Games and Information*, Clarendon Press, Oxford, 1973.

Hintikka, J.: (1974) 'Quantifiers vs. quantification theory,' *Linguistic Inquiry* 5, 153–177.

Ioup, G. L.: (1975) *The Treatment of Quantifier Scope in Transformational Grammar*, unpublished Ph.D. dissertation, City University of New York.

Jackendoff, R. S.: (1972) *Semantic Interpretation in Generative Grammar*, MIT Press, Cambridge, Massachusetts.

Johnson-Laird, P. N.: (1975) 'Models of deduction,' in R. J. Falmagne (ed.), *Reasoning: Representation and Process*, Lawrence Erlbaum Associates, Hillsdale, N.J.

Kaplan, D.: (1969) 'Quantifying in,' in D. Davidson and J. Hintikka (eds.) *Words and Objections*, Reidel, Dordrecht.

Koster, J.: (1979) 'Conditions, empty nodes, and markedness,' *Linguistic Inquiry* 9, 551–593.

Lakoff, G.: (1965) *Irregularity in Syntax*, Holt, Rinehart and Winston, New York.

Lasnik, H.: (1975) 'On the semantics of negation,' in D. J. Hockney, (ed.) *Contemporary Research in Philosophical Logic and Linguistic Semantics*, Reidel, Dordrecht.

Lasnik, H. and J. J. Kupin: (1977) 'A restrictive theory of transformational grammar,' *Theoretical Linguistics* 4, 173–196.

Martin, E. Jr.: (1978) 'The psychological unreality of quantificational semantics,' in C. W. Savage (ed.) *Minnesota Studies in the Philosophy of Science*, Vol. IX, University of Minnesota Press, Minneapolis.

May, R. C.: (1977) 'The grammar of quantification,' unpublished Ph.D. dissertation, MIT, Cambridge, Massachusetts.

Miller, G. A.: (1956) 'The magical number seven plus or minus two: some limits on our capacity for processing information,' *Psychological Review* 63, 81–97.

Napoli, D. J.: (1974) 'The No Crossing filter,' in M. W. La Galy, R. A. Fox and A. Bruck (eds.) *Papers from the Tenth Regional Meeting of the Chicago Linguistic Society*, Chicago Linguistic Society, Chicago.

Quine, W. V. O.: (1956) 'Quantifiers and propositional attitudes,' *Journal of Philosophy* 53, 177–187.

Reinhart, T.: (1976) *The Syntactic Domain of Anaphora*, unpublished Ph.D. dissertation, MIT, distributed by Indiana University Linguistics Club.

VanLehn, K. A.: (1978) 'Determining the scope of English quantifiers,' unpublished M.A. dissertation, MIT, Artificial Intelligence Laboratory Report AI-TR-483.

Vendler, Z.: (1976) *Linguistics in Philosophy*, Cornell University Press, Ithaca, New York.

NUEL D. BELNAP, JR.

QUESTIONS AND ANSWERS IN MONTAGUE GRAMMAR

This paper is built on Bennett (1979) (henceforth QMG). QMG was drafted by Bennett to be a joint paper by the two of us; we held a number of discussions on the issues raised therein, but none of the changes on which we agreed or the differences which we wished to mention were committed to paper before his untimely death. It is my ultimate plan to bring out a jointly authored version of QMG containing both agreements and differences. The central portion of this paper, Section 3, on quantification into questions, represents an area of agreement: Section 3 is motivation of and minor alteration of some of the constructions suggested in QMG. The rest of the paper divides up as follows. Section 1 is a brief discussion of the role of Montague grammar (Montague, 1974) in a theory or system of natural language processing (by man or machine). Section 2 discusses various aspects of the concept of "answer." Section 3, as mentioned above, builds on QMG to give a theory of quantifiers whose scope is wide with respect to question-words. Section 4 discusses one question word, *which*, in the singular, indicating how QMG could be altered to agree with the suggestions made in Section 3. Section 5 defends the view that different question-words should be assumed to behave differently – it is argued that the contrary assumption is false.

1. MONTAGUE GRAMMAR AND NATURAL LANGUAGE PROCESSING

Belnap and Steel (1976) (henceforth LQA) addressed itself to the elaboration of a *good* formal apparatus for the asking and answering of questions, being in this respect unabashedly normative. It also took itself to be throwing some perhaps weak light on questions and answers in natural language, but that was not its purpose. There is in contrast the descriptive job of how questions and answers actually work in a natural language, say English, an undertaking to which some linguists and philosophers are increasingly turning. And among the various methodologies one might employ, there is that due to Montague. For present purposes, i.e., for the purpose of guiding this discussion, I wish to think of the following as essential to the Montague approach.

(1) An account of "meaning" is to be provided by translation into a formal "logician's language" such as Montague's IL. The target language should be

S. Peters and E. Saarinen (eds.), Processes, Beliefs, and Questions, 165–198.

rich enough to do whatever job is required, whether that richness is provided by "possible worlds" or not. In any event, it should have a mathematically rigorous semantics. The Strategy of the Target Language is not essential on technical grounds, but it is my view that perspicuity suggests it; for by this means one obtains an overview of the resources commanded by a particular semantic scheme. One gets this overview from study of the target language and its semantics.

(2) With respect to the fragment for which a Montague account is claimed, the translation is to be completely rigorous – no loop holes, no being satisfied with a few examples, no invocation of "and similarly." The standard of rigor is that of contemporary mathematical logic.

(3) At least for the reason (2) above, obtaining such a translation presupposes an absolutely formal grammatical analysis, so that the translation of larger pieces is strictly determined by the translation of smaller pieces and how they are combined. The grammatical analysis is *not* to be "homemade," but just as rigorous as the semantics itself – i.e., just as rigorous as mathematical logic.

(4) There should be as much of what Hausser calls "surface compositionality" as possible. That is, in stating the compositional rules, one should as much as possible restrict attention to surface rather than "deep" features.

There are some negative points.

(5) I take it that there is *no* requirement that the type (in the sense of type-theory) of the translation have any intuitive significance. E.g., it is quite irrelevant that people do not think of terms as signifying properties of properties; if such a translation is theoretically fruitful, by all means invoke it. It is true that Montague theorists ordinarily or always translate English sentences into the type of sentences of IL but even this seems to me unnecessary; e.g., the same purposes could be served if they were translated into symbols which were of a type to name propositions. The point is that, on my view, the chief problem the Montague approach should be taken as solving is the embedding problem – the derivation of the meaning of composite expressions from their parts. And whatever has to be invoked to solve that problem can be treated like the postulated features or kinds of physical science (spin, charm).

(6) I do not myself take the total absence of transformations to be The essence of the Montague approach. Presumably to say as much is to weaken point (3), even though it will remain in the spirit of the enterprise to limit the role of transformations, as much as possible deriving larger pieces by direct surface combination.

(7) A last negative point: (1) does not on my account demand a translation into IL itself. In fact I have the view that the language ML^{ν} of Bressan (1972) or a variant thereof, would on the whole permit simpler (equivalent) translations. Further, it does not to me seem essential to the enterprise that the target language be typed; on this I do not have any fixed views, but can well imagine that over all simplicity might be served by choosing the intensional type-free set theory of Bressan (1973-74).

What, then, is the role of a Montague theory in natural language? I think that there are two quite different ways a formal theory of language can be involved with processing of natural language – whether by computer or by brain. The first and most obvious is that the processor *use* the formal representation in its processing. If the processor is a brain, then we are talking about the "psychological reality" of the formal representation. If the processor is a computer, we are talking about making recommendations as to the most efficient way to get the language processed. Evidently one might have formal representations in *some* sense "equivalent" which nonetheless differed as to their psychological reality, or as to their efficiency, so that the differences were important in spite of the "equivalence."

But at least with respect to the computer case, and I think also with regard to people-processors, there is another possible role for a formal representation of language. I can make my point best by backing off from the particular case of language processing, considering instead the more general question of describing tasks for the computer (I come back to people later). I want to say and to urge that it is *good* to have descriptions of these tasks which are largely independent of how the task is to be carried out. One wants, that is, a success criterion *not* tied to any realization of a procedure for attaining that criterion. Let us call such an account *procedure-independent*.

For example, it used to be thought (and probably some people still think this) that the only proper formal definition of a high-level computer programming language (e.g., FORTRAN) is in terms of a "compiler" for that language, a compiler which would take a program in the high-level language and produce a machine-level procedure capable of carrying out the program. In contrast, I think that what is needed in addition is a procedure-independent account of the high-level computer language; for only then does it make sense to judge a compiler as "correct," "efficient," etc. Only then does it make sense to speak of two compilers for the "same" high-level language. Further, it is useful to have definitions of high-level languages which ignore at least in some respects limitations on the computer – so that one will not in language-design be biassed by possibly wrong-headed expectations of what will turn out (perhaps) to be manageable or not. Of course this can be carried too far, and represents a matter for refined judgment; I only want to say that there is a procedure-independent aspect of the matter, an aspect needing attention and defense.

The analogy holds good, I think, for processing natural language. One wants a procedure-independent account of what counts as good processing. And the more the account is free of the language of processing itself, the greater chance there will be of avoiding the bias which can be introduced by building into the language-description one's own expectations as to the best methods of processing.

I think this is equally true of formal descriptions of natural language as used by people. One would like a description free of guesses as to how people process language, a description which makes no pretense whatsoever of "psychological reality." The only claim that has to be made is that it gets "the meaning" right. And to the extent that meaning is caught by "truth-conditions" (it is no part of my thought that we need to be committed to the view that truth-conditions capture all meaning, but only that they are a necessary part of meaning), a formal truth-conditional account of natural language is a Good Thing. And though it is perhaps sufficiently obvious, let me note explicitly that the reason one wants a *formal* account is that one wants to have clear and precise measures as to how well a proposed processing scheme suffices for the purposes at hand.

Here, I think, is one role for Montague grammar and semantics. For this job, the *only* constraints are (1) that it Get English Right in a formal way, and (2) that it be *seen* to get it right. Not of course for all English, and perhaps not for any of English in all respects – but for whatever respects are claimed, and for whatever fragments are claimed.

2. ANSWERS

What is the linguistic task in the vicinity of questions? Part of it is certainly to describe the syntax and semantics of direct and indirect questions, including such relations between the two as there may be, and though this section is about answers, I wish to devote a few sentences to stating my views on this relation. The reason I wish to do this is because I have been said to be associated with those who would take indirect questions as primary and understand direct questions through them. I regret having been sufficiently obscure so as to lead readers to this opinion, for in fact my instincts (and my views are little more than that) push me to regard direct questions as primary and to understand indirect questions in terms of them. But I hasten to add that this talk of "primary" has nothing to do with transformation – I have no views as to whether one sort can be obtained by transforming the other sort, or whether they should instead be generated independently. At bottom the firmest conviction I have is this: that with doubtless a few exceptions, indirect and direct questions in English stand in a one-to-one correspondence, with the correspondence being syntactically recognizable, and with corresponding members having precisely the same semantic meaning. The second most firm conviction is that an indirect question is a nominalized interrogative, nominalized because of the love of English for the verb-noun construction, and not in order to make any meaning-change. Hence, in the sequel I shall not care whether my examples are direct or indirect, and I shall freely talk of answers to indirect questions.

As for answers, the first question here, as I see it, is

Q1. whether linguistic theory should as well describe "the" question-answer relationship.

But in spite of the relative inattention paid to this problem by all but the most recent work of linguists, it seems to me that almost the only basis for not including this task as part of linguistic theory would be the view that there is no stable, determinate question-answer relationship to describe. In fact, however, our ability to distinguish responses which on linguistic grounds can count as answers seems to be about as well entrenched as our ability to distinguish what counts as a sentence:

(1) *Which person kicked Sam?* (a) *John.* (b) *It was John.* (c) *John did.* (d) *John kicked him.* (e) *He was kicked by John.* (f) *John kicked Sam.* (g) *The person who kicked Sam was John.* (h) *John alone kicked Sam.* (i) *His brother.* (j) *He did.* (k) **He* (l) **Sam kicked John.* (m) **He kicked John.* (n) **John is the person Sam kicked.* (o) **China is populous.* (p) ? *Nobody.* (q) ? *Somebody.* (r) ? *Someone with red hair.* (s) ? *I don't know.* (t) ? *Ask Sam.*

Allowing that we have this competence, however, does not quite settle the question; for some may nevertheless think the question-answer relationship should be treated by that part of linguistics (textual – or perhaps contextual – analysis) which more generally addresses itself to explaining how and why conversations fit together, a part which some think is nowhere near ready to be developed in any rigorous way. My own view is that some parts of the problem of the question-answer relationship are likely to prove far easier than the more general problem and may well and fruitfully be attacked with present techniques. Part of this view is that we can often tell the difference between *appropriate response* and *answer*; e.g., I should think everyone would agree that (s) or (t) is an appropriate response without being an answer. The status of (p)–(r) I leave open, at least for now.

There is however an important second question, even granting that Q1 gets a "yes":

Q2 What part of linguistic theory should undertake the account of the question-answer relationship?

There are a number of possibilities.

Q3 Is there an intersting context-and-semantics-free syntactic theory of answers?

Q4 Is there an interesting context-free semantic theory of answers?

Clarification: by "context" here I do not mean the features of context which we now thoroughly understand by present techniques (speaker, auditor, etc.) of what Montague called "pragmatics," but is better called "indexical semantics"; I mean instead to refer to those features of context which we all know are there but do not yet know how to describe in any rigorous way. I would explicitly include purposes, institutional or social settings, etc., about which we can say many wise and wonderful things without however having a tidy theory.

About Q3. It seems to me that in fact syntax should provide us with an interesting theory of answers: to (1) the phrase (k) *He* is syntactically bad and (j) *He did is* syntactically fine (I do not know why). On the other hand, it seems unlikely that syntax alone can provide a *full* theory of answers. I want to say that whether or not (j) *He did* counts as an answer to (1) depends on what the denotation of *he* is taken to be, and that that is a matter for semantics (including contextual semantics). In the linguistic theory of questions and answers which we have so far worked out, we have not offered a syntax of answers, but *only* a semantics – that is, we have offered views about what the meaning of an expression must be to count as an answer, but we have not offered any about what the expression must look like. This is not to be taken as a defect of the Montague program, but only an indication of something that needs doing. Hausser (1976a) for example, offers both a syntax and semantics of answers. I disagree, however, with the fact that his theory does not distinguish what I should call "answers" from what I should call "appropriate responses" – as noted below, Hausser lumps (a) above with (p)–(r).

As to Q4, it seems clear that much can only be said about answerhood on the contextual level. This is notoriously true for *why*-questions, but also holds for more straightforward questions; Bolinger (1978) is a good source of evidence for this claim. Still, it is my belief that in fact much that is of interest can be said about the question-answer relationship in syntax-cum-semantics without retreating to the overgrown terrain of context. And the research program I advocate for the present stage attempts precisely that.

2.1 *Short or long*? As (1) illustrates, there are both "short" and "long" answers to questions. This fact has led to theories of the semantic representation of questions of two quite different types: those which take the short answers as in some sense primary, and those which take the long answers as primary. According to Hausser (1976), the primary responses to (1), of those listed, are (a) *John* or (p)–(r) *nobody, somebody, somebody with red hair*. Tichy (1977) is also a short-answer man, but would presumably count only (a). No one but Hausser is as specific, but it would seem that theories of the Hamblin or Karttunen types would make the full sentences primary; Karttunen might pick (f) *John kicked Sam* as primary, and it is reasonably clear that QMG would opt for (g) *The person who kicked Sam is John*. Hausser advertises his view by choice of terminology, calling the short answers "irredundant" and the long "redundant." Hamblin 1958 also builds his (opposing) view into his terminology by calling the short ones "coded answers."

There is more than one issue revealed by this debate. First, should short or long answers be primary? I confess that I don't care. I believe that any full language description should include accounts of both, and I don't care if one is "derived" from the other, or if the two sorts of answers are taken as on all fours (but of course related). In particular, it seems to me worth noticing that long answers hardly (if ever) occur in natural discourse; and *also* worth noticing that answers to questions are statements or propositions, expressible in a context-free way only by full sentences. We need both. (I use the "short/long" terminology so as not to load the question of primacy.)

Of substance is the question as to *which* short expressions should count as short answers, and *which* long expressions should count as long answers, as well as the question as to which long answer ought to be correlated with each short answer. I will treat these matters later.

2.2 *Real answers*. I'll follow Belnap and Steel (1976) in marking the linguistic/extra-linguistic distinction with "nominal" and "real," and assume their arguments that both nominal and real answers are wanted in a full theory of questions. The Montague framework is naturally suited for the development of multiple theories of real answers just because the intensional logic on which it is based is so richly supplied with abstract entities of various types. On the Hausser scheme, real answers are functions of a certain kind, functions which (roughly) map the meaning of interrogatives into propositions. Thus the extra-linguistic meaning of the nominal answer *John* will (roughly) map the meaning of *Who is a poet*? into the meaning of *John is a poet* and map the meaning of *Who kicked Sam*? into the meaning of *John kicked Sam*. On the Tichy scheme, the answer is an entity, and the question does the mapping; namely the question takes the set of all possible worlds as domain, and for each such world, the question delivers as value an entity of the appropriate type. Thus, the meaning of *Who kicked Sam*? might take the real world into the meaning of *John*. One of the fundamental differences between the Hausser and Tichy schemes is that the latter has built into its very foundation the presupposition that, for every question, there is exactly one full and complete true answer. The presupposition is that every question is what LQA called a "unique-answer question." I am so convinced of the falsity of this presupposition that I propose to call it *The Unique Answer Fallacy*. The counter-examples I have in mind include *Where is a place at which I can get gas on a Sunday*? *Who are some of your friends*? *What's the age of one of your children*? *What's in the basket*? To each of these, there are multiple answers, each of which is full and complete and true. Note that to the last both *some apples* and *three apples* count as full and complete; see below, Section 5.

On the Hamblin (1958), (1973) scheme, real answers are propositions; a question denotes the set of all its possible (propositional) answers. The Bennett (1977) scheme which preceded QMG also had real answers as propositions; however, a question was made to denote, at a world, not all possible answers, but just true ones at that world. (Bennett was following Karttunen, whom we discuss below.) The effect of this choice of Bennett, which was in effect carried over into QMG, was to make answerhood contingent; but the only contingency of answerhood is derived from truth. Perhaps this comes over most clearly as follows. We can give an account of what counts as a *possible* answer to a question. On the Bennett scheme, the answers to a question at a world are just those propositions which are possible answers, and are true at that world. According to the Hamblin scheme, in the spirit of the "absolute questions" of LQA, answerhood is noncontingent: the answers to a question at a world are always all the possible answers, not just the true ones. It is pretty clear that, given a certain Assumption, there is little choice between these views – each is (almost) translatable into the other. The Assumption, which the Montague framework allows to be clearly stated, is that if a proposition is an answer to a question in any world at all, it is also an answer in every world in which it is true. This assumption clearly holds for the QMG scheme, in some sense of 'clearly'. I mean that it is subject to rigorous proof, and that the proof has been carried out (in fact by Thomason) for some of the cases, but not in detail for all. Without the rigor of the Montague scheme it would not be possible to verify the Assumption at all.

Even with the Assumption, there is one substantive, though minor, difference between the two accounts of answer: the Hamblin scheme, and LQA, allow inconsistent answers, while the Bennett scheme does not. Thus Bennett gives only two possible answers to *Did Mary wear the red hat, the blue one, or the one which is both green and not green*? LQA would have thought there were three answers, one inconsistent. In my opinion not much hinges on this difference, though I do believe that it is in fact possible to answer a question with an inconsistency. Everyone allows answers which are wildly implausible, so why not answers which are inconsistent? Their absence, then, seems an artifact of Bennett (and also Karttunen and QMG) choices on this point, so that I would choose differently.

There is a more radical possibility for making answerhood contingent. Consider *Which man in the room is holding a martini*? and a candidate short answer, *Fred*. Everybody agrees that if Fred is a man in the room, then *Fred* represents a possible short answer: if he isn't holding a martini, we've got a false possible answer, and if he is holding a martini, a true one. But what if Fred does not even fall under the subject-term of the interrogative? What if Fred is not a man in the room? It is possible to have intuitions which suggest that in these circumstances, *Fred* doesn't represent an answer to the question at all – it's not just that it is false, but that unless Fred is a man in the room, it isn't even an answer to the question, any more than (say) *China is populous*. To cater to such intuitions would require a relativizing of answerhood to worlds in a much more radical way than the one chosen by Bennett (and Karttunen and QMG); but at this point in time, the suggestion has not been worked out in detail for English (see Belnap, 1972, for its realization in connection with a formal language of questions and answers). It would likely cohere with a reworking of Montague which quite generally gave different semantic roles to "subject" and "predicate" (old fashioned senses), as in Gupta (1978) and (in a different way) Hausser (1976b).

I said above that Bennett followed Karttunen; and indeed for both, the denotation of a question at a world is a set of true propositions. But this very similarity can be (and I think has been) a source of confusion. For on the one hand, the members of the Bennett (and Hamblin) sets are (full and complete) answers, while on the other hand, the members of the Karttunen set are not themselves answers. Rather, the Karttunen question denotes "the set of propositions which in that situation *jointly* constitute a complete and true answer to the question" (1976); my italics). That is, although Bennett and Karttunen both have a set of true propositions as the denotation of an interrogative or indirect question, the two sets do not play the same role; for Bennett the set is a set of answers; for Karttunen, the set is itself the answer, while its members must be taken *jointly* for complete answerhood. (Sometimes Karttunen himself talks as if the propositions in the set were answers, e.g. when he is relating his work to Hamblin in Karttunen (1976); but the more studied formulations are always as the one quoted; and so is the *use* of the apparatus. I might mention that when Bennett and I were working together, neither of us clearly saw the difference in the schemes, thinking ourselves closer to Karttunen than in fact we were.)

What about the choice between the Bennett and the Karttunen schemes? It *does* make a difference. In fact, Karttunen questions always have a unique answer, because (a) obviously denotation is unique, and (b) the answer is itself the denotation. Note the use of "the" in the Karttunen quote above – "*the* set of propositions . . . " Hence he commits (in my judgement) The Unique Answer Fallacy, and cannot handle questions to which there are multiple full and complete true answers. The Bennett scheme is therefore richer, since it can do that easily.

Of course, if I am wrong about The Data and in fact there are in English no questions other than those with a unique answer, the criticism is weakened. But I still would make it, for the Karttunen decision builds into the foundation of one's way of understanding questions that there *couldn't* be a language with an interrogative form which asked (for example) for examples: *What's an example of a prime between 10 and 20*? was the favorite example of LQA.

The upshot is that among schemes which let interrogatives denote sets of propositions, I prefer Bennett to Karttunen strongly, because Karttunen commits The Unique Alternative Fallacy (I hope you're not put off by the repetitive rhetoric here; after all, it is only Rhetoric). And I prefer Hamblin to Bennett weakly, because Bennett cannot permit inconsistent answers.

But what I really hanker for is the scheme mentioned above which makes answerhood contingent in a much more radical way than either Bennett or Karttunen.

Now for QMG. With respect to comparisons with the above, it goes along with Bennett. But in order to allow quantification into questions, there is a technical difference: on the QMG scheme, questions denote not sets of propositions per se, but sets of "open propositions," which are mappings from sequences of individuals into propositions. The sequences are in effect, à la Tarski, "assignments of values to the variables." The election of open propositions instead of plain ones was forced by deep and important but still technical reasons arising out of the desire to handle the aforementioned quantification into questions. But the spirit remains that of the Bennett scheme described above.

2.3 *Nominal answers*. Every complete theory of questions ought also to have some views about nominal (linguistic) answers. In the Montague framework, this means at least: nominal answers must be linguistic entities which (under translation) denote real answers. The QMG scheme, as it stands, gives no more information than that about nominal answers; and indeed even that much is only implicit. The following is designed to make the QMG theory of nominal answers explicit; comments come after.

First note that the types of translations of English sentences in QMG are open truth-values of IL, i.e., functions from sequences of individuals into truth-values; and translations of English interrogatives are of the type of sets of open propositions (sets of functions from sequences of individuals into propositions). So let φ' be the QMG translation in IL of English declarative φ, and let ψ' be the QMG translation of English (direct or indirect) interrogative ψ in IL. φ' (in IL) will then denote an open truth-value and ψ' (in IL) will denote a set of open propositions. Then two definitions of "φ is a logically possible answer to ψ" suggest themselves.

First definition. φ is a *logically possible answer to* ψ just in case the only thing that stands between it and answerhood is truth; i.e., whenever φ is true, the open proposition it expresses counts as an answer to ψ. Also, it must be consistent. Technically, $\exists s\varphi'(s)$ must be consistent, and for every indirect interpretation A of the QMG fragment, A-assignment g, and point of reference $\langle w, t\rangle$, if $\exists s\varphi'(s)$ is true with respect to A, w, t, g, then so is $\psi'(\lambda s[{}^{\wedge}\varphi'(s)])$.

Second definition. φ is a *logically possible answer to* ψ just in case it is possible that the open proposition it expresses is an answer to ψ; technically: $\psi'(\lambda s[{}^{\wedge}\varphi'(s)])$ is consistent.

By the Assumption discussed a little while ago, these two definitions are equivalent. And since it is hard to choose between them, we have additional evidence that a scheme which does not allow proof of the Assumption is probably defective.

While I am on this topic, I offer one more bit of evidence. On the QMG scheme, there are two natural definitions of the *presuppositions* of a question. One is: propositions or sentences which are implied by every possible answer. Another is: propositions or sentences which must be true if the question is to have some true answer. Only if the Assumption is true do these two equally plausible candidates turn out to be equivalent.

Example. With reference to QMG, let *A* and *B* be sentences of the fragment. Then *A* & –*B* and –*A* & *B* are logically possible answers to *whether A or B*. And every other logically possible answer to this question is logically equivalent to one of these. Also, *Fred kicked Sam* is not, but *the person who kicked Sam is Fred* is, a logically possible answer to (1) (allowing for small additions in the fragment).

2.4 *The distributivity principle and test.* There are a number of verbs like *know, remember*, and *tell* which take as complements both indirect questions (nominalized interrogatives) and nominalized sentences (e.g., *that*-clauses). Now consider: to know whether China is populous is to know some answer to the question as to whether China is populous; to remember which person kicked Sam is to remember some answer to the question as to which person kicked Sam; to tell Peter what time it is is to tell Peter some answer to the question as to what time it is. I want to generalize; to do so I use substitutional quantification in-and-out-of quotes. (Belnap and Grover, 1973) Let "IQ" range substitutionally over indirect questions and let "P" range substitutionally over sentences.

DISTRIBUTIVITY PRINCIPLE. For each IQ, to *know* IQ is to *know* some answer to the question as to IQ. Ditto for *remember, tell*, etc.

This principle is perhaps not exactly true (see for instance Powers, 1978), but it is a pretty good approximation. I call it the "distributivity principle" because it distributes the *know* (etc.) "inside" the question and onto its answers (see QMG's meaning postulates). And it leads to the following necessary condition for answerhood:

DISTRIBUTIVITY TEST: For any P and IQ, let the following inference fail:

Sally knows that P

Sally knows IQ

Then "P" is *not* an answer to "IQ"; or, in indirect discourse, that P is not an answer to the question as to IQ. The same holds with other names in place of *Sally*, and verbs such as *remember* and *tell* in place of *know*. The same holds for the direct question (interrogative) corresponding to the indirect question "IQ".

The fact that the inference does hold is not enough to guarantee that "P" is an answer to "IQ"; for example, "P" might obviously entail some answer to "IQ" without itself being such an answer. I only claim that the fact that it doesn't hold is enough to *rule out* a candidate "P" as an answer to "IQ".

I note that for our purposes we may equate the failure of the inference with the consistency of the following:

Sally knows that P *but Sally doesn't know* IQ.

If that is consistent, then "P" is not an answer to "IQ".

EXAMPLES. *Peter knows that China is populous but he doesn't know which person kicked Sam.* This is consistent, so *China is populous* is not an answer to *which person kicked Sam*? *Mary remembered that a redhead kicked Sam, but Mary didn't remember which person kicked Sam.* This is consistent, so *a red head kicked Sam* is not an answer to the question. *Peter knows that the person who kicked Sam is John but Peter doesn't know who kicked Sam.* This is inconsistent, which makes it likely (but doesn't guarantee) that *the person who kicked Sam is John* is an answer to the question.

3. QUANTIFYING INTO QUESTIONS

Belnap (1972) suggested a formalism for making interrogatives out of (open) interrogatives by quantification, just as quantifiers can make declaratives out of (open) declaratives. Bennett (1979) argues that the phenomenon of quantifiers having wide scope with respect to *wh* worlds actually happens in English, citing the triple ambiguity of

John wonders where two unicorns live.

There is of course (1) the reading such that John, for each of two (actual)

unicorns, wonders where they live, and (2) the reading such that he wonders where the single place is where two unicorns live. Neither of these require quantification into interrogatives. (3) The third reading, which makes *two unicorns* wide with respect to *where* but still inside *wonder*, is the one such that John is envisaging each unicorn living in a different place. If *wonder* meant *wants to know* (it doesn't), then the third reading is the one which would scope *two unicorns* between *wants* and *know*: John wants it to be that he knows for each of two unicorns, where it lives.

An even clearer argument for the necessity of treating some quantifiers in interrogatives as having wide scope (but not having declaratives as their scope) comes from *depend* examples such as

> *What the average grade is depends (only) on what grade each student receives*

Obviously the scope of *each* cannot be the whole declarative; for it is not true that for each student, the average grade depends (only) on what grade that student receives. Nor can the scope of *each* be inside the *what*, for that would presuppose that each student received the same grade. Instead, one has to look at *what grade each student received* as a closed unit – an indirect question which is a complement of *depend* – in which *each* is wide with respect to *what*.

The strength of this argument depends, incidentally, on a thesis (Karttunen) to which I am much attached: no theory of questions is worthwhile unless it can account for both direct and indirect questions, and indirect questions in *every* mode of embedding. This is a historical remark; there was a stage at which the Åqvist-Hintikka epistemic theory was helpful even though it could not account for embeddings of indirect questions in *ask, wonder, tell*, etc., much less inside *depend* or *matter*. But at the present stage, the epistemic theory is of only limited usefulness – as a theory about English interrogatives, as opposed to a theory as to how much erotetic logic can be found inside epistemic logic, which is an entirely different and unrelated matter.

QMG makes an interesting application of quantification into queries to produce an argument against the identification of direct questions with *I ask you* plus an indirect question (the performative analysis). For the fact is that the direct question

> *Where do two unicorns live*?

has *two* readings, depending on varying the scopes of *two unicorns* and *where*, while

> *I ask you where two unicorns live*

has *three* readings, including the one where *two unicorns* has widest scope, so that the truth of the sentence implies the actual existence of unicorns. Since 3 ≠ 2, the two forms of speech are not semantically interchangeable.

This ambiguity of quantification into questions leads, not unexpectedly, to an ambiguity with respect to cross-sentential anaphors. Consider:

> *Let us pretend that there are two unicorns. And let us first ask where they live.*

Where each lives, or where they all live together?

These cases, it seems to me, force the view that English permits derivation of interrogatives from interrogatives by quantifier introduction (what I call "quantification into questions"). One more clear case, and a distinctively erotetic one at that: *Mary asked Bill where two unicorns live* or *Mary asked Bill what each of his children's age was* must have readings in which the quantifiers have middle scope – neither the whole declarative (because that would imply a falsehood, the existence of unicorns), nor inside the *wh* (which would imply Mary's concern for a single dwelling place for the two unicorns, or a single age for the children). Other cases are not so clear, e.g., *John knows where two unicorns live*. Undoubtedly Hintikka should be in a position to throw light on the difference or identity between the wide and middle scope in this case, since his apparatus is geared to distinguishing what happens when quantifier scopes are wide or narrow with respect to *know*. But at present his program cannot help directly, because his game-theoretical semantics does not allow *any* categorematic meaning to *where two unicorns live*. That is, it is not enough simply to trot out a couple of formulas in epistemic logic which are then claimed to correspond to the two readings. What further is required is information as to how these formulas are related to the *structure* of the English sentence, information such as that provided by the Montague program.

Having established (as I think) the necessity for quantification into questions, I regret being forced to report that catering to this feature of English interrogatives requires a good deal of complication. I do not think the complication is avoidable except by denying the phenomenon, which I suppose some will do.

Let me try to outline the central idea, using a device or two to oversimplify. First the syntax. (Undoubtedly there are some contraints on quantification into questions; but I don't know what they are and so say nothing about them.) What I am explicating is the introduction of quantifier words into interrogatives (direct or indirect). The derivation of these is from three components: a quantifier word (determiner), a common noun phrase, and an (open) interrogative (direct or indirect). Also one needs to know at which variable the quantification is being introduced. An example will suffice:

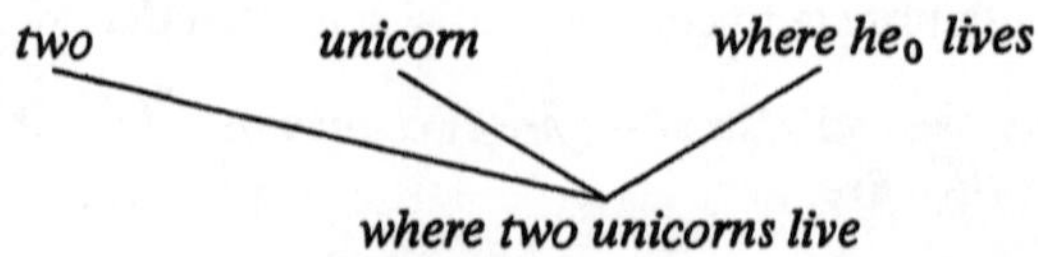

Two could be replaced by any other quantifier word such as *each, a, the, at least one*. The common noun phrase could be complex. (The reason the quantifier word and the common noun phrase enter into the derivation separately is that we appear to need the meaning of the latter, as well as the meaning of *two unicorns*, to get the right meaning for *where two unicorns live* – looking ahead, the separate need for the common noun occurs in clause (2b) of the example on p. 182. I note here that it is not certain that appearance is reality; there is a possibility, arising out of considerations revolving around *what*-questions, that the meaning of *two unicorns* is enough. But the matter is complicated, and I postpone consideration of it for another occasion.)

Now the semantics. The central idea is that an answer to the derived question must answer the ingredient open question (with respect to he_0) for two unicorns; that is, for two unicorn-values of he_0, the answer must tell us where these values live. More generally, if an interrogative is derived according to the above pattern from a quantifier word, common noun, and interrogative open at he_0, then each answer to it must provide answers to the ingredient open interrogative for "quantifier-word common-noun" values of he_0. Thus, answers to *where at least one unicorn lives* must tell us, for *at least one unicorn*, where he lives; answers to *where each unicorn lives* must tell us, for *each unicorn*, where he lives; and answers to *where a unicorn lives* must tell us, for *a unicorn*, where he lives. And this makes sense regardless of whether the interrogative is direct or indirect (nominalized).

One example of some interest is a quantification into a *whether*:

whether the king of France is bald

derived from

the; *king of France*; *whether* he_0 *is bald*

On the above recipe, an answer must tell, for *the present king of France*, whether he is bald; so that since there is no present king of France, the question cannot have any true answers. It is not, that is, a "proper yes-no question" (LQA) even if we use the Russell (and Montague) theory of *the*.

There are a number of choices to be made at this point for carrying out this vaguely arm-waved scheme. One of the most important ones, made already by QMG, is that an answer must not only provide an answer for two unicorns (for example), but must in effect say that it does. This we might call the "internal" view of answerhood. The choice renders answerhood noncontingent up to truth. For example, let A be an answer if it says where a and b live, and *also* says that $\{a, b\}$ is a set of two unicorns, so that in effect it is saying of itself that it is telling us where two unicorns live. This is the "internal" view, and we can see that A will tell us where two unicorns live in any world in which it is true, so that answerhood will be noncontingent "up to truth". In contrast, suppose we make A say only where a and b live, and put as an *external* constraint that to be an answer, $\{a, b\}$ must be a set of two unicorns. Given that the unicornhood of a and b is a contingent matter, we can see that this view – the external view – would make answerhood much more radically contingent: there could be worlds in which A is true, but not an answer (since $\{a, b\}$ could be not a set of two unicorns, even though A truly told us where a and b live).

I think the external or contingent view of answerhood needs exploring in detail, but the first thing to do is get at least one view laid out in full splendor; so this other task is left for another occasion, and I confine myself to the internal view, as in QMG.

As an intermediate state between the total arm-waving above and the full IL formalism below, I offer a simplified and also slightly distorted picture of what is going on, a picture drawn in quasi-formalism and quasi-English, with use-mention confusions thrown in. Switching examples, consider

ψ = *whom two redheads love*

as coming from *two*, *redhead*, and

φ = *whom* he_0 *loves*

by quantifier introduction. What we are after is the set ψ' of answers to ψ; ψ' will be a set of propositions. We are given the set of answers to φ. But evidently because of the presence of he_0, in φ, these answers have in some sense to be "open", and for this reason we must suppose defined not merely what it is to be an answer to φ, but what it is to be a y-answer to S with respect to he_0, where "y" tells us what value to give to he_0. A y-answer to φ with respect to he_0 will then be a proposition. By an *answer to* φ *with respect to* he_0 we mean a y-answer to φ, for some y, with respect to he_0.

We demand of each answer to ψ the following. It must be a proposition O such that

(1) O is true

and there is a property of individuals **P** and a function-in-intension f from individuals to propositions such that O says (where $^{\vee}f$ is the extension of f, and $^{\vee}\mathbf{P}$ of **P**):

(2a) two redheads are members of $^{\vee}\mathbf{P}$,

and for any y, if y is in $^{\vee}\mathbf{P}$, then

(2b) y is a redhead, and
(3a) $^{\vee}f(y)$ is a y-answer to φ (= *whom* he_0 *loves*) with respect to he_0, and
(3b) $^{\vee}f(y)$ is true.

This may be understood as follows. Each answer O is "based on" a property **P** of individuals and a function-in-intension of f from individuals into propositions. O must of course be true, by (1). Further, by (2a, b) $^{\vee}\mathbf{P}$ must be constituted by two redheads – these are the entities for which O provides an answer to *whom* he_0 *loves* with respect to he_0. The function $^{\vee}f$ is what tells us what true (by 3b) φ-answers (by 3a) go with each entity in $^{\vee}\mathbf{P}$. So altogether O does in fact truly answer φ (with respect to he_0) for two redheads, and tells us it is doing so. The following is the right picture to have in mind of a typical answer O:

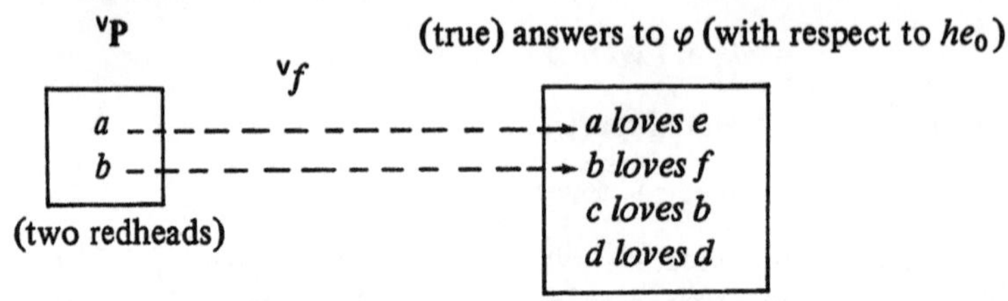

(I have written *a loves b* for *the person who loves b is a*, for brevity.)

I hope you can see that this idea generalizes immediately to (a) any quantifier word in place of *two*, (b) any common noun phrase in place of *redhead*, and (c) any open interrogative in place of *whom* he_0 *loves*. For example, a picture of an answer to *whether the present king of the Belgians is bald* is as follows:

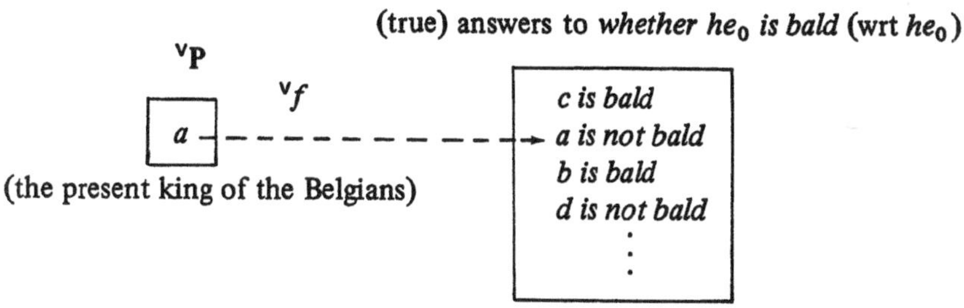

Still, the above won't do as it stands – complications are concealed by the simplicity of the example.

The first complication is that we need the concept of an "open proposition" to be an answer to an interrogative with a free variable, e.g., *whom* he_0 *loves*. If our answers were linguistic, then we could use for answers to this the familiar category of open sentences, e.g., *the person* he_0 *loves is b*, but we need an answer as an abstract entity with which to do our Montague calculating. Nor can we assume that he_0 is our only variable, or that there is only one. The evident solution (as Thomason explained) was to represent what are in effect assignments of values to the various he_n *inside* IL by means of sequences of individuals – the *n*-th member of the sequence being (in effect) the assignment of he_n – and then to define an *open proposition* as a function from sequences to propositions (which of course are sets of worlds, or mappings from worlds to truth-values). By themselves such entities aren't much, but for answers to open questions we gather them into sets – and one can see that a "set of open propositions" can do entirely different work than an "open set of propositions." For the latter, a single fixing of the value of the variable fixes a set of (plain) propositions. But the former allows the "variable of" each open proposition to be fixed independently. It is in the abstract realm as if one had a set of open sentences such as [he_0 *loves a*, he_0 *loves b*, he_0 *loves c*, he_0 *loves d*], where one had a binding operation on the set which could give the various he_0's *different* values; and a look at our picture above of a typical answer to *whom two redheads love* will cause you to see that such is exactly what is required.

The second complication depends on this: whenever one needs open whatsems (i.e., functions from sequences of individuals to whatsems) of any type in a Montague scheme, one is likely to need open whatsems of every type, for one must reflect in a uniform way the presence of the he_n in phrases of all types. And so it happens here. But after all, though this is a technical complication, it is not one in spirit; for the extension of e.g., the open common noun phrase *woman who loves* him_0 *ought* to be a function from sequences of individuals (capable of fixing the value of the variable) into sets of individuals. It is only an accident, as it were, that has heretofore allowed a simpler treatment.

When we introduce these complications, and try to say everything in strict Montaguese, we get the following. (This represents a slight variation on the details of QMG.)

To fix the types of our variables, we give the type of the extension of the variable as follows (also consult QMG):

x, y:	individuals
n:	nonnegative integers
s, r:	sequences of individuals (thought of as, in effect, assigning the n-th member of the sequence to the variable him_n)
P:	sets of individuals
$\mathbf{P}$:	properties of individuals (so $^{\vee}\mathbf{P}$ is a set)
C:	open sets of individuals; i.e., functions from sequences into sets – the type of the translation of common nouns.
O, N:	open propositions: functions from sequences into propositions (i.e., into functions from worlds to truth-values)
Y:	set of open propositions
X:	property of open propositions (so $^{\vee}X$ is a set of them)
f:	functions-in-intension from individuals into open propositions; $^{\vee}f$ is a function from individuals into open propositions.

Also one bit of notation, which we merely describe, but which is formally definable in IL (see QMG):

$s[x/n]$ is that sequence of individuals which is like s everywhere except at n, and which has x as its n-th entry.

This notation can be used in defining another concept.

$$M[y/n] = \lambda r \cdot M(r[y/n])$$

Think of the open proposition M as a "propositional function," i.e., a mapping from individuals into propositions. This will be "true enough" if for every sequence s, $M(s)$ depends only the n-th member of s. Then $M[y/n]$ can be usefully thought of as the (ordinary) proposition which results when M (thought of as a propositional function) is applied to the individual y. (This is formally not quite accurate, since $M[y/n]$ is itself an open proposition; but when $M(s)$ depends only on the n-th member of s, $M[y/n]$ will be a *constant* open proposition, which may, near enough, be identified with its value for any s.)

I shall omit brackets wherever it seems reasonable, and also add them from time to time. I shall follow Church's use of dots: a dot is a left parenthesis, whose mate is "as far away as possible," either at the end of the expression or at the end of the parenthetical part within which the dot occurs. I shall also use horizontal strokes to indicate matching brackets (when things get tough).

One change from QMG is to give each quantifier-word a categorematic translation – not to be cute, but to highlight (1) that quantifier-words work alike throughout the fragment, and (2) that they have exactly the same categorematic meaning when introduced into interrogatives as they do when introduced into declaratives – though of course the "introduction rules" are different. I take (2) to be important – the quantifiers are *not* ambiguous as occurring in declaratives and in interrogatives, and this treatment shows it.

The translations of the three quantifier-words of QMG are as follows (these are standard, and it is obvious others could be added on a like pattern):

$$a' = \lambda C \cdot \lambda s \cdot \lambda P \cdot \bigvee x \cdot C(s)(x) \wedge P(x)$$
$$every' = \lambda C \cdot \lambda s \cdot \lambda P \cdot \bigwedge x \cdot C(s)(x) \rightarrow P(x)$$
$$the' = \lambda C \cdot \lambda s \cdot \lambda P \cdot \bigvee x \cdot [\bigwedge y \cdot C(s)(x) \longleftrightarrow \cdot y{=}x] \wedge P(x)$$

The following simply says that to say an open proposition is true is to say its extension is satisfied by some sequence:

$$True(O) \longleftrightarrow \bigvee r[{}^{\vee}O(r)]$$

In the following, think of Y as a question. Then we may read "$Ans\,(N, Y, y, n)$" as "N is a y-answer to Y with respect to the n-th variable."

$$Ans\,(N, Y, y, n) \longleftrightarrow \bigvee M \cdot Y(M) \wedge N = M[y/n]$$

That is, whenever the members of Y can be thought of as propositional functions, N can be thought of as the result of applying one of them to y. Again, $Ans(N, Y, y, n)$ may be read: N is a y-answer to Y with respect to n (or, with respect to the n-th sequence position); thus, N may be thought of as answering Y "for" y. For instance, if Y is the pair of open propositions correlated with *he*$_0$ *walks* and *he*$_0$ *doesn't walk*, so that Y is correlated with *whether he*$_0$ *walks*, and if y is the entity correlated with *John*, then $Ans(N, Y, y, O)$ just in case N is in effect one of the propositions expressed by *John walks* or *John doesn't walk*. (A little more accurately: N must be an open proposition having one of these propositions as its constant value.) For it is good to think of *John walks* as answering *whether he*$_0$ *walks* "for" John; of *Bill walks* as answering it "for" Bill; etc.

We now have enough definitions to present the semantics of quantification into interrogatives. First we use the availability of categorematic quantifier words to gather the syntactical rules S12–S14 into a single rule, using "P_{SQ}" for the set of singular quantifier words, "P_{CN}" for common noun phrases, and "P_{IQ}" for indirect questions (nominalized interrogatives); and also "B_{CN}" for basic common nouns:

S12–14. If $_n$ is a numerical subscript, $\alpha \in P_{\mathrm{SQ}}$, $\eta \in P_{\mathrm{CN}}$, and $\varphi \in P_{\mathrm{IQ}}$, then $F_{11}(_n, \alpha, \eta, \varphi) \in P_{\mathrm{IQ}}$, where $F_{11}(_n, \alpha, \eta, \varphi)$ comes from φ by performing the following operations: (i) replacing the first occurrence, if there is one, of *he*$_n$ or *him*$_n$, whichever is first, by the concatenation of α and η (adjusting to *a* or *an*, if required); (ii) replacing all remaining occurrences of *he*$_n$ or *him*$_n$ by *he*, *she*, or *it*; or *him*, *her*, or *it*; according as the gender of the member of B_{CN} that occurs first in η is masculine, feminine, or neuter.

I note the following change from QMG: φ there had to be in P_{BQ}, the family of "basic questions," which have not in QMG been subject to the introduction of a *which with preposition*. I do not fully understand this feature of QMG, and may therefore be making a mistake. But I do not think I am, since I also believe in other changes which would totally abandon QMG's requirement for basic questions as a category additional to that for indirect questions; these concern multiple *wh*'s, Section 4 below.

Finally the semantics corresponding to this syntax:

T12–14. If $_n$ is a numerical subscript, $\alpha \in P_{\mathrm{SQ}}$, $\eta \in P_{\mathrm{CN}}$, and $\varphi \in P_{\mathrm{IQ}}$; and if α, η, φ, translate into α', η', φ' respectively, then $F_{11}(_n, \alpha, \eta, \varphi)$ translates into the following term denoting a set of open propositions:

$$\begin{array}{ll} & \lambda O. \\ (1) & True(O) \wedge \\ & \mathrm{V}P\mathrm{V}f \cdot O = \lambda s \cdot {}^\wedge . \end{array}$$

(2a) $\alpha'(\eta')(s)({}^{\vee}\mathbf{P}) \wedge$
$\wedge y \{ [{}^{\vee}\mathbf{P}](y) \rightarrow$
(2b) $\eta'(s)(y) \wedge$
(3a) $Ans([{}^{\vee}f](y), \varphi', y, n) \wedge$
(3b) ${}^{\vee}[[{}^{\vee}f](y)(s)] \}$

It will not do to try to explain this line by line; instead, I have numbered the lines for comparison with the example worked out above on p. 182 – the example gives the real explanation of what is going on.

A penultimate word. Early Karttunen, and Karttunen-Peters, did not allow for quantification into questions, but Karttunen and Peters (1979) treats the topic explicitly and informatively. Their treatment is, however, limited *a priori* by their foundational commitment to unique-answer questions (which constitutes, you recall from Section 2.2, their committing the Unique Answer Fallacy). Thus, they are able to treat *What grade is deserved by each of your students*? because this question expects a uniquely true answer – it is what LQA called a "complete list question"; and up to order and such like, there can be exactly one complete list of students together with the grade each deserves. (I am assuming the disambiguation which takes *each of your students* as having wide scope.) But they do not discuss interrogatives like *What grade is deserved by two or three of your students*? with *two or three of your students* having the wide scope. My view is that they do not discuss such questions solely because of the foundational commitment mentioned above. Further, I think that were they to include them, Karttunen and Peters, like QMG, would have to introduce complications tantamount to open propositions and their cousins; but I am not so certain of this that I would care to bet.

A final word. We have treated quantifier-phrases as, essentially, producing a new interrogative when introduced into an interrogative. Elsewhere of course quantifier-phrases produce declaratives, which evidently leads one to suppose that one will need clauses which treat their introduction into imperatives as producing imperatives, and even to imagine that they might be needed elsewhere. For example, *the average grade depends on the grade of each boy* gives the appearance of requiring that *the grade of each boy* be a unit, with *each* having wide scope in it – derived, I suppose, from *each boy* and *the grade of* him_0. But perhaps instead *the grade of each boy* should be looked on as a disguised indirect question, a nominalization of *what is the grade of each boy*? Either way, there are subtleties needing attention.

4. MULTIPLE *which*

Everyone with a theory of questions relying on logical techniques of some kind is fascinated by multiple *wh*-questions such as *which woman loves which man*, for it is precisely formalism which can handle the complications induced by such questions. Such theorizers generally take considerable pride in the way their theories treat multiple *wh*-questions. Still, it seems sure that such questions are almost entirely absent from any *real* corpus, (R. Lang, personal communication) so that (a) it is not all that important that a theory be able to treat them, and (b) we *must* recognize that our data about them is miniscule.

On the other hand, we do seem to be able to parse them and to make a certain amount of sense out of them; we tend to understand them, and to know how to answer them, at least to a rough approximation. (See Bolinger, 1978, for a rich source of data interestingly worked over.) So it is good to try to treat them. (A *logic* of questions which tries to go beyond ordinary language should *certainly* treat them. See LQA.)

The only question I should like to address concerning them is whether we should take them as arising by introduction of the *wh*'s one at a time, or whether the *wh*'s should be thought of as being simultaneously introduced. That is, should the tree for *which woman loves which man* be the first or second of the following?

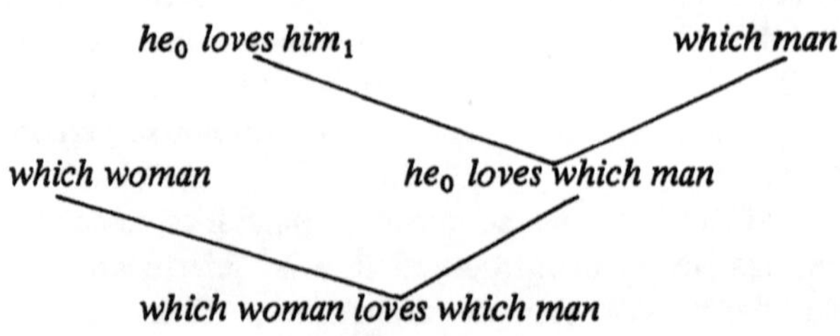

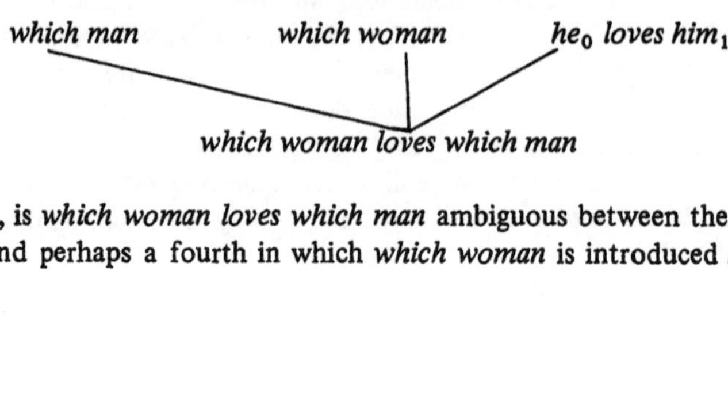

Or, thirdly, is *which woman loves which man* ambiguous between these two readings, and perhaps a fourth in which *which woman* is introduced *before*

which man? My present view is that the only correct theory is that of simultaneous introduction: the question is asking for a unique pair such that first member of the pair is a woman and loves the second, who is a man. It presupposes that there is exactly one woman-man pair with the woman loving the man. QMG took a different position, insisting that the only correct theory is that of one-at-a-time introduction. Then the presupposition would be that there is exactly one woman such that she loves exactly one man, a different story entirely. (Bennett never departed from this view, even in the face of explicit efforts at counter-persuasion. For this reason, I think the one-at-a-time view should be borne carefully in mind.)

One's intuitions concerning this may correlate with intuitions about multiple introduction of quantifiers. Consider *exactly one woman loves exactly one man*. On a standard Montague view, this has two readings, one of which is that exactly one woman is such that she loves exactly one man. But I think it has a reading on which it means precisely that there is exactly one man-woman pair, the woman loving the man. Out of *three bosses gave gifts to three secretaries*, I get just three givings, not at least nine, and *one boss gave a gift to one secretary* gives me only one gift-giving, ruling out the possibility that some of the bosses gave gifts to a number of secretaries. Think of the following. Father: *Was there any kissing at the party last night*? Daughter: *Oh, Daddy, one boy kissed one girl*. Mother (normal): *Good*. Father (logician): *So how many did the rest of them kiss*?

In any event, though this introduces complications over and beyond those in QMG in certain directions – namely, the need for rules governing multiple introduction of *which*'s – it leads to a simplification in another direction – the apparatus of basic questions was needed only (I think) to make sure that no *which*'s were introduced after the *which* occurring (by preposition) first in the question. (I *think* this was also Karttunen's only motivation for "proto-questions".) That is, QMG let *which*-introduction lead from basic question to basic question, unless preposition occurred, in which case an indirect question was created. And QMG allowed no *which*-introduction into indirect questions. But if repeated *which*-introduction is prohibited, then one can (I think) eliminate the category of basic questions altogether. *Which*-introduction (possibly multiple) can be directly into declarative sentences (instead of into basic questions) and can result directly in indirect questions (instead of basic questions), with preposition taking place upon introduction.

This altered format would tend to explain something otherwise mysterious – the impossibility of *which* and its friends (immediately) inside *whether*. The explanation would be this. First, our main hypothesis, that *wh*-introduction always has declaratives as its input and questions as its output, so that if there is more than one *wh*-word governing a question, the *wh*-words will have to be introduced simultaneously. Second, that *whether* is a kind of *wh*-word. And third, that (as far as I can see) there is no way to make semantic sense out of introducing *whether* and another *wh*-word simultaneously.

With respect to the first hypothesis, *of course* there is no trouble about *which man knows which woman loves John*; but those two *which*'s do not govern the same question. Nor on similar grounds is there trouble about *whether John knows which man Mary loves*. It is only the cousins of *whether Mary loves which man* that seem outrageous – with the usual exception of echo questions. And even then we ought to be careful about the conclusions we draw – it is not true that *which* cannot bind a position inside *whether*, but only that *which* cannot be introduced into a *whether*-question. If a declarative intervenes, all is well. That is, *which man is such that you asked me whether Mary loves him* is fine, coming from *which, man*, and he_0 *is such that you asked me whether Mary loves* him_0. (I suppose this is what *whether Mary loves which man* "means" when used – in the proper context – as an echo question by stressing *which*.) But this is straightforwardingly an introduction of *which* into a declarative.

With respect to multiple *wh*'s, one ought to cite Bach-Peters questions as examples which appear to quite require simultaneous introduction. Thomason has emphasized this. I have in mind examples like *which man that she loves finds which woman that he loves*. It seems impossible to get this by one-at-a-time introduction; and surely easy with multiple introduction, for it is asking for the pair $\langle a, b \rangle$ such that a is a man, b is a woman, b loves a, a loves b, and a finds b.

Thomason (1977) has supplied an exact syntax and semantics for this form of multiple introduction, as well as forms with *the* and *a*, and has a strong and therefore interesting hypothesis about how *which, the*, and *a* must be ordered in such multiple introduction. I subscribe to and recommend Thomason's theory.

The point, incidentally, is not that the semantics required is extra-heavy – ordinary first-order techniques are all that are called for. The point is that if semantics is to follow syntax, then the syntax must permit multiple *wh*-introduction, and not derive everything by one-at-a-time introduction, as in Montague. For example, the above example must come syntactically as follows:

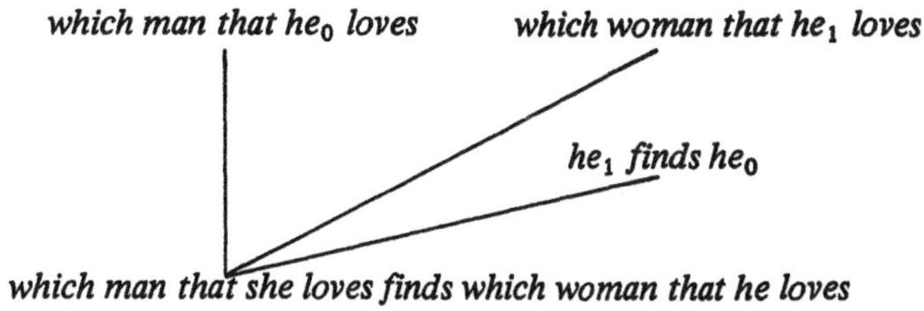

I do not have views on the syntax of multiple *wh*-questions, e.g., as to when *which*-introduction is possible and when not, and as to how the preposing is to be worked out properly. But when all the *wh*'s are singular *which*'s, and the introduction is syntactically possible, I think the semantics is straightforward. I also *think* that for singular *which*'s the semantics is independent of which *which* is preposed: *which woman loves which man* has the same semantic value as *which man which woman loves*; certainly it comes out that way on this theory.

But nothing follows from this about multiple *wh*'s where some are singular *which*'s and some are not; perhaps *which women love which man*? asks for a (unique) man for each woman, while *which man do which women love*? asks for a single man for all the women. These ought also be compared with the passives, *which man is loved by which women*? and (if it's English) *which women is which man loved by*?

I want now to proceed to the formal account of the introduction of multiple *which*, but first it seems best to indicate how the elimination of basic questions from QMG changes the QMG rule for the introduction of a single singular *which*. What follows corresponds most closely to S17 of QMG, and I so label it.

S17. If $_n$ is a numerical subscript, $\eta \in P_{\mathrm{CN}}$ (category of (singular) common noun phrases), $\varphi \in P_{\mathrm{T}}$ (declaratives), and φ contains an occurrence of either he_n or him_n, then $F_{16}(_n, \eta, \varphi) \in P_{\mathrm{IQ}}$ (indirect questions), where $F_{16}(_n, \eta, \varphi)$ comes from φ by performing the following operations in order: (i) replacing the first occurrence of he_n or him_n, whichever is first, by *which* η; (ii) replacing all remaining occurrences of he_n or him_n by *he*, *she*, or *it*; or *him, her*, or *it*, respectively, according as the gender of the member of B_{CN} (basic common noun) that occurs first in η is masculine, feminine, or neuter; (iii) preposing the occurrence of *which* η just inserted.

The semantic rule is that of T17 (= T11) of QMG, adjusted for the input being a declarative instead of an interrogative.

T17. If $_n$ is a numerical subscript, $\eta \in P_{\mathrm{CN}}$, $\varphi \in P_{\mathrm{T}}$, and φ contains an occurrence of either he_n or him_n, and η, φ translate into η', φ' respectively, then $F_{16}(_n, \eta, \varphi)$ translates into

$$
\begin{array}{l}
\lambda O. \\
\quad True(O) \wedge . \\
\quad \vee x \cdot O = \lambda s \cdot \wedge . \\
\quad\quad \wedge\, y \cdot [\eta'(s)(y) \wedge \varphi'(s[y/n])] \longleftrightarrow y = x
\end{array}
$$

EXAMPLE.

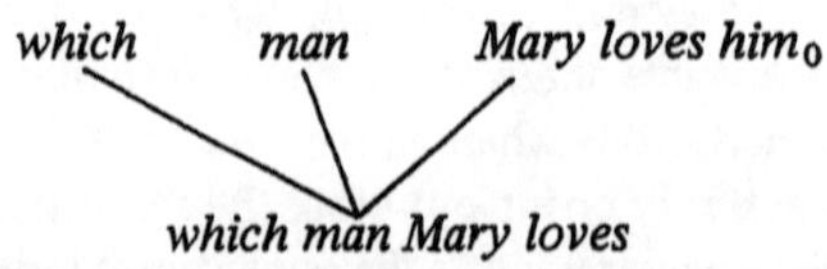

A logical answer to this will be equivalent to a sentence having the form *the man such that Mary loves him is John*. I believe this is "the" proper reconstruction of the short answer, *John*. I reject that *Peter knows that Mary loves John* implies *Peter knows which man Mary loves*; the case I have in mind has Mary loving many men, so that no one can know which man Mary loves, the question having no true answer. So by the Distributive Test, *Mary loves John* is not an answer. I explain the temptation to take the implication as holding by the observation that *Peter knows that Mary loves John* does indeed imply *Peter knows which man Mary loves* in the presence of an extra premise guaranteeing that the question has a true answer, that its presupposition is fulfilled; e.g., an extra premiss like *someone knows which man Mary loves* or even *there is a true answer to the question as to which man Mary loves*.

Of a piece with my narrow view of answers to *which*-questions is the ruling out of the substitution of just any miscellaneous term for *John*. I don't count *a redhead* or *the neighbors' son* as even short logically possible answers (though of course they are "appropriate responses"), invoking at this point the Distributivity Test. *Peter knows that the man such that Mary loves him is a redhead* is evidently consistent with *Peter doesn't know which man Mary loves*. The case for *the neighbors' son* is weaker; if this is used rigidly, as they say, then it would be acceptable, for rigidity is the essence of the Montague variable which figures in the translation. But if *the neighbors' son* is used in a wiggly way, it is not acceptable. Still, there is much disagreement about this, and one wants the various theories all formulated with care.

I note that these results are intended only for *singular which*. I also have views on plural *which* (see QMG, Section 5) and on other *wh*-words, but aside from a brief mention in Section 5 below, I omit them here. In any case, I think theories of singular *which* should not be tested by appeal to either plural *which* or by appeal to other questions-words, for I doubt that these other question-words are in fact "forms of" *which*. On my view, their answer-forms are not or might not be the same as those for *which*; so that unless one wants to explicitly argue from the data that they are, it is bad methodology and linguistic obfuscation to support a theory of singular *which* by appeal to these other question-words. For example, in considering *which man Scott is*, it will not do to substitute the possibly different question, *who Scott is*.

Now finally, for the technical unpacking of multiple *which*. As I said, I do not have a syntax for you, so that I can only give you the semantics.

Let $n_1, \ldots, n_m$ be numerical subscripts; let $\eta_1, \ldots, \eta_m \in P_{\text{CN}}$ (singular common noun phrases), and $\varphi \in P_{\text{T}}$ (declarative sentences). Let $\eta_1, \ldots, \eta_m$, φ translate as $\eta_1', \ldots, \eta_m', \varphi'$. Then the result of introducing *which* $\eta_1, \ldots,$ *which* η_m into φ at $n_1, \ldots, n_m$ is the following expression denoting (as is proper) a set of open propositions. I use "s^*" to abbreviate "$((\ldots(s[y_1/n_1])[y_2/n_2])\ldots)[y_m/n_m]$".

$$\begin{aligned}&\lambda O.\\ &\quad True(O) \wedge\\ &\quad \vee x_1 \ldots \vee x_m \cdot O = \lambda s \cdot {}^\wedge \cdot\\ &\qquad\quad \wedge y_1 \ldots \wedge y_m \cdot [\eta_1'(s^*)(y_1) \wedge \ldots \wedge \eta_m'(s^*)(y_m) \wedge\\ &\qquad\qquad \varphi'(s^*)] \longleftrightarrow \cdot\, y_1 = x_1 \wedge \ldots \wedge y_m = x_m\end{aligned}$$

I note that nothing extra is required for Bach-Peters questions; they already all come out right.

(But universality cannot be claimed for the above; Karttunen-Peters are surely right that not all multiple singular *which*-questions presuppose a unique m-tuple. For example, *which boy is assigned to which room*? can be used to ask for a *list* of pairs.)

5. DIFFERENT *wh's* SHOULD BE TREATED DIFFERENTLY

The bold or simple generalization that all *wh*'s can be treated alike has now had a long enough run for its money. The time has come to recognize that each question-word must be treated on its own, and that furthermore there can be more than one use of the same *wh*-word. All this is obvious enough, provided one pays attention to answerhood as-it-really-is and doesn't try to bend the facts to fit a false theory. And also its truth is widely recognized, but also widely ignored, which is the purpose of my coming down on the side of the angels.

For one thing, contrary to QMG, it is false that the following always hold (and true that they sometimes hold): *where* = *which place, who* = *which person, what* = *which thing*. Take *where is John going*? or *where John is going*, or (echo form) *John is going where*? Here *where* takes the position of an adverb, not, like *which place*, the position of a term. *Which place is John going*? ain't good grammar. *Where John is going*, then, should come from

where; John is going adverb$_0$,

with *adverb*$_0$ a variable which is presumably also available for quantification by *everywhere* and *somewhere*. Exactly how the semantics should go for this form of *where*-introduction has not been fully thought out, and so I do not offer a Montague clause. But I do have two questions to raise. First, is *where John is going* the same as the bastard-English, *which adverb is such that John is going* (*that adverb*)? That is, can we copy the Montague clause for *which*-introduction, but let the range be the appropriate type for adverbs instead of the type of individuals? I doubt it, chiefly because I think *which*-questions can have only one (true) fully complete answer whereas we can have both *where John is going is to the building at State at Main* and, nonequivalently, *where John is going is to a movie* – both as fully complete true answers. Second, is *where John is coming from* the same as *which place John is coming from*? I doubt it.

Who is perhaps the worst, but as in the case of *where*, I shall only raise some questions. It is incredible that Hintikka should have taken *John knows who Peter is* as a kind of well-understood English phrase on which to *base* philosophical reflections, for *who Peter is* and its direct form *who is Peter*? are radically ambiguous. (There are many who have a different opinion on this matter, but they are wrong, and seem to me to have obtained their opinions not by studying the data, but instead by wishing to save their theories. Still, I tell you of this, for you, too, may have a theory you wish to save.) The first clue as to ambiguity is syntactic: there are a number of possible sources for *who is Peter*?:

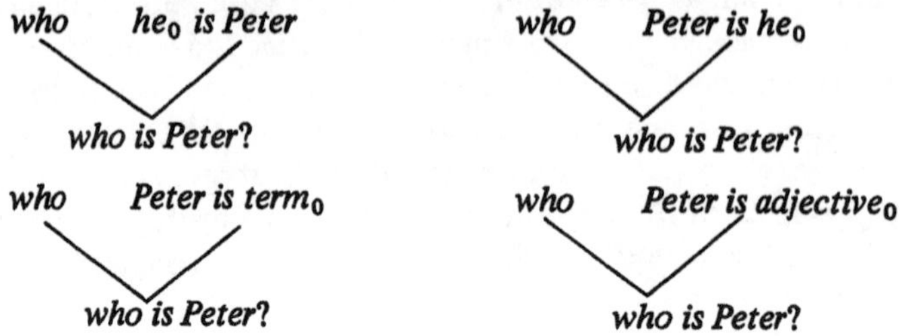

That is, we can distinguish between the echo-question *who is Peter*? and the echo-question *Peter is who*? (either side of *is* may be questioned), and also in the latter case, the syntactic category of *who* may be thought to be proper-name-like, or term-like, or adjective-like, since all of these may sensibly follow *is*. We should not assume that any of these derivations give rise to precisely the same question as any other. But as a matter of fact, it seems to me the top two are equivalent, and that when questioning he_0, reading *who* as *which person* is all right: *which person Peter is* can have as answers either *that man over there is Peter*, or *Peter is that man over there*, and it doesn't matter which. The bottom left entry might have as an answer *Peter is a bricklayer* – which cannot be a (full) answer to *which person Peter is*, since the following is consistent (distributivity test): *John knows that Peter is a bricklayer, but John doesn't know which person Peter is*. Compare, with the bottom left sense in mind: *John knows that Peter is a bricklayer, but John doesn't know who Peter is*.

Upshot: it is a dangerous oversimplification to assume that *who* is just *wh* + animate. And it is even more dangerous to assume we understand exactly what it means in either direct or indirect questions, especially when combined with *is*. And in working out a theory of questions, one ought never to substitute *who* for *which person* in giving examples, unless the substitution is somehow independently justified.

I turn now to *which color*. Consider first *which color Mary likes*. Here I think our ordinary account of *which* works: a middle-size answer is *Mary likes red*, in which we note that *red* is being used as a proper name, not as an adjective – the grammar tells us this. But contrast *which color hair Mary has*. It seems to me the middle-size answer to this is surely *Mary has red hair*, with echo-question *Mary has which color hair*?, so that because the questioning of an adjective position instead of an individual position is at stake, the ordinary account will not work. Evidently what is wanted is a theory based on the determinable/determinate (*color*/*red*) distinction. Perhaps such a theory is not so hard to some by; I think it is *needed* for an accurate account of such questions, and that taking *color* as an ordinary common noun will give the wrong results. (The QMG long answer to the second example might be *the color which Mary's hair is is red*; that's O.K. – but note that the *which*-clause presumably still has to be derived from *Mary's hair is* $adjective_0$, not from *Mary's hair is* he_0.)

Lastly, I come to *what*. *What* sometimes is used exactly like *which*, being introduced with a common noun: *what dog Mary likes* seems to me indistinguishable from *which dog Mary likes*. In its grammatical role as a determiner, then, I do not distinguish *what* from *which* (though this is to be taken as a hypothesis, quite subject to falsification; indeed, contrary evidence would not surprise me, and might please me).

But like *who*, *what* can sometimes occupy the position of a term (instead of a determiner): *what is in the basket, what broke up the party last night*. The simplest conjecture is that in these cases, *what* is *which* + inanimate; equivalent, that is, to *which thing(s)*. The conjecture is false. Compare

(a) *what is in the basket*
(b) *which things are in the basket*

The former but not the latter can be *fully* answered by

(c) *three applies*

Evidence: (c) is not an answer to (b) by the Distributivity Test, for the following is consistent: *John knows that there are three apples in the basket (and nothing else), but John doesn't (fully) know which things are in the basket*. But the following is surely inconsistent, suggesting that (c) is in fact an answer to (a): *John knows that there are three apples in the basket (and nothing else), but John doesn't (fully) know what is in the basket*. So (a) and (b) do not pose the same question.

Hausser thinks that any term can be used as a short answer to (a); I do not, rejecting by the Distributivity Test such candidates as *few apples, none of Mary's apples, at most five apples*, while accepting *a few apples, all of Mary's apples, at least three apples*. I do not think a theory of *what* easy to come by, and require of any such theory that it distinguish these cases. One appealing conjecture is that all and only existence-entailing (or presupposing) terms can be short answers to what-questions. Sometimes I think *most of Mary's apples* or *many apples* (Partee's suggestions) might be counterexamples, but mostly I don't. These are particularly easy on the ear as part of a list: *What is in the basket? A few bananas and most of Mary's apples*. It does seem likely, however, that the list of suitable terms has somehow further to be narrowed; *something shiny* (or *mysterious*; David Lewis, conversation) clearly won't do as short answers, by the Distributivity Test. Perhaps each term must be formed from a sortal in the sense of Gupta (1981), together with an existence-entailing (or presupposing) quantifier. Then *something shiny* would be ruled out because *thing* is not a sortal. Thomason has wondered (in conversation) if the terms which can answer *what*-questions are the same as those which can be referred to anaphorically across sentence boundaries; this may well be largely true but isn't quite right (nor, let it be emphasized, did Thomason conjecture that it was). For *something* is a paradigm case of an antecedent for cross-sentential anaphoric reference: *Bill saw something on the lawn. It was larger than a cash register*.

A difficult part of treating *what*-questions is getting the "and nothing else" part right. That it *must* be got right is clear from the Distributivity Test, for *John knows that there are three apples in the basket* is consistent with *John doesn't (fully) know what is in the basket*. In this particular case "and nothing else" could be added by saying "everything in the basket is an apple," but it is not quite so clear how to generalize. I do in fact have some views on this, partly due to Thomason, but leave them for another occasion.

There is a very great deal more to say about these matters. But I shall be happy if the chief point has come through: the data strongly suggest that it is now time to refine our theories of English questions by treating each of the different *wh*-words *separately*.. If later generalizations appear, fine; but if we start by supposing that all the *wh*-words work alike, we shall tend to overlook some marveously interesting features of our language.

University of Pittsburgh and
Indiana University

ACKNOWLEDGEMENTS

I am indebted not only to Bennett, as recorded at the beginning of this paper, but heavily to Richmond Thomason. I have also received much benefit from lengthy discussions with each of Roland Hausser, Lauri Karttunen, Stanley Peters, and Pavel Tichy.

REFERENCES

Belnap, Nuel D. Jr.: (1972) 'S-P interrogatives,' *Journal of Philosophical Logic* 1, pp. 331–346.

Belnap, Nuel D. Jr. and Dorothy L. Grover: (1973) 'Quantifying in and out of quotes,' in Hughes Leblanc, ed., *Truth, Syntax, and Modality*, North-Holland, Amsterdam, pp. 17–47.

Belnap, Nuel D. Jr. and Thomas B. Steel Jr.: (1976) *The Logic of Questions and Answers*, Yale University Press, New Haven and London.

Bennett, Michael: (1977) 'A response to Karttunen on questions,' *Linguistics and Philosophy* 1, pp. 279–300.

Bennett, Michael: (1979) *Questions in Montague Grammar*, Indiana University Linguistics Club, Bloomington.

Bolinger, Dwight: (1978) 'Asking more than one thing at a time,' in Henry Hiz, ed., *Questions*, D. Reidel, Dordrecht, pp. 107–150.

Bressan, Aldo: (1972) *A General Interpreted Modal Calculus*, Yale University Press, New Haven and London.

Bressan, Aldo: (1973–74) 'The interpreted type-free modal calculus MC,' *Rend. sem. mat. Univ. Padova* 49 (1973), pp. 157–194, 50 (1973), pp. 19–57 and 51 (1974), pp. 1–25.

Gupta, Anil: (1981) *The Logic of Common Nouns: An Investigation in Quantified Modal Logic*, Yale University Press, New Haven and London.

Hamblin, C. L.: (1958) 'Questions,' *Australasian Journal of Philosophy* 36, pp. 159–168.

Hamblin, C. L.: (1973) 'Questions in Montague English,' *Foundations of Language* 10, pp. 41–53.

Hausser, Roland R.: (1976a) 'The logic of questions and answers,' (preprint).

Hausser, Roland R.: (1976b) 'Presuppositions in Montague grammar,' *Theoretical Linguistics* 3, pp. 245–280.

Hausser, Roland R. and Dietmar Zaefferer: (1978), 'Questions and answers in a context-dependent Montague grammar,' in F. Guenthner and S. J. Schmidt, eds., *Formal Semantics and Programatics for Natural Languages*, D. Reidel, Dordrecht, pp. 339–358.

Karttunen, Lauri: (1976) 'Syntax and semantics of questions,' *Linguistics and Philosophy* 1, 1–44. Also in Henry Hiz, ed., *Questions*, D. Reidel, Dordrecht, 1978, pp. 165–210.

Karttunen, Lauri: 'Questions revisited,' (undated preliminary draft).

Karttunen, Lauri, and Stanley Peters: (1976) 'What indirect questions conventionally implicate,' *CLS 12: Papers from the 12th Regional Meeting of the Chicago Linguistic Society*, Chicago Linguistics Society, Chicago, pp. 351–368.

Karttunen, Lauri, and Stanley Peters: (1979) 'Interrogative quantifiers,' (incomplete first draft), mimeographed.

Montague, Richard: (1974) *Formal Philosophy*, edited with an introduction by R. H. Thomason, Yale University Press, New Haven and London.

Powers, L.: (1978) 'Knowledge by deduction,' *Philosophical Review* 87, pp. 337–371.

Thomason, Richmond: (1977) 'Multiple quantification, questions, and Bach-Peters sentences: some preliminary notes,' xeroxed holograph.

Tichy, Pavel: (1977) 'Questions, answers and logic,' *American Philosophical Quarterly* 15, pp. 275–284.

WILLEM J.M. LEVELT

LINEARIZATION IN DESCRIBING SPATIAL NETWORKS

The topic of this paper is the way in which speakers order information in discourse. I will refer to this issue with the term "linearization", and will begin with two types of general remarks. The first one concerns the scope and relevance of the problem with reference to some existing literature. The second set of general remarks will be about the place of linearization in a theory of the speaker.

The following, and main part of this paper, will be a summary report of research of linearization in a limited, but well-defined domain of discourse, namely the description of spatial networks.

1. SCOPE AND RELEVANCE

One of the design characteristics of spoken language is its strict temporal ordering, or left-to-right structure. This property may not be convincingly present at the level of phonemes, but it certainly holds at the level of clauses: There is no way to co-articulate clauses; they have to be produced one after another. Since most speech in everyday life involves more than single isolated clauses, it is the rule rather than the exception that a speaker has to make decisions on the ordering of clauses. Such decisions, moreover, are not trivial. There are, in most circumstances, many conceivable ways of ordering the information to be expressed in discourse, but the speaker chooses one ordering rather than another, and this is most probably not a random choice. This choice problem may not be so apparent if the information has a very strict linear structure itself. If somebody reports an accident he has witnessed, a main part of the discourse will reflect the temporal order of the events that took place. Or if one describes a meal (Byrne, 1977), it is reasonable to begin with the first course, and to end with the last one. But, again, these cases are more the exception than the rule. Often, informational structures have no intrinsic linear order. Take apartment descriptions. Linde and Labov (1975) had informants describe the layout of their apartments. Such layouts are two-dimensional structures. They have to be mapped on a linear order of clauses in such a way that the listener can, within certain limits, reconstruct the two-dimensional picture. This mapping involves what I will call a

S. Peters and E. Saarinen (eds.), Processes, Beliefs, and Questions, 199–220.

linearization-strategy, and it appears from Linde and Labov's work, that these strategies are quite systematic. In almost all cases, the informants' strategy is a kind of *tour:* they start at the front door, and move through the apartment room by room. At choice points they take one branch first, and, after finishing it, jump back to the last place of choice in order to select a next branch. This means that the tour is a quite abstract one: these jumps cannot be performed physically. They are mental switching operations which may reveal something important about discourse planning. Another similar case is the way in which people describe their living rooms. Again, an at least two-dimensional structure has to be mapped on a linear order of clauses. Veronika Ullmer-Ehrich (1981) in our institute has found that a main strategy of the subjects in describing their living rooms is to make what we call a *gaze tour*. They position themselves at the door, and gaze along the walls in either left-to-right or inverse fashion. They describe the pieces of furniture one-by-one in the order of the gaze tour. Speakers can often be the captives of their linearization strategy. Several of the informants entirely forgot to mention the furniture in the middle of the room, perhaps because the focus of gaze only followed the walls.

These cases are still relatively simple for the speaker. But what about explaining games? How would one explain the game of chess to somebody who is uninformed? The informational structure is so multidimensional that speakers are not able to set up a linearization strategy which guarantees full transmission of the relevant information. We found that discourse planning is quite chaotic here; the only way, apparently, is to teach the listener while playing.

Several forms of linearization are strongly interactive. The listener's reactions may become highly important for the speaker's linearization. This is, for instance, very apparent from an analysis of discourse planning in the Watergate-tapes (Linde and Goguen, 1977). But also in more monological forms of discourse planning, the listener's role is important. After all, the speaker wants the listener to understand a particular informational structure. He therefore has to take into account the listener's presumed foreknowledge and processing capacities. This will turn out to be an essential issue in the analysis of spatial network descriptions.

Let me finish this set of general remarks by mentioning one other set of linearization studies in the literature. There are at least three empirical studies on how people give road directions (Klein, 1981; Wunderlich, 1981; Munro, 1977). Also here, the speaker makes a tour from source to goal, a tour which is laid out via a system of landmarks. These, and all other cases of spatial discourse I have seen, are full of deictic devices, which, in their turn, depend strongly on the linearization strategy chosen.

2. THE PLACE OF LINEARIZATION IN A THEORY OF THE SPEAKER

The ubiquity of linearization in everyday language use does not imply that it involves a unified psychological mechanism. If we manage to cut up the speaker's nature at its joint – and I think a theory of the speaker has to do that – it is not self-evident that linearization will come out as a separate limb, or bone. Since, however, a theory of the speaker does not exist, all serious candidates for joints and bones are worth considering. The main distinction I would like to propose for a theory of the speaker (following Kempen, 1977) is between the processes involved in the genesis of the *ideas* underlying speech, and the processes involved in the choice of linguistic *forms* for their expressions. The first set of processes, which may be called *conceptualizing*, may be conceived of as the set of non-linguistic preliminaries to producing or sustaining an utterance. It should include, among other things, the development of communicative intentions, the selection of the appropriate information from the knowledge base, and the linearization of this information. The second set of processes, *formulating*, give linguistic form to the generated

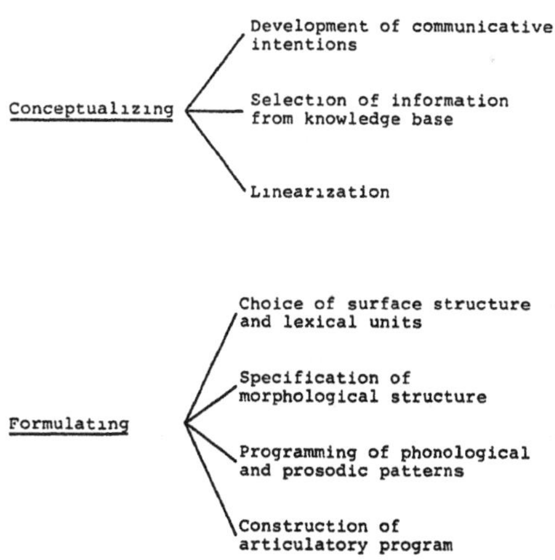

Fig. 1. Processes involved in speaking.

intentions and contents. Among the activities involved will be the choice of surface structure and of lexical units, the specification of morphological structure, the programming of phonological and prosodic patterns, and the construction of an articulatory program. I would like to see as much as possible work done by the conceptual preliminaries, so that the formulating mechanism can operate in a highly automatized fashion on highly specified conceptual input.

In this conception, linearization has to do with the conceptual preliminaries only, i.e., it is a non-linguistic process. It is, therefore, no surprise that linearization can be observed in other human behavior as well, e.g. in walking through a museum, or in playing music.

Even if linearization is a purely conceptual issue, it need not be a unified process. If linearization is fully determined by the content of the discourse, it would still make no sense to study linearization as a relatively autonomous process. But, in my view, there is reason to suppose that linearization shows functional properties which are independent of the knowledge base, and which may turn out to be fairly general for different types of discourse. These properties, I would like to claim, come forth from the economy of short term memory. The present approach is, therefore, orthogonal to content analysis explanations of discourse structure. I will now try and make these claims more concrete by working in some detail through a case of linearization in a simple well-defined domain.

3. THE DOMAIN OF DESCRIPTIONS

The spatial structures I have worked with are gridlike networks as displayed in Figure 2. They consist of nodes and arcs, and are always connected. The nodes are colored dots of degree 1, 2, 3 or 4, i.e. they have one to four arcs, and are, correspondingly, called single, dual, triple and quadruple nodes. The arcs are equally long, and are arranged either horizontally or vertically. It is helpful to distinguish three types of structure in this domain: The first type is the *linear* structure. It consists of a string of dual nodes, with two single nodes at the ends (see Figure 2a). The second type is *hierarchial*. It contains triple or quadruple nodes (as in Figure 2b). These nodes will, of course, be choice points for the subject who has to describe the network. The third type of structure is the *loop* (see Figure 2c). It creates all sorts of special problems in linearization, as we will see shortly.

In the experimental situation, the subject is visually presented with a network, and is required to describe the network into a tape recorder, beginning

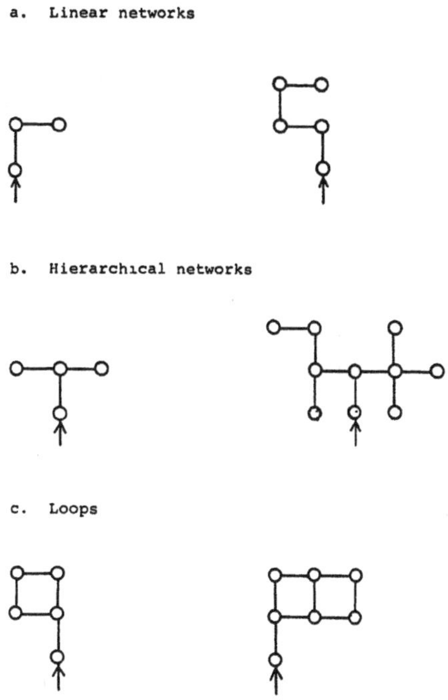

Fig. 2. Examples of networks used.

at the arrow, in such a way that the listener will be able to draw the network from the tape. It is further mentioned to the speaker that the listener has seen the same example networks as the speaker, so that he knows the domain of spatial structures under concern.

By choosing this domain, I hoped, on the one hand, to capture some of the important aspects of other spatial domains, like city maps, apartment lay-outs, electric circuits, etc, and on the other hand, the domain would allow for a precise formulation of a linearization model, which could then be tested experimentally. I would now like to present two such models. The first one is a bit more speaker-oriented, the second one more listener-oriented, or "cooperative".

4. A SPEAKER-ORIENTED MODEL OF LINEARIZATION

The first model was constructed so as to capture the main features of what

Linde and Labov observed in their study of apartment descriptions. A description is like a tour, i.e. the moves preserve maximal spatial connectedness. Jumps only occur back to unfinished choice points, and it seems that not only moves, but also jumps are as small as possible, namely back to the last choice point. Whatever the nature of the model, it should fulfill the requirement that it generates at least one complete description for every network in the domain.

I have designed an augmented transition network (ATN) that will do just that. It is given in Figure 3. The ATN consists of four states and a set of transitions between them. In some cases different transitions lead to the same change of state. In the Figure these are collapsed into one arc for the sake of visual simplicity. Each of the transitions has one condition-action pair associated to it. If the condition of a transition is fulfilled, the transition may be made under simultaneous execution of the action.

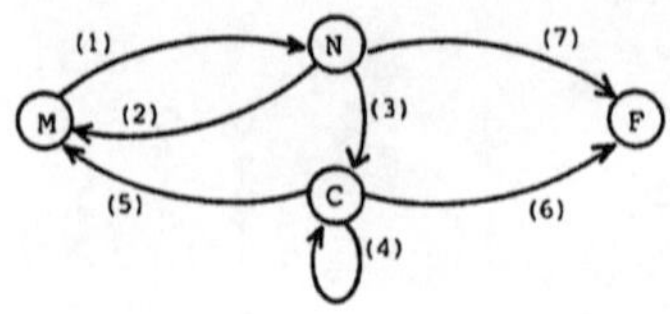

Transition	Condition	Action
(1a)	network entrance	make entry statement reduce valence of entrance node by 1.
(b)	other than network entrance	(select* and) describe move, reduce val. of node left and of node entered by 1.
(2a)	node val =1	describe node
(b)	node is loop entrance and val >1	describe node
(3)	node valence >1	describe node
(4)	node valence >1	seek M/F
(5)	node valence =1	-
(6)	node valence =0	-
(7)	node valence =0	describe node

*enter loop if loop has been recognized at transition (2).

Fig. 3. Speaker-ATN for network descriptions (speaker-oriented).

The network can recursively call itself, as we shall see in a moment. This is a necessary device for dealing with choice points. This recursive property requires a push-down store which keeps the addresses to which the ATN has to pop back after finishing an embedded operation. We must assume that the ATN has something like a semantics, i.e. the operations are performed under reference to the network under concern. One way to put this is that the ATN moves a pointer over the spatial network, and that the actions refer to the information at the pointer. More specifically, the various "describe" actions (see Figure 3) should be true for the information at the pointer. Finally, the ATN keeps a register of so-called node-valences. Intitially, the valence of the node is its degree: 4 for quadruple nodes, 3 for triple nodes, etc. Every time a node is entered or left, the valence of the node is reduced by 1. Semantically, this amounts to marking these entries and exists of nodes.

If the network is linear, as in Figure 2a, it is easy to see how the ATN works. Starting in state M (the initial or move state), the ATN will oscillate between states M and N (the node state), and it will describe the successive nodes and arcs by performing the actions that correspond to transitions 1b and 2a. When it finally meets a single node, i.e., a node which after being entered has valence O, transition 7 is made, and the final state F is reached. In short, the ATN predicts that linear networks are described in a connected way from beginning to end.

If a structure is hierarchical, as in Figure 2b, the recursive power of the ATN has to be used. If, in state N, the pointer is at a choice point, i.e. with valence > 1, transition 3 has to be made, by which the ATN reaches the choice state C. From here it can only make transition 4, i.e. it has to transverse the network from M to F as an embedded action. The choice state is stored on the push-down store, which means, semantically, that the address of the choice point is stored, while the ATN proceeds to describe one of the branches from the choice point. If such a branch is linear, it is automatically described by oscillating between states M and N, until the end of the string, and there-with state F is reached. Control transfers back to C. If the choice node has only one valence left, transition 5 will be made, and from state M, the final branch from the choice node will be described. If two valences are left, another push operation (transition 4) will be performed, etc. This way of dealing with hierarchical structures means that the ATN will always return to the last unfinished choice point, and will never skip.

Really complicated is the situation with loops. The ATN can handle them in two ways. The first one is what I would like to call the dumb way. Consider the loop on the left in Figure 2c. The ATN enters the choice point. It will be in state N, and will transit to state C, since the valence of the node is greater than 1 (transition 3). From the choice state it will enter the loop in subroutine-mode, i.e. with the choice address on store. Upon returning to the same node, it finds that the node has valence zero, which is the condition for transition 7 to the final state. Since the push-down store is not empty, control shifts back to state C. The node valence, however, is still zero, so that transition 6 is made, and the final state is reached with empty store. The dumbness of this procedure is that (a) unnecessary storage is involved, and (b) several additional computations have to be made at the end.

The clever way is to recognize the loop, and *not* store the choice point at entering the loop. This is the condition for transition 2b. The ATN just keeps oscillating between M and N, without recursion, and therefore without storage. One could say that a timely recognized loop can be "linearized", or "unfolded". In this way the number of actual choice points can be reduced.

I have a proof (see Acknowledgement) that this ATN generates at least one complete description for every network in the class.

It may be clarifying to see the ATN at work for an actual description obtained in the experiment to be reported furtheron. Figure 4 gives the network described, the (Dutch) description, its English translation, and its breakdown according to the ATN of Figure 3.

Clearly the ATN of Figure 3 is non-deterministic, since it does not prescribe which arc has to be taken first at a choice point. I will return to this after presentation of the second ATN.

In order to complete the discussion of this ATN let us consider the listener's role. The listener can also be modelled as an ATN. The ATN should be able to draw the spatial network on the basis of the description generated by the speaker-ATN. The corresponding listener-ATN is presented in Figure 5. It is an almost complete image of the speaker-ATN. In fact, it functions exactly in a matching fashion as long as the clever loop-procedure is not used. If the clever way is used by the speaker, the listener-ATN will perform the equivalent of the dumb procedure. Only if the speaker were to mention that he is entering a loop (which is not done by the speaker-ATN, but which could easily be added), could the listener also be clever. Apart from this loop-issue, the storage requirements for speaker and listener form a perfect match.

This latter fact means that, if the network gets complicated, the load on the listener may become quite substantial, only because of multiple embeddings of choice-points. The next ATN is designed to make the speaker a bit more cooperative, so that the listener has an easier task to perform.

Network

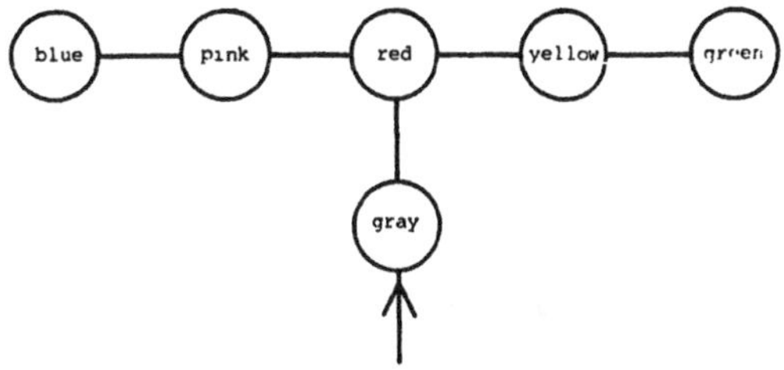

Description

We beginnen bij grijs.
Van grijs kun je naar boven naar rood.
Van rood kun je naar rechts naar geel
en nog verder naar rechts naar groen.
Je kunt vanuit rood ook naar links,
dan kom je eerst bij roze terecht,
en nog verder naar links,
dan kom je bij blauw.

English translation and ATN-breakdown

Statement	Transition
We begin at	(1a) entry statement
gray	(2a) describe node
From gray one can go up to	(1b) describe move
red	(3) decribe node
	(4) seek MF, stack state C.
From red one can go right to	(1b) describe move
yellow	(2a) describe node
and still further right to	(1b) describe move
green	(7) decribe node
	unstack and return to state C.
	(5) -
From red one can also go left, then you first reach	(1b) describe move
pink	(2a) describe node
and still further left, then you come to	(1b) describe move
blue	(7) describe node

Fig. 4. Analysis of actual description according to speaker-oriented ATN of Fig. 3.

5. A LISTENER-ORIENTED MODEL OF LINEARIZATION

The load on the listener is caused by the recursiveness of the speaker-ATN. Would it be possible to build a non-recursive speaker? From listening to one subject in a pilot study, I got the idea that this could be done. That subject did not *jump* back to the last choice point, but she *moved* back, step by step. So the return from green to red in Figure 4 would be described as follows:

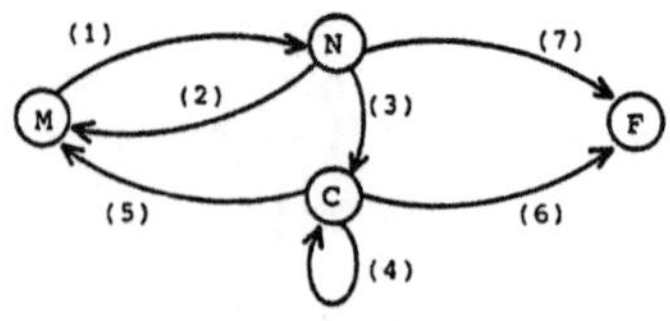

Transition	Condition	Action
(1a)	entry statement	draw entry arc
(b)	move description	draw arc from node
(2a)	node descr., val =1	draw node to arc, mark arc exits
(b)	node descr., val >1 and loop mentioned	draw node to arc, mark arc exits
(3)	node val >1	draw node to arc, mark arc exits
(4)	node val >1	seek M/F
(5)	node val =1	-
(6)	node val =0	-
(7)	node val =0	draw node

Fig. 5. Listener-ATN to ATN of Fig. 3.

"From green back again to yellow, and from yellow again to red". Inspired by this procedure, I designed an ATN which can be called listener-oriented, for reasons that will become clear shortly. It is presented in Figure 6.

This ATN consists of two networks. The top one generates description of arcs and nodes, it could be called the "move-network". The bottom one is the "return-network". It generates the return from end-nodes, by mentioning in reverse order the nodes and arcs that had been described before. The ATN is non-recursive, and has, correspondingly no push-down store. Instead, it has a so-called "unfinished node counter". Every time the move-network meets a node with valence > 1, i.e., a choice node with at least two unfinished arcs, the counter value is increased by 1, and one of the arcs is entered (see transition 2b). So, the address of the node is not stored, but only the fact that somewhere there is an unfinished choice node. The ATN proceeds through the network, oscillating between M and N, counting unfinished choice nodes, until it reaches a node of valence 0. It will then transfer control to the return-network, which proceeds by oscillating between R and N′, until it meets a node with valence 1 or 2, i.e., an unfinished choice point. If only one arc is still to be done, the ATN enters it, and reduces the counter-value by 1,

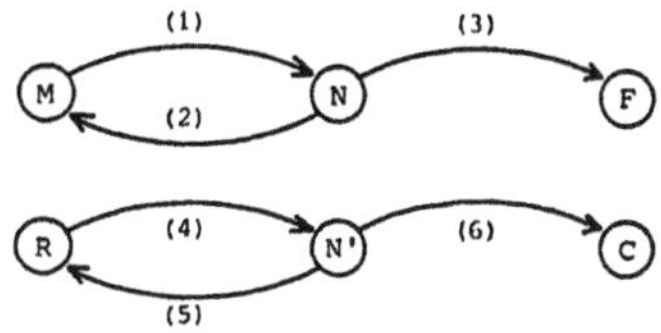

Transition	Condition	Action
(1a)	network entrance	make entry statement, reduce val. of entrance node by 1.
(b)	other than network entrance	(select* and) describe move, reduce val. of node left and node entered by 1.
(2a)	node val =1	describe node
(b)	node val >1, non loop	describe node, UNC n = n + 1
(c)	loop entry	describe node
(d)	node valence =0, and UNC n>0	describe node, seek R/C
(3)	node valence =0 and UNC n=0	-
(4)	node valence =0	mention return move along non-r-marked arc, r-mark arc
(5)	-	mention node
(6a)	node val =1	mention node, UNC n = n - 1
(b)	node val =2	mention node

*if loop, enter loop

Fig. 6. Non-recursive speaker-ATN (listener-oriented).

since there is one fewer unfinished choice node. If there are two open arcs left, the count is obviously not reduced. The return-network, prohibits returning twice along the same arc, which is a necessary but unimportant technicality. Loops are hard for this ATN. Without going into details, it should be remarked that loops can only be handled in a way corresponding to the clever procedure of the earlier ATN, i.e., a loop *has* to be recognized by the speaker.

For the listener, this speaker-behavior is really very easy. The corresponding listener-ATN is presented in Figure 7. A listener without short-term memory would still be successful, so to speak.

Though this pair of networks is far easier in terms of memory load than the former pair, a price has to be paid. Firstly, the descriptions will be up

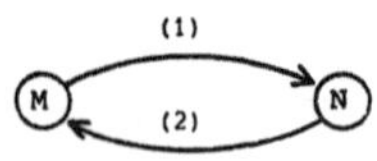

Transition	Condition	Action
(1a)	entry statement	draw entry arc
(b)	move description	draw arc from node
(c)	return move mention	more along drawn arc
(2a)	node description	draw node to arc, mark arc exits
(b)	node mention	check node

Fig. 7. Listener-ATN to ATN of Fig. 6.

to 50% longer, due to the return moves. Secondly, if loops are missed, completeness of description is no longer guaranteed.

Like the former speaker-ATN, the present one is non-deterministic. At choice points the speaker can go one arc or another. I would now like to discuss some principles of choice, which can probabilistically predict which arc will be chosen at choice points. These principles are of a *local* and of a *global* nature.

6. LOCAL CONSTRAINTS ON CHOICE

The purely local situation at a choice point is always one of four possibilities. They are given in Figure 8. The first three situations are binary. In each case, there is one degree of freedom for predicting the choice probabilities. The fourth situation allows for six possible orders of choosing the different arcs, i.e., there are 5 degrees of freedom. A simple theory of local constraints can be designed to describe these 8 degrees of freedom in total with just two parameters. According to this theory, a speaker would, firstly, decide whether he will go straight or not. The probability of going straight, s, is the first parameter. For all cases that the subject cannot or will not go straight, a further decision is taken whether to go right or left, if that choice is still open. The second parameter, then, is the probability r of choosing right. These two parameters will predict all cases in Figure 8. I will return to this in discussing the experimental results.

Node type	Order	Probability
	straight → right	s
	right → straight	1 - s
	straight → left	s
	left → straight	1 - s
	right → left	r
	left → right	1 - r
	straight → right → left	s·r
	straight → left → right	s(1 - r)
	right → straight → left	(1 - s) r s
	right → left → straight	$r(1 - s)^2$
	left → straight → right	(1 - s)(1 - r)s
	left → right → straight	$(1 - s)^2 (1 - r)$

Fig. 8. Four local choice situations.

7. GLOBAL PRINCIPLES OF CHOICE

Local constraints derive from the structure of the choice node itself. Global constraints emerge from structural properties of the network as a whole. My conjecture is that such global principles of choice are quite general in nature and will apply to linearization in quite diverse domains of discourse.

The various global constraints on choice can be derived from one underlying principle, which I will call the

Principle of minimal effort. Everything else being equal, speakers will prefer to give descriptions which minimize the number and duration of elements on store, and the length of the description. There will be a preference for using structural information whenever it can be instrumental to such minimization.

The first global constraint we derive from this principle of minimal effort is depicted in Figure 9. The constraint can be formulated as follows:

GC1: Everything else being equal, the probability that from a choice node a shorter branch is described before a longer branch is greater than 0.5.

The figure shows a choice situation, and a table of the elements on store if the first (speaker-oriented) ATN linearizes in one way or the other. Clearly, there is a longer duration of storage if the long branch is taken first. The prediction, therefore, is that the shorter branch will have a higher probability to be taken first.

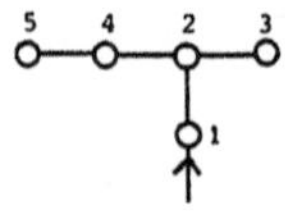

Number of elements on store (speaker ATN of Fig.3)	
Seq. (a)	1 → 2 → 3 → 4 → 5
n	0 0 1 0 0
Seq. (b)	1 → 2 → 4 → 5 → 3
n	0 0 1 1 0

Fig. 9. Duration of load for two linearizations of network.

The listener-oriented speaker will make the same choice, but for a different reason. For him, there is no difference in storage, but clearly the description will be longer if the long branch is described first; this would namely involve a longer return move.

The second global constraint has to do with the number, not the duration of items on store. Contrary to the first constraint, it is only valid for the speaker-oriented ATN.

GC2: Everything else being equal, the probability of branches with fewer embedded choice points to be described before branches with more embedded choice points is greater than 0.5.

The constraint is illustrated in Figure 10. It presents the storage load for

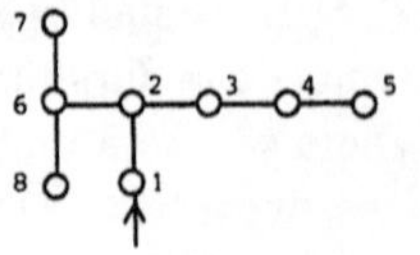

Number (n) of elements on store (Speaker-ATN of Fig.3)	
Seq. (a)	1 → 2 → 3 → 4 → 5 → 6 → 7 → 8
n	0 0 1 1 1 0 1 0
Seq. (b)	1 → 2 → 6 → 7 → 8 → 3 → 4 → 5
n	0 0 1 2 1 0 0 0

Fig. 10. Size of load for two linearizations of network.

going either right or left first. Maximal storage load for the ATN of Figure 3 is, apparently, less if the linear branch is done before the hierarchical one. Though for this figure the *average* load is the same for the two linearizations, the *maximal* load should be the correct measure, since our short term memory does not resist a continuing but slight load. It is more like a bottle-neck: it breaks down at moments of overload.

It should be noted that this second global constraint is formally identical to Yngve's depth hypothesis. In a similar fashion, it predicts that linearization creates maximally right-branching discourse structures. I believe that this is a very general and fruitful hypothesis about linearization in a large variety of discourse domains.

I mentioned that the listener-oriented ATN would not show this global constraint. The reason is simple: it does not involve any storage.

A last global constraint I want to make is that speakers prefer to be clever in dealing with loops:

GC3: Everything else being equal, the probability that, at choice points, loops are described before other branches is greater than 0.5.

This constraint is examplified in Figure 11. We have seen that the clever

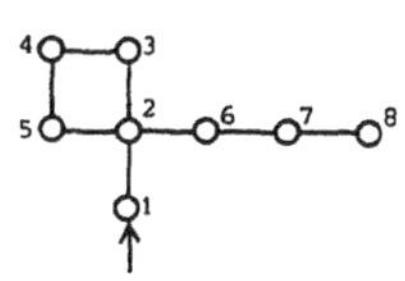

Number (n) of elements on store (Speaker-ATN of Fig.3)

Seq. (a)	1 → 2 → 3 → 4 → 5 → 6 → 7 → 8
n	0 0 0 0 0 0 0 0
Seq. (b)	1 → 2 → 6 → 7 → 8 → 3 → 4 → 5
n	0 0 1 1 1 0 0 0

Fig. 11. Size of load for two linearizations of a loop.

procedure is to "unfold" the loop. In that case, no storage of the choice node is necessary, but the requirement is that the loop is done first. This can all be seen in the table of storage load in the figure.

This constraint is a probabilistic one for the first speaker-ATN. For the listener-oriented ATN it is a deterministic requirement, since this ATN only allows for the clever procedure.

8. SOME EXPERIMENTAL FINDINGS

Let us now turn to some of our experimental findings. For the sake of brevity. I will not present the full details of experiment and results here. It should suffice to say that I constructed 53 different networks in order to test the ATNs, and the probabilistic constraints. We had correspondingly, 53 subjects who described all these networks in different orders.

The characteristic difference between the ATNs is that the first one predicts *jumps* back to choice points, and the second one return *moves*. It turned out that of our 53 subjects 33 were exclusively jumpers, 16 were exclusively movers, and only 4 both jumped and moved. It seems, therefore, that there are two very consistent linearization types. The next question is, of course, whether the two ATNs correctly predict other aspects of linearization for these two types of subject. In the following, I will therefore report the results for "jumpers" and "movers" separately. I will proceed as follows. Firstly, I will give some data on linear, hierarchical, and loop structures. Then I will mention some results on local constraints. And finally, the global constraints will be considered.

The experimental set contained 7 *linear networks*. They are given in Figure 12. Both ATNs predict full connectivity here. There is not a single case in the data where the description is discontinuous: all follow the network from node to node.

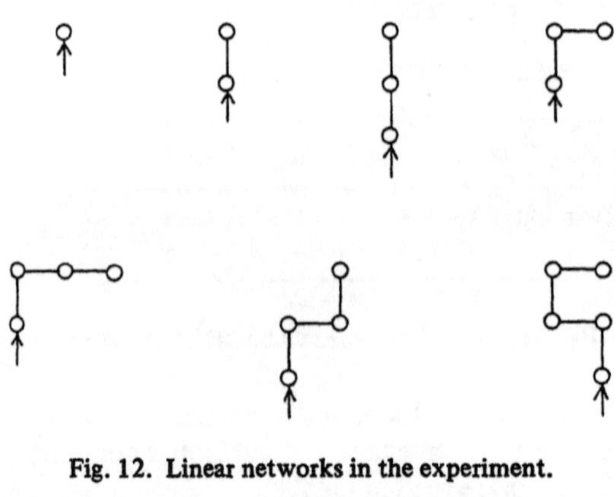

Fig. 12. Linear networks in the experiment.

There were various *hierarchical networks* in the set. One network was especially designed to test the last-in-first-out property of the push-down store. That is, it tested whether the subject always returns to the last unfinished node. This should be true for both ATNs, although for different reasons. The pattern, given in Figure 13, is embedded 7 times.

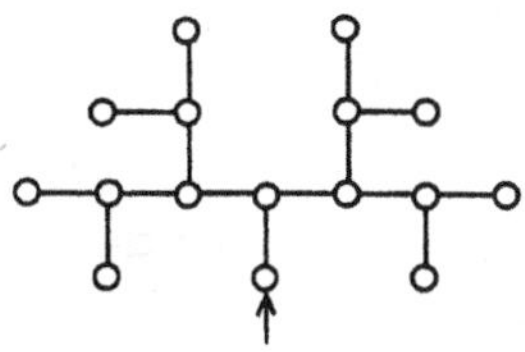

Fig. 13. Multiply hierarchical network.

Of the 33 jumpers, only 3 show deviations in the return order of choice points. Two of these make just one reversal of order, and one subject makes two such inversions.

The 16 movers show no violations whatsoever, which is of course a consequence of strictly adhering to the moving-strategy.

Since the property is quite essential to both ATNs, these results give substantial support to a major feature of their design.

Loops, finally, create problems for both jumpers and movers. The loops used in the experiment are depicted in Figure 14. I will only give a summary of the results for these networks.

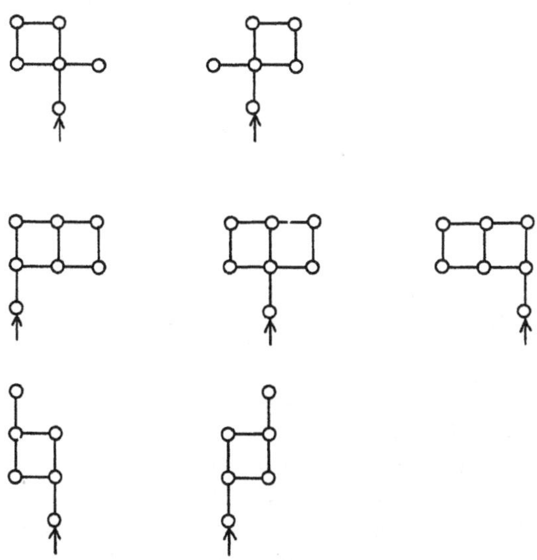

Fig. 14. Loops used for testing ATNs.

Movers, it turns out, only do what their ATN predicts in 50% of the cases. In no less than 33% of the cases, they follow the order predicted, but stop short of a *complete* description. In only 17% of their descriptions does the order really violate the ATN predictions. As expected (see section 5) loops make movers very error-prone.

Jumpers linearize, as predicted by their ATN, in 65% of the cases. In 8%, they stay incomplete, and in 27% of the cases, their order contradicts predictions from the ATN. This is substantial, and requires, in my view, some further theoretical work.

The *local constraints* were tested with the networks in Figure 15. I made a least square estimate for the two-parameter model, and tested the fit by χ^2.

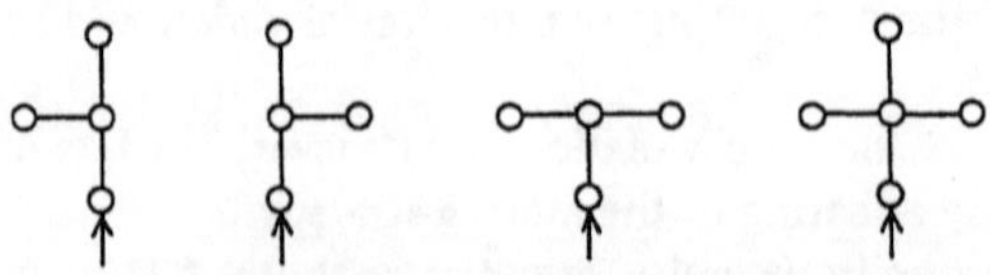

Fig. 15. Networks used for testing local constraints.

Neither jumpers nor movers showed any significant deviations from the model (.50 > p > .30 and .30 > p > .20, respectively). But the two types differed in their first "straight-on" parameter. Jumpers were more inclined to go straight first ($s = 0.52$) than movers ($s = 0.38$).

The *first global constraint* (*GC1*), short branches before long branches, was tested with the patterns in Figure 16. The constraint was strongly confirmed for both jumpers and movers for all patterns except 16(e) and (f). It could be the case that the local straight-on decision has precedence over global constraints, but this has to be further studied.

The *second global constraint* (*GC2*), Yngve's depth hypothesis, was tested with the networks in Figure 17. For jumpers, it was strongly confirmed for all networks, except 17 (c) and (d). It seems that jumpers do seek the least complex branch first, but don't distinguish very much between embedding and form complexity.

The movers, as predicted in section 7, do not follow the constraint for any of the networks. But a surprising additional finding is that they show the inverse for all patterns, i.e. they seem to *seek* complexity. This was not predicted and requires further theoretical analysis.

The *third global constraint* (*GC3*), finally, which predicts that loops have precedence, was tested with the patterns in Figure 18. Jumpers enter the loop first in 68% of the cases, movers do so in 80%. This seems promising, but care

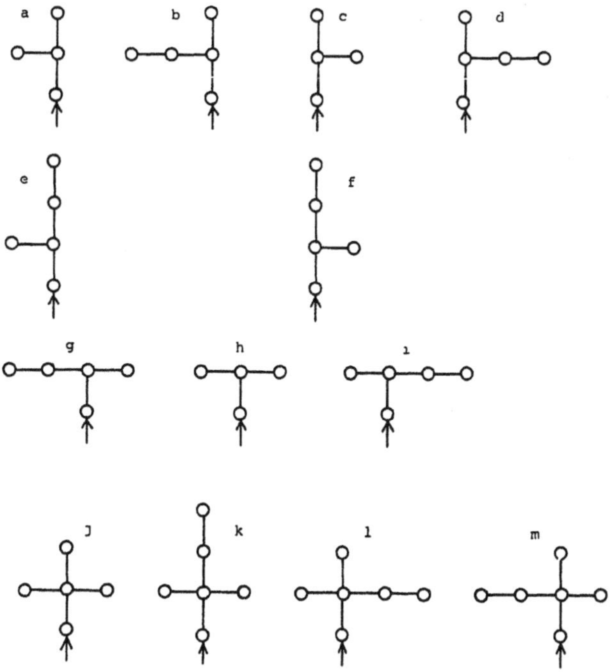

Fig. 16. Networks used for testing first global constraints (GC1).

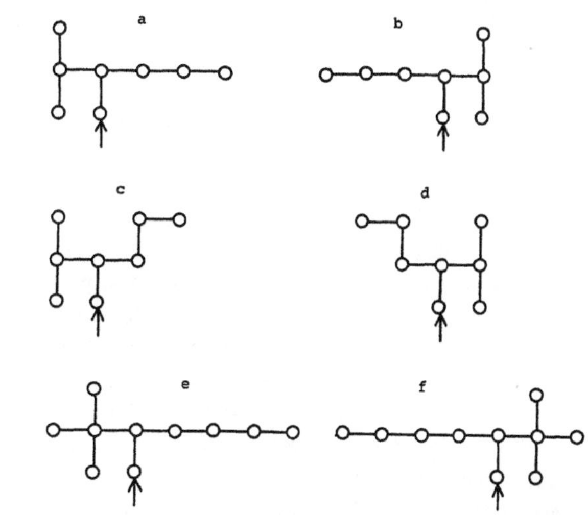

Fig. 17. Networks used for testing second global constraint (GC2).

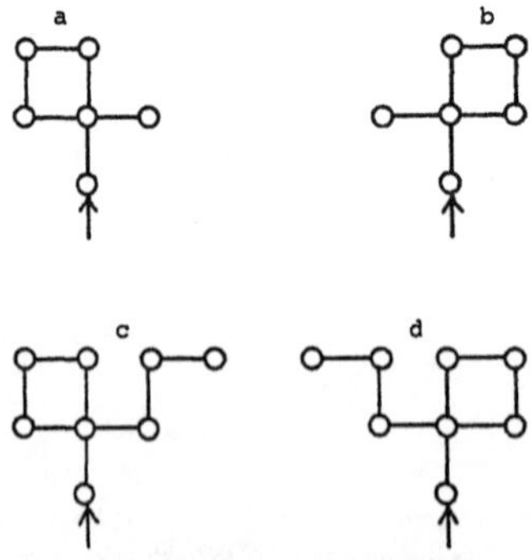

Fig. 18. Networks used for testing third global constraint (GC3).

is necessary in the choosing of an acceptable null-hypothesis. It is not reasonable to put H_0 at 50%, since the speaker can always choose between three arcs, two of which enter the loop. If H_0 is set at 67%, only movers show a slight tendency to prefer the loop. It seems, then, that the clever procedure of "unfolding" the loop is not very popular with our subjects.

9. CONCLUDING REMARKS

It would have been surprising to find that the ATN-models worked in all cases. But up to the level of hierarchical spatial structures, they are in almost faultless correspondence to the speakers' behavior. It should be noted that this correspondence does not depend on the particular format of the ATNs, but on a few general construction principles: connectivity of moves in both ATNs, first-in-last-out storage of choice nodes in the speaker-oriented ATN, no such storage but connected return moves in the listener-oriented ATN. It should not be difficult to realize these same principles in other ways: in the speaker-oriented ATN one could, for instance, reduce the push-down store and the node valence register to a single mechanism (as suggested by Dr. Hendrix during the conference), and similar changes can be made in the listener-oriented ATN without affecting any of the predictions made, and thus without affecting the empirical fit. For loop-structures, however, both ATNs are less accurate, and so will be other variants built according to the same principles. The main deviations from the ATN predictions are, apart from incompleteness, the "cutting up" of a loop, thus treating it as a hierarchical 2-branch structure. Why is it that speakers find it hard to deal with loops in a connected way? Psychologically, this may have to do with difficulties subjects encounter in maintaining their original deictic orientation while turning through a loop. This suggestion (made by Dr. Partee at the conference) should be followed up since it might lead to an additional construction principle in linearization models (cf. Levelt, 1981).

Taken together, the results so far underline the basic importance for discourse generation of principles such as preservation of connectivity, first-in-last-out treatment of choice points, and a general minimal effort principle based on short term memory economy. My conjecture is that these functional principles of linearization are not limited to this particular domain, but apply more generally to other types of discourse as well. (See J. Mandler, 1978, who shows the working of similar principles in the retrieval of stories.) The combination of a first-in-last-out principle, and minimization of memory load predicts a prevalence of hierarchical right-branching structures in discourse, an interesting property to look for.

Max-Planck-Institut für Psycholinguistik, Nijmegen

ACKNOWLEDGMENT

I am grateful to Wilma Silvius who ran the experiments, and analyzed the protocols. Dr. R. H. Jeurissen, Department of Mathematics, Nijmegen University, provided a completeness proof for a set of linearization devices, including the ATN of Fig. 3. Finally, thanks are due to Dr. Tony Ades who suggested changes and improvements, of which several were realized in this final version of the text.

REFERENCES

Byrne, R.: (1977) 'Planning meals: problem solving on a real data-base,' *Cognition* 5, 287–332.

Kempen, G.: (1977) 'Conceptualizing and formulating in sentence production,' in S. Rosenberg (ed.), *Sentence Production: Developments in Research and Theory*, Erlbaum, Hillsdale.

Klein, W.: (1981) 'Some aspects of route directions', in R. J. Jarvella and W. Klein (eds.), *Speech, Place, and Action. Studies of Language in Context*, Wiley, Chichester.

Levelt, W. J. M.: (1981) 'Cognitive styles in the use of spatial direction terms', in R. J. Jarvella and W. Klein (eds.), *Speech, Place, and Action. Studies of Language in Context*, Wiley, Chichester.

Linde, C. and W. Labov: (1975) 'Spatial networks as a site for the study of language and thought,' *Language* 51, 924–939.

Linde, C. and J. A. Goguen: (1977) 'Structure of planning discourse,' unpublished manuscript.

Mandler, J.: (1978) 'A code in the node: The use of a story schema in retrieval,' *Discourse Processes* 1, 14–35.
Munro, A.: (1977) *Speech Act Understanding*, Dissertation, 1977, U.C. San Diego.
Ullmer-Ehrich, V.: (1981) 'The structure of living space descriptions', in R. J. Jarvella and W. Klein (eds.), *Speech, Place, and Action. Studies of Language in Context*, Wiley, Chichester.
Wunderlich, D. and R. Reinelt: (1981) 'Telling the way', in R. J. Jarvella and W. Klein (eds.), *Speech, Place, and Action. Studies of Language in Context*, Wiley, Chichester.

INDEX OF NAMES

INDEX OF SUBJECTS

FSC
www.fsc.org
MIX
Papier | Fördert
gute Waldnutzung
FSC® C083411

Kolibri 360 GmbH
Ferdinand-Jühlke-Straße 7
99095 Erfurt, Deutschland
produktsicherheit@kolibri360.de